THE SILENT REVOLUTION

THE INTERNATIONAL CENTER FOR ECONOMIC GROWTH is a nonprofit research institute founded in 1985 to stimulate international discussions on economic policy, economic growth, and human development. The Center sponsors research, publications, and conferences in cooperation with an international network of correspondent institutes, which distribute publications of both the Center and other network members to policy audiences around the world. The Center's research and publications program is organized around five series: Sector Studies; Country Studies; Studies in Human Development and Social Welfare; Occasional Papers; and Reprints.

The Center is affiliated with the Institute for Contemporary Studies and is headquartered in Panama; the administrative office is in San Francisco, California.

For further information, please contact the International Center for Economic Growth, 243 Kearny Street, San Francisco, California, 94108, USA. Telephone (415) 981-5353; Fax (415) 986-4878.

THE SILENT REVOLUTION

THE INFORMAL SECTOR IN FIVE ASIAN AND NEAR EASTERN COUNTRIES

_____ *Edited by* _____

A. Lawrence Chickering
and
Mohamed Salahdine

An International Center for Economic Growth Publication

ICS PRESS
San Francisco, California

AMK 0478 - 4/2

Inquiries, book orders, and catalog requests should be addressed to ICS Press, 243 Kearny Street, San Francisco, California 94108. Telephone: (415) 981-5353; fax: (415) 986-4878. To order call toll-free **(800) 326-0263** in the contiguous United States.

Cover design: Ben Santora.
Cover photograph: Salahuddin Azizee.
Interior photographs: Raymond Collet and Mohamed Salahdine (Morocco); Associated Newspapers Ltd. and Hemaka Dias (Sri Lanka); Maitree Ungphakorn (Thailand); Salahuddin Azizee (Bangladesh).
Copyeditor: Peter Hayes.
Production editor: Heidi Fritschel.
Index: Shirley Kessel.

Distributed to the trade by National Book Network, Lanham, Maryland.

Library of Congress Cataloging-in-Publication Data
The silent revolution : the informal sector in five Asian and Near Eastern
    countries / edited by A. Lawrence Chickering and Mohamed Salahdine.
        p.   cm.
    "An International Center for Economic Growth publication."
    Includes bibliographical references and index.
    ISBN 1-55815-163-X. — ISBN 1-55815-162-1 (pbk.)
    1. Informal sector (Economics)—Morocco. 2. Informal sector
(Economics)—Philippines. 3. Informal sector (Economics)—Sri
Lanka. 4. Informal sector (Economics)—Thailand. 5. Informal sector
(Economics)—Bangladesh. I. Chickering, A. Lawrence.
    II. Salahdine, Mohamed.
    HD2346.M8S58 1991
    330—dc20   91-25370
                                                                        CIP

Contents

Preface

In many developing countries, where jobs in officially licensed enterprises are scarce, much of the population makes a living by working outside the official tax and regulatory systems. These people, who make up the informal sector, are innovators, skilled at surviving, and sometimes prospering, in a highly regulated environment. Although the informal sector is an important source of jobs, income, and even housing, its participants lose their full rights as citizens by operating outside the legal economy.

In April 1989, economists from Bangladesh, Egypt, Morocco, the Philippines, Sri Lanka, and Thailand traveled to Peru to observe the work of Hernando de Soto, whose 1989 book *The Other Path* brought international attention to the plight of informal sector participants. The International Center for Economic Growth then asked these six economists to analyze the informal sector in their own countries, examining the relevance of de Soto's approach. The results, except for the study of Egypt, which could not be completed in time for publication, appear in this volume.

The contributors' conclusions provide important lessons for policy makers in developing countries. The country studies show how governments, which often view the informal sector as a problem to be solved by law enforcement and regulation, actually ensure its continuation through misguided policies.

If developing countries are to advance along the development path, they must bring informal sector participants into the legal economy, to share in both the benefits and the costs of formal economic activity. We expect *The Silent Revolution* to bring a new understanding of the role of the informal sector in the development process to both scholars and policy makers.

Nicolás Ardito-Barletta
General Director
International Center for Economic Growth

Panama City, Panama
September 1991

Acknowledgments

We would like to thank a number of people who helped this project at various stages. William P. Fuller, president of the Asia Foundation, must get our first thanks for helping initiate the project while he was still at the Asia Bureau of the U.S. Agency for International Development (AID) and for continuing to give encouragement after he left it. Hernando de Soto and the staff of the Instituto Libertad y Democracia (ILD) extended us extraordinary hospitality during our study-group trip to Peru in the spring of 1989 and gave us invaluable help by briefing us on the history and progress of their work there and organizing a visit to a number of informal housing projects and businesses. David Hagen, Gary Vaughn, and Lance Marsten from the Private Sector Development office of AID's Asia Bureau all provided help at crucial times. Beth Cypser (AID, Cairo Mission) and Joan Walsh (AID, Dhaka Mission) provided equally crucial assistance with communications and other difficulties in Egypt and Bangladesh, respectively. AID's Morocco Mission also provided important assistance.

Nicolás Ardito-Barletta, Robert Hawkins, Jerry LaPittus, Rolf Lüders, and Nancy Truitt provided valuable comments on the manuscript, and Heidi Fritschel and Peter Hayes did an almost superhuman job editing it.

A. LAWRENCE CHICKERING
AND MOHAMED SALAHDINE

Introduction

Since the beginning of the 1970s, the informal sector—or underground economy, as it is commonly known in the industrial countries—has been a subject of increasing attention for scholars and policy makers searching for answers to the challenges that face many developing countries. At first, attempts to understand the large numbers of individual workers and firms doing business "off-the-books," outside of the official, "formal" economy took a negative view. The initial studies, beginning with a 1972 study by the International Labor Organization (ILO), saw the sector as essentially dysfunctional—a problem that needed fixing. But as the failure of the prevailing bureaucratic model of development became clear, a new attitude toward the informal workers and their potential role in development began to appear.

The bureaucratic model sees development—to borrow an analogy from physics—in Newtonian terms, viewing society as a machine and seeking to perfect the machine in an effort to make development happen. This theory has thus tended to focus on what it came to regard as the optimal economic conditions, related to resource endowments, demographic rates, and appropriate technology, among other economic variables. All attention to poverty and the poor focused on dysfunction —or "what the poor lacked." This focus led, in turn, to a regulatory, bureaucratic approach to poverty with an emphasis on "fixing" the poor.

According to this model, the poor in developing countries were a passive and dispirited people, whose dysfunction prevented real self-improvement. Their only hope, therefore, was for state or foreign aid that would provide various social services, including training, health services, housing, and so on. As confidence in this model declined, however, observers in developing countries began to notice something quite different. Faced with a lack of job opportunities in the formal sector, many of the poor were surviving by working for themselves or for family members. Operating outside of the rules and regulations of the formal economy, these businesses were providing a wide variety of important goods and services. The reason for the poverty of these people did not seem to be lack of entrepreneurial initiative.

The effects of the bureaucratic model of development and the role of the informal sector became the subject of heated debate following the publication of Hernando de Soto's 1987 study of the informal sector in Peru, *El Otro Sendero* (published in English as *The Other Path*) (de Soto 1989). De Soto argued that government institutions and policies, supported by an implicit coalition of traditional conservatives and socialists, were systematically excluding the poor from full participation in the economic and social life of Peru. He also argued that people in this excluded "informal sector" were being held back from employing their entrepreneurial skills to improve their own lives, and that they represented a resource that could make an important contribution to economic and social progress.

De Soto's book set off a debate both about Peru and about the role of the informal sector in developing countries everywhere. If he was correct about Peru, the next, obvious question was whether his analysis described that country uniquely or whether it represented an important new theory about developing countries generally. This study was initiated to help answer that question, exploring in several Asian and Near Eastern countries many of the issues and questions he raised in Peru.

The roots of the informal sector problem can be found in the bureaucratic model of development, which focuses on government promotion of large-scale enterprise and advanced technology as the essential tools in a successful development strategy. This model, accepted and followed by many policy makers in developing countries and some scholars until the early 1970s, was influenced by the belief that development depended on transforming traditional society, which theorists believed was retrograde and therefore a "problem" that policy should aim to "overcome." This model looked to bureaucratic enterprises to replace traditional economic and social structures with modern (post-traditional) ones.

This development model was highly Western, rationalistic, and organizational. It had a weak concept of individuals and of citizenship.

It also devalued local community, seeking instead to build a national community linked to nationalism and the nation state.

By playing down the role of individuals in development, the policies associated with bureaucratic industrialization aimed to impose development from the top down. They paid little or no attention to individuals or firms. Unfortunate in itself, this approach brought with it another unfortunate by-product: it often turned into an engine for generating class privileges, both for people lucky enough to get jobs in the bureaucracy administering the whole process and for those lucky enough to get jobs in favored (subsidized) sectors. These sectors, in which enterprises are heavily regulated (if not actually owned) by governments and receive subsidies and other special treatment, often become monopolies living off the public purse.

The bureaucratic/industrialization theory dominated the thinking of some theorists and many policy makers in the 1950s and 1960s, but by the mid-1970s its failures were becoming apparent. The principal difficulty was that it produced contradictory social and economic results. In particular, the dichotomy that was believed to exist between the "modern" and "traditional" sectors seemed less and less relevant as a means of explaining the economic and social structures that were actually emerging in most developing countries.

This dichotomy seemed especially irrelevant compared with another, increasingly evident dualism between the official, formal economy of large enterprises subsidized and encouraged by official government development policies and a second, "real" economy of small entrepreneurs operating beyond the formal economy and its supporting governmental institutions and policies. In the formal economy, the commitment to large-scale industrialization tends to shield enterprises from competition, and they employ relatively small numbers of people. In the other economy, informal enterprises operate in a free, unregulated market. They are dynamic and competitive, and they employ a large and growing fraction of urban populations. In this setting, government subsidies to large enterprises divert resources away from the informal economy and thus actively discriminate against it.

The problems in the industrialization model were especially evident in its failure to account for and accommodate the ongoing exodus from rural areas in developing countries. This exodus bore no relation either to the growth and evolution of large-scale enterprises or to the patterns of visible employment. The industrialization model regarded high percentages of self-employment and employment in small enterprises as indicators of poverty and economic failure. Thus, both theory and policy neglected the mass of microenterprises that has come to employ between 35 and 65 percent of the labor force of most developing countries and produces 20 to 40 percent of gross domestic product (GDP).

In 1972 the International Labor Organization (ILO) initiated inquiry into the informal sector and described it as a large group of enterprises characterized by unobstructed, easy entry into markets; use of local resources; family ownership; small-scale operations; use of appropriate technology with high labor intensity; reliance on training provided outside the formal education system; and operation in unregulated, competitive markets. The approach recommended was basically a social welfare one, stressing training to provide skills.

Since the ILO initiated its inquiry, the bureaucratic model of development has lost much of its following. Although the policies of many developing countries are still based on it, the reason is more political than intellectual. Experience has shown that societies are not Newtonian machines. It has shown that development policy cannot succeed if it focuses on regulating both individual behavior and economic variables from the center (aside from interventions strictly necessary to protect public health and safety). In contrast, post-Newtonian development theory focuses on *nonmaterial* factors—creation of an *environment* for releasing the energies and creativity of ordinary people to work for self-government in economic, social, and political life. This theory has inspired studies of the informal sector that seek to understand how government institutions and policies influence the incentives of participants in informal markets.

Recent studies have shown that microenterprises and the informal sector can be among the most dynamic and healthy sectors in developing economies. As such, they fill an essential role in providing jobs for large numbers of urban workers and adapting both to general patterns of economic growth and to negative shocks. Not only do the informal sector's entrepreneurs survive in the face of government-subsidized large-scale industrialization; their flexibility and adaptability have allowed them to provide essential goods and services on which large-scale, modern manufacturing enterprises depend (Webb 1975:2), such as clothing, weaving, woodwork, repair services, and production of small machines. They can provide these goods and services because of their competitiveness, their proximity, and their low unit costs.

This "real" (that is, unsubsidized) economy diffuses itself organically into diverse pores of the formal economy in myriad production, distribution, and service sectors; and it does so often in the face of masses of bureaucratic regulations. In ideal circumstances, these rules would serve legitimate public regulatory functions, protecting public health and safety. In reality, however, many of them do not serve the public interest in any significant way. They tend to become their own end, inexorably building on themselves, while multiplying transaction costs and obstructing the creativity of many of the most entrepreneurial people in developing countries—who are also often the poorest.

Although it is out of favor among economic theorists, the bureaucratic/industrialization approach to development continues to exercise strong influence over policy makers in many developing countries. In doing so, it has the effect of creating exclusive preserves for large enterprises and the wealthy people who own and control them, protecting many of them from real entrepreneurship and risk taking. This is a tragic mistake that denies many people with genuine entrepreneurial talent the opportunity to improve their own lives. It denies them full participation in the economic and social life of society, while depriving the overall economy of their entrepreneurial talents.

Besides the important functions that informal activities perform for the economic system, the spontaneous enterprise of informal entrepreneurs provides remarkable socioeconomic training in and preparation for modern (post-traditional) forms of social and economic life. In fact, the creative, individualistic activities found in the informal sector almost certainly provide a better social and psychological introduction to the rationalist individualism characteristic of modern economic life than do the large bureaucratic, hierarchical structures promoted by development theory and policy.

Providing an environment conducive to entrepreneurship requires establishing economic and legal institutions that define the rights and responsibilities of economic actors. Such institutions define the basic terms of economic and social relations among whole peoples. Encouraging entrepreneurship means creating a more open, competitive environment for the economy as a whole. As the former Eastern bloc governments have come recently (and dramatically) to understand, the most important institution for establishing such an environment is the right of private property, which creates clearly defined interests that will encourage people to take risks.

These reforms will redirect the entrepreneurial energies of those in the formal sector away from the mercantilist patterns of the present toward more productive activities, and they will greatly expand the dynamic and creative potential in microenterprises and the informal sector.

The case studies in this book are concerned with a series of questions and issues relating to this dynamic world of informal microenterprise: How important is the informal sector in economic and social life? Who is in it? Which model better describes it—the bureaucratic/ Newtonian model or the self-governing/entrepreneurial one? Why do individuals and firms choose to remain informal, off-the-books, avoiding both the costs and benefits of participation in the official, formal economy? How is informality affected by policy? What policy reforms might be enacted to encourage this dynamic sector?

The question of reforms involves several very different issues. One aspect of reform entails repealing policies and regulations that obstruct entrepreneurship and enterprise without serving any legitimate public regulatory purpose. A second kind of reform involves cessation of policies that assist and allocate resources to certain "favored" sectors (especially large enterprises), thus implicitly discriminating against people in other sectors (especially microenterprises). Finally there are reforms that involve public or private efforts to empower people to contribute to economic and social development. The best examples of this are programs that provide credit to small entrepreneurs, such as the Bank Rakyat Indonesia, ACCION in Latin America, and the Grameen Bank in Bangladesh (see Muzammel Huq and Maheen Sultan's chapter herein on the latter). Other examples might include programs that encourage self-governing institutions to expand the informal workers' participation in all dimensions of political and social life, as well as control over their own lives.

Additional questions concern the political implications of the growing self-awareness of the informal sector for policy makers and the policy environment. And finally, the contributors to this book explore how people in the informal sector actually live and work—how they exist in the economy, cut off from the main financial and legal institutions that facilitate commerce. Through individual portraits of people who work in the sector, the contributors reveal what the informal sector is—who is in it and why. These vignettes show more clearly than any abstract discussion a sector whose health and vitality are far more important than the dysfunction and pathology often emphasized in regard to it.

The Experience of Peru

The background and guide for these investigations is the work of Hernando de Soto and the Instituto Libertad y Democracia (ILD) and their ground-breaking studies of the informal sector in Peru. De Soto's extraordinary findings, summarized in his best-selling book *The Other Path*, greatly accelerated concern about the informal sector in the 1980s. In the book, de Soto documents the existence of an enormous informal sector—50 percent of the labor force working full-time, with another 10 percent working part-time, off-the-books. Together, they produce nearly 40 percent of Peru's GDP. In particular, de Soto found that 47 percent of construction and 95 percent of public transportation in the capital city of Lima are informal. Of the city's

331 markets, 57 were constructed by the government; the other 274 were constructed informally.

In analyzing why such a large fraction of Peru's labor force would choose to operate outside and beyond the law, de Soto concluded that the reason was the excessive regulation imposed by the enormous bureaucratic state, which was effectively excluding Peru's informals from full participation in the country's economic life. His most-cited finding was drawn from his simulation of registering a small garment business with two sewing machines. Working six hours a day, he found it took 289 days and several bribes to go through all of the government departments and bureaus and comply with all of the regulatory requirements. The same procedures took three-and-a-half hours in Florida and four hours in New York. He concluded that most small businesspeople and entrepreneurs judge that the costs of participating in Peru's formal economy exceed any possible benefits. So they work off-the-books.

Another of his findings, which was equally dramatic, concerned the difficulties of gaining title to undeveloped land. The issue is important because the willingness to invest and improve land is very much dependent on the owner's having secure title. In Peru, when de Soto began his studies in the early 1980s, it took an estimated six years and eleven months, working eight hours a day, to complete the 205 bureaucratic steps—involving fifty-one different departments and bureaus—to get secure title.

In choosing to be informal, people give up the benefits of formal institutions established to facilitate commerce. They lose access to formal credit markets; to courts, which can enforce impersonal contracts; and to formal insurance institutions and pension benefits. De Soto even concluded that since the Peruvian government collects more than half of its tax revenues from informal sources, the informal sector pays more taxes than the formal sector in that country.

Beyond these specific conclusions and the policy recommendations they imply, de Soto's work has larger ideological and philosophical implications, which have changed the nature of the political debate in Peru and may do so in other places. He argues, for reasons analogous to a famous remark that Chesterton once made about Christianity, that the debate between "capitalism" and "socialism" has had no meaning in Peru. The problem, Chesterton said, was not that Christianity had been tried and found wanting, but that it had been found difficult and not tried. Despite claims to the contrary from all sides, de Soto argues, there has been almost no capitalism in Peru. Its bureaucratically protected private sector is *mercantilist*, not capitalist; the only real capitalists in the country, he concludes finally, are the informals and the poor.

This argument implies that Peru's economic and political system has been the practical handmaiden of an implicit coalition between the oligarchic mercantile class on the right and the socialists on the left—both fighting for centralization of power and authority, and all on behalf of the "the people."

Given these conclusions, it is easy to see how de Soto has exerted great influence on the economic and political debate across the political spectrum in Peru. A year or more before the presidential election in the spring of 1990, all political parties in that extremely polarized country had embraced his conclusions about the importance of opening economic and social opportunities for the informal workers. The Marxist Alfonso Barantes announced in April 1990 that he wanted de Soto as his running mate; the conservative candidate Mario Vargas Llosa wrote the foreword to de Soto's book; and after the election de Soto became one of the closest advisers of the winner Alberto Fujimori.

As observers watched these extraordinary events unfold in Peru, they increasingly asked to what extent de Soto's analysis might describe conditions in other places. For if it did, it would change the way we look at the interaction between politics and economics in developing countries. If his was a general theory, applicable to many countries, it would become possible to develop an economic and social theory of development that would integrate both equality and growth into a common vision, one that could stimulate an extraordinary and unique political consensus behind it.

The project that led to this book aimed at a preliminary investigation of the role of the informal sector in six Asian and Near Eastern countries. Inspired in conversations with the Asia–Near East Bureau of the U.S. Agency for International Development (AID), the project was designed to review de Soto's methodology for use in other countries, to refine the methodology (as necessary), and then to apply it to a cross section of countries in Asia and the Near East. The countries we chose are Bangladesh, Egypt, Morocco, the Philippines, Sri Lanka, and Thailand. All except Egypt are represented here. (The study of Egypt, by Samir Toubar, was not completed in time to go to press with the rest of the book. We do, however, discuss his findings in our conclusion.)

Because the comparison with Peru was at the heart of our objective, the project began with a five-day trip to Peru by the contributors to visit the ILD, hear presentations on its analysis of different problems and issues, and visit different informal sector industries and firms as background to developing a research design. In a series of seminars, the ILD staff focused especially on business registration, housing, and broad issues of rule making in governance. Our site visits took us to several housing projects, a small machine tool factory, and a factory for making souvenirs. We then traveled to Washington, where we participated in a two-day seminar with AID officials and outside experts to define a research and publication project that would explore in other countries the principal issues investigated by the ILD in Peru.

The Problem of Definition

The first issue in designing this project was one of definition. The history of concern about the informal sector has been greatly confused by multiple definitions of the term.

We have mentioned the ILO's definition. Many other studies rely on similar multicriteria definitions, wherein the informal sector is distinguished from the formal sector by labor intensity, minimal employment of capital or technology, minimal legal barriers to entry, and clientele of limited solvency (Hugon and Deblé 1985; Charmes 1986). The purpose of studies using such definitions is to examine the informal sector at the macroeconomic level.

In such approaches, employment in modern enterprises is compared with total labor-force participation rates to reveal informal sector employment. Jacques Charmes, for example, estimated total employment in the Maghreb's informal sector by adding together five categories of employment—independent workers, some assistants, apprentices, and employers and wage earners of enterprises having fewer than five employees. He then compared the result with full labor-force participation rates and concluded that 57 percent of the nonagricultural work force in the Maghreb was employed informally (Charmes 1986).

Similarly, S. V. Sethuraman (1976) distinguishes five different employment sectors—industrial production, construction, transportation, retail trade, and services—in proposing criteria for membership in the informal sector. By his criteria, a production unit in the construction industry belongs to the informal sector if it fulfills one or more of the following eight conditions:

- It employs no more than ten people (including part-time and occasional workers).

- It avoids social regulations.

- It does not work at fixed hours.

- It employs workers from the household of the head of the enterprise.

- It has an itinerant nature or occupies provisional premises.

- It does not use electrical or mechanical energy.

- It does not use credit from formal institutions.

- It employs workers with fewer than six years of schooling.

Other researchers group informal activities in three categories according to the degree of complexity of their accounting systems: enterprises with no accounting system, those with a rudimentary accounting system, and those with an elaborate system. These three levels are correlated with levels of development and size of production units: the more accurate and controlled the accounting system, the greater the indication that a firm is fulfilling conditions of passage into the modern, formal sector.

Finally, we must mention the Marxist vision, which proposes a functional definition of the informal sector. In the Marxist view, informality is the product of the unequal development of capitalism in nonindustrialized urban areas. Far from disturbing the system, the informal sector, in the Marxist view, plays an essential role in providing a low-wage reserve of labor. Exerting downward pressure on wages, informal activities encourage payment of substandard wages and contribute to maintaining capitalist power over the poorer classes (Morice 1983; Charmes 1982; Hugon and Deblé 1985).

It is interesting to note that all of these definitions reflect the same "modernist," Newtonian rationalism, which sees healthy development in large, rationalistic enterprises and sees only pathology and dysfunction in the small, unplanned activities that are described by these views of the informal sector. All of these criteria portray popular enterprises in the informal sector as confused economic activities, which are neglected in large economic aggregates and which are only weakly integrated into the labor market (see Vekemans and Ismael 1969; Vekemans, Giusti, and Ismael 1970). In this essential respect, the Marxist and non-Marxist views of the informal sector begin to converge.

Choice of definition is obviously crucial in selecting strategies for reform. Without a clear definition, it is impossible to be clear about what "the problem" is, or what to do about it. In general, definitions tend to focus on either functional attributes (size or complexity of operation, for instance) or legal status. Those who choose functional attributes tend to worry about the informal sector as an expression of poverty, and their policy responses often focus on providing various forms of direct assistance to the sector. Those, like de Soto, who focus on legal status—with enterprises operating outside formal legal and financial institutions defined as informal regardless of size or complexity—tend to worry about institutional issues. The latter see the informal sector as evidence of institutional failure and focus their proposals for reform on improving the institutional setting. They seek to encourage participation in the larger economic and social life of the society, especially in the rule-making process, and aim to make the government more open and accountable.

These two approaches often see poverty in different ways. The first group, emphasizing pathology and dysfunction, sees the poor as a *proletariat*, requiring help. The second group, epitomized by de Soto, tends to see the poor as *entrepreneurs*, needing only policies that do not discriminate against them. There is one approach that borrows from both of these: credit programs, such as the Grameen Bank, described in Chapter 6, which offer direct help, but in a manner based on acceptance of the self-governing, entrepreneurial capacities of even the poorest people.

The two different approaches described above highlight the ultimate question about the locus of the problem: is it the dysfunctions and pathology of the informal sector or the institutions of the larger society that limit informal entrepreneurs' opportunities to work for their own economic and social progress?

If one sees informality as pathology, then recommendations for help inevitably come with prescriptions for centrally planned assistance. The great virtue of Hernando de Soto's work in Peru has been to bring to light a new vision of poverty and the poor. If his vision is correct (or to the extent it is), an important way will have been found to provide opportunities to the poorest sectors of most developing countries for their integration into the economic and social mainstream. No miracle cure to development will have been found, but important impediments may then be cleared to encourage development by working, saving, and investing. The chapters that follow explore these and other issues.

The Structure of the Studies

Because of the difficulty of trying to produce useful comparative results, we, as coeditors, developed a detailed memorandum outlining the topics we hoped each contributor would address.

We asked contributors to begin with the issue of definition. Most contributors adopted a definition based on legal status, but Chapter 6 also defines informality on the basis of firm size and income level. We then asked for a summary of conclusions about why people choose to be outside the formal economy. And we asked if there had been an increase or reduction in the size of the sector and for possible explanations.

Next, we hoped to give a "human," personal picture of the informal workers—who they are, how they got where they are, their capacities, and their potential. So we asked the contributors to conduct personal interviews with people in the informal sector in their country and to record the highlights. This discussion is made more vivid by the photographs that appear in the book.

We then sought to address the thorny issue of measurement. Given limited resources and methodological problems, we asked authors to investigate the available literature to come up with broad magnitudes of employment and productivity in the informal sector. Our purpose was to understand how the informal sector relates to the formal economy and especially to see whether the informal sector represents a significant phenomenon in these countries, or whether it is actually marginal and insignificant.

Estimating the size of the informal sector again raises the problem of definition. In Peru the ILD found that certain sectors, such as transportation, were commonly assumed not to be in the informal sector because bus drivers need a license plate and a driver's license. But since the law outlaws private provision of public bus service, even licensed private buses must operate informally. (Informal drivers acquire routes by invading them.)

The larger issue here is the extent of regulation in society. If a society is entangled in bureaucratic rules, it is likely that people will obey some regulations and ignore others. But this makes such people ultimately vulnerable if the state (perhaps prodded by an individual) decides to punish them. The only way to avoid this situation is to have simple rules and laws that expedite compliance and operate from the underlying presumption that people should be free to do what they want unless there is some good reason why they should not. Many countries, including Peru, proceed from the opposite presumption.

The next section of each chapter analyzes the causes of informality—why people remain informal—which are substantially related to the costs of being formal. We encouraged the participants to use, as much as possible, the same methodology as the ILD used in Peru. This meant considering first the costs (in time and money) of registering (or making formal) a small business, like the small garment factory used in the ILD's simulation. It also meant evaluating the costs of staying in business—that is, of complying with the regulatory requirements associated with legal, formal status.

We also asked the contributors to consider the tax issue. How important is tax avoidance? What taxes do informal workers pay or not pay? Informal enterprises tend to pay excise and sales taxes, which are most of the tax bite in developing countries; but they tend not to pay income taxes, which are relatively unimportant in those countries.

Informal workers also tend to have to pay bribes in lieu of taxes. This discussion addresses the argument that most people are informal only because they want to avoid taxes.

After considering the costs informal workers choose to avoid by staying out of the formal sector, the contributors research and quantify the costs of remaining informal. Probably most important are exclusion from formal legal and credit institutions and the difficulty of gaining title to land. Quantifying such costs involves estimating, as the ILD did in Peru, how long it takes for informal sector participants to gain legal title to unimproved land. By preventing people from gaining title to land, informality may keep them from acquiring collateral that would allow them to get credit. A major source of credit used to start new businesses comes from home mortgages, which require a clear title to land. Titles are especially necessary for the poor with small businesses, who have severe difficulties getting unsecured loans.

Next, we asked the authors to consider political and institutional issues. Specifically, we asked them to consider the problem of discrimination against the informal workers and poor people generally, in the light of how rules are made in their countries. Are there many opportunities for people to express their views on rules and regulations between elections? In Peru, for example, the overwhelming majority of rules in that country are made not by legislatures with accountability to voters, but by bureaucratic fiat. We wanted to understand the political implications of the institutional processes the contributors described.

Finally, we encouraged them to propose solutions, separated into two broad categories. The first category includes "negative" reforms, which would remove or eliminate barriers that have the effect of excluding the informal workers from full economic and social participation in their country. These reforms would reduce the high costs of formality and thus encourage full participation in the formal sector. Besides asking authors for a current agenda for reform, we also asked them to discuss any policy reforms that have been enacted in the past to reduce informality.

The second is made up of "positive" reforms, which would transform old institutions or create new ones to provide real services that the informals and the poor are not getting at present. We asked what key institutional change or series of changes would empower informal workers to gain control over their own lives? Examples include credit to small borrowers, such as is made available by the Grameen Bank, or decentralized, competitive, self-governing institutions to deliver public goods and services, such as in health or education.

Finally, we asked the contributors to consider the political implications of all of these issues—what political forces support the current policy mix in their countries? How might those forces change if, as in Peru, the informal sector developed a self-conscious understanding of its problems and possible solutions?

Although the contributors did not address these issues to the same extent or in the same way, their chapters shed extraordinary light on topics of great interest. The results of their investigations follow.

The Informal Sector in Morocco:
The Failure of Legal Systems?

To the best of our knowledge, no systematic study exists of Morocco's informal sector. The Moroccan Ministry of Planning uses the International Labor Office's 1972 definition of this sector based on multiple criteria, but it is of little use in understanding this complex phenomenon (Salahdine 1985, 1988a, b). Many existing studies of education, training, and employment provide interesting information on labor, but they do not illuminate the existence of informal employment, nor do they provide an analytical system that would help evaluate the size and importance of informal labor (Ministry of Planning 1980–1989). The Moroccan Ministry of Economic Affairs and Office of Statistics have only just begun to take an interest in the issue and to ask questions about how to study it. They are especially interested in understanding the size and importance of the informal sector and how to integrate it into the country's national income accounts.[1]

While awaiting more rigorous definitions of the informal sector, different government ministries and departments have adopted crude definitions, usually based on firm size, capitalization, and unclassified professional categories, including apprenticeship or employment in a family business.[2] According to one definition drawn from these criteria, the informal sector accounted for 69 percent of active urban employment in 1971 and 75 percent in 1982. Although informal activities predominate in all sectors, by this definition 85 percent of all workers employed in the service and trade sectors would be informal, as would 73 percent of artisans. Moreover, the average annual increase in employment in the informal sector (6.9 percent) would be twice that in the formal sector (3.3 percent).

These extremely high figures reveal the importance of the informal sector in Morocco. Nevertheless, these numbers are based on calculations that suffer from serious methodological weaknesses. First, they include businesses that are difficult to classify as informal even if they employ no more than ten persons (for example, medical offices, law firms, and accounting services; pharmacies; wholesale and jewelry businesses). If lack of legal registration serves as the hallmark of informality, size of a business may or may not reveal registration status. Many businesses with fewer than ten employees are registered (and thus are not informal), and many larger businesses are operated off-the-books. Second, these numbers are based on statistics on licensed businesses and do not take into account statistical gaps and inconsistencies. Third, and most important, these numbers do not include mobile economic activities not registered according to official commercial regulations. Thus, a serious effort to understand the informal sector must do more than merely count small artisanal units that are visible and prosperous and have their own premises. Defining the informal sector in this way enormously understates its importance, especially in a country in which artisanal activities are age-old and well regulated.

The informal sector is most important as a development and policy problem when it is defined as unregistered activities undertaken outside and beyond the reach of official regulations, and often carried on from the home, with no official business location. Nevertheless, these activities contribute a great deal to economic and social progress. They are especially appealing to rural immigrants and working-class entrepreneurs, satisfying survival needs and providing opportunities for entrepreneurship.

But the informal sector also reveals the difficulties that arise when the state tries to implement rules taken from other legal systems, rules that are the product of other distinct histories. The relationship between a people and its laws—a people's concept of legality—is the crucial factor in determining the contours of the informal sector. Unfortunately, current legislation in Morocco does not conform to working-class realities or to the fundamental interests of small-scale entrepreneurs.

The state's tardiness in addressing this issue is related to the difficulties it has encountered in gathering precise information on activities that, from the state's perspective, are important primarily because they have escaped social accountability and state control. But to neglect these informal activities, and to fail to understand the connection between these micro-units, the artisan sector, and the national and international economic systems because of methodological difficulties or material costs, is to avoid real contact with a problem of tremendous importance. This shortcoming is all the more harmful because these economic activities are not merely transitional; they are a long-term component of the Moroccan economy.

This chapter examines the informal sector as a full, legitimate, and crucial partner in the development of the Moroccan economy. In particular, it looks closely at the informal transportation industry and the informal construction industry, which primarily builds working-class housing. Because both of these activities make an important contribution to the Moroccan economy, they highlight the economic and social significance of the informal sector and the state's attitudes toward and policies on the sector. Finally, this exploration will suggest important institutional and policy reforms that would encourage informal employers and workers to attain full formal participation in Morocco's economic and social life.

Method of Inquiry

Ideally, these two informal industries would be examined by selecting a random sample representing the characteristics of the whole population. Unfortunately, a complete list of informal truckers or clandestine builders from which to draw a sample was not available. Likewise, interviewing all the informal truckers in a given geographical area was not possible. Even had it been, the inquiry would have taken on a bureaucratic and administrative character that would have hindered the attainment of its objective.

The method chosen was the open-ended interview. This method of in-depth interviewing was not without its problems, however. It was a slow, deliberate process, requiring several visits, often just to say hello or confirm an idea or a thought. In this way, trust developed between interviewer and interviewee. It was recognized that distrust on the part of interviewees does not always take the form of an explicit refusal to answer questions but may translate into erroneous and deceptive information.

Because questionnaires may create suspicion and fear in interviewees, considerably distorting the relationship between interviewer and subject, we talked to the interviewees informally, without transcribing or recording their remarks. It was only after the interview that we proceeded to reconstruct the discussion in order to evaluate it and draw out the principal themes.

Unauthorized Transport of Goods

Since July 1985, when the private sector began to transport passengers—a service previously controlled exclusively by the state—professional carriers have also shown growing interest in the informal transport of merchandise. This has led to heated debate in the government and within Parliament on the subject. Some observers believe that the public system for the transport of goods is threatened by privatization as well. Others think that the official monopoly of the National Office of Transport (ONT) in the goods transport sector should be called into question. Underlining the need to adapt transport to user needs and to the system of production and trade, the independent weekly *La Vie économique* has called on the state to deregulate the transportation system. Finally, other observers accuse the parallel system for the transport of goods of fostering the regression and anarchy found in the transport sector. The few truckers sanctioned by the Ministry of Transport denounce the informal transport of goods as a dangerous phenomenon that should be excluded from the transport market.

To understand the signficance of this controversy, one must review the framework of the regulations for the transport of goods in Morocco. According to these regulations, the ONT is the sole charter agent for the transport of goods in Morocco (royal decree of November 12, 1963, and Official Bulletin No. 2914, September 4, 1968, p. 899). Created in 1963 as the Central Transport Office, this public establishment theoretically has a monopoly over the chartering and coordination of ground transport. In carrying out its obligatory function, the ONT designates the trucker or truckers who will serve the users of public tranport. Indeed, transporters are not allowed to carry goods for a third party unless they possess a loading form issued by the ONT.

Article 24 of the November 1963 royal decree establishing the ONT specifies sanctions for all persons who compete with the ONT in its role as the sole charter agent of truck transport. Article 24 forbids even opening an office for the loading of trucks without the prior authorization of the Ministry of Transport. Anyone wishing to open a goods transport agency must register and obtain a special authorization card for each vehicle used by the firm. A request for an authorization agreement must be filed with the provincial governor's office, which, after noting its opinion, sends the request to the Ministry of Transport. The ministry transmits the request to its Public Transport Service in Rabat, which then submits it to the Technical Commission on Transportation. If the commission approves the agreement, it then decides on the number, nature, and capacity of the vehicles authorized, as well as their area of operation. The commission, which makes decisions based on majority vote, is composed of the prime minister and representatives of the following government departments: the Ministries of Transport, Equipment, Interior, Justice, Finance, Post, Telephones and Telecommunication, Tourism, and Agriculture and the Department of Ground Transport. The authorization agreements are valid for seven years and renewable under the same conditions required for their original issuance. The prescriptions of the agreement can be suspended, modified, or withdrawn by the Technical Commission on Transportation (article 4 of the royal decree of 1967).

Finally, article 4 of the royal decree of 1967 stipulates that anyone running a firm for the transport of goods that is not appropriately registered or that uses an unauthorized vehicle is liable to a fine of between 120 and 1,200 dirham (although, in fact, the unauthorized transport of goods dominates the goods transport market).

Transport regulations distinguish between two kinds of vehicles: those with permits for circulation (APCs), and those without permits for circulation (SPCs). A circulation permit is required when the contents of a truck weigh more than 8 metric tons. The permit notes the weight, nature, and itinerary of the goods each vehicle is authorized to transport. To obtain a permit, a private trucker must file both a request attesting to his turnover and a registered copy of the truck lease with the director of ground transport in the Ministry of Transport, who decides whether to grant the permit. If the permit for circulation is refused by the director, the petitioner can appeal to the Ministry of

One form of informal transport is the horse cart for hire.

Transport, but only during the one-month period after he is notified of the decision. Article 7 of the royal decree supporting the law of August 5, 1968, lays down penalties for all violations of these legal provisions. They include fines as well as seizure and sale of the vehicle.

The fleet of SPCs (without permits for circulation) is estimated at 200,000, carrying a total payload of more than 300,000 metric tons. The slowly increasing number of APCs (with permits for circulation) is just over 6,000, carrying a total payload of 150,000 metric tons.

Despite its purported monopoly over the transport of all Moroccan goods, the ONT is in fact confined to freight generated by administrative and public establishments, or only 19.3 percent of goods transport. Thus, illegal transport may be three times as great as official transport.

An examination of the modes of transport by product transported reveals that unauthorized carriers dominate the transport of foodstuffs and perishable foods. Freight transported by the ONT includes mainly bulk materials—primarily minerals—which constitute 85 percent of its tonnage, 75 percent of its total kilometers, and 76 percent of its turnover. This specialization of the ONT, and its neglect of nonbulk loads, explains in part the importance of informal transport.

What should be done? Should the clandestine transporters of goods be accorded legal status through the provision of circulation permits for certain goods in certain regions? Should the public transport sector be restructured and privatized to better serve user needs, and should the ONT's right to serve as the sole charter agent for public transport be withdrawn? Or should the role of the office be reinforced by giving it more resources to crack down on informal transporters to remind them of the existing rules and regulations? Although choosing one of these options is essential, Morocco, caught between an official discourse favoring privatization and the omnipresence of the state, is at a crossroads. It is finding it difficult to take the first step to implement policies that would privatize and deregulate its economy.

Until such a step is taken, the informal, and theoretically illegal, transportation of goods is tolerated, and clandestine transporters pass through the web of official regulations, taking over the roads and quietly dividing strategic territories in the cities among themselves. They carefully choose where to park their vehicles, often through a judicious economic calculation. Discretion is essential to avoid the authorities and still to park in a location of high potential demand, picking up the business resulting from the failure of the official transport system. Moreover, to retain these valued parking spots in major cities, many vehicles pay off the authorities daily. Some even strike up relationships with the authorities, but this should not minimize the stakes of the game and the tension maintained by the administration and the bureaucracy between the police and the transporters.

Almost all the truckers interviewed were rural migrants with no academic training. But the severity of their needs had taught them to confront difficult and unexpected situations. The typical illegal transporter is about forty years old, with a face marked by a lack of sleep and exposure to sun, and with an uncultivated manner.

Eager for freedom, practically adventurers, most truckers had not practiced another urban trade before acquiring their trucks. Their trucks were bought with cash, the price ranging from 80,000 dirham (US$10,000) to 150,000 dirham (US$18,500), but at times reaching 200,000 dirham (US$25,000). More recent entrants into the trade, of course, paid more for their trucks. These high initial costs reveal that the acquisition of a truck is a real barrier to entry into the profession, all the more because only about 25 percent of drivers seek to overcome this problem by purchasing used trucks. Used trucks are not prized, and the rare acquisition of this type of truck is made through the informal communication—the Arab "telephone system"—in parking areas.

As for the source of start-up capital, interviews with twenty transporters revealed that financing is obtained primarily from the sale of a small property such as land or a house (60 percent) or from a family member in the form of a loan (25 percent). Other sources of capital are personal savings (10 percent) and loans (5 percent). Often insolvent and in a precarious situation because of their illegal status, transporters cannot benefit from the official banking system, which addresses, before all else, the needs of large enterprises and rarely those of small enterprises—and then only when they possess guarantees and collateral.

Most truckers operate independently and own their vehicles. Drivers' fees are a fixed but minimal percentage (usually 6 percent) for each trip and usually do not cover maintenance of the truck or goods. The distance to be covered and the weight of the goods determine in part the price of the trip. For the 120 kilometers (75 miles) between Rabat and Meknes, for example, the price can vary between 350 dirham (US$44) and 1,500 dirham (US$188). The nature of the merchandise is taken into consideration as well. Not insured against theft or damage, informal carriers avoid or charge extra for the transport of fragile or perishable goods. But in the end, the price is set according to the type of customer: regular customers receive the market price; occasional users are charged more.

Steadily increasing but unavoidable costs that also affect the transport sector are the high vehicle-insurance fees, which range from 6,000 dirham (US$750) to 8,000 dirham (US$1,000) per year, depending on the age and type of vehicle. Dependent on the international market for their equipment and fuel, transport activities also suffer from the repercussions of price increases. Between 1987 and 1989, the price of diesel fuel rose 18 percent, insurance went up 35 percent, and the price of other materials rose by 50 percent. Transport revenue, however, remains unstable, and half the truckers interviewed claimed not to have saved for later investment. Consequently, cushions against vehicle depreciation or repairs are practically nonexistent. Even worse, most of the vehicles owned by those interviewed are barely running, the average age of their trucks being eight years.

Informal carriers thus must take into account many factors in setting their prices because of the competitive nature of the sector. In a healthy, competitive market, however, the drivers who prevail are those who know the most appropriate route for each type of good and those who are able to avoid the routes taken by the official carriers and to evaluate the attitudes of the police along the route. Paradoxically, despite the problems just outlined, almost all the carriers interviewed (92 percent) remain committed to the transport sector and do not wish to leave it. Their one gamble is that they will be able to save for repairs to their trucks, a risky bet in that regulatory constraints are excessive and unavoidable.

Still, all the people interviewed who use informal carriers praised the truckers' availability, flexibility, competitive prices, and the provisions for payment that they extend to their regular customers in such sectors of the economy as agriculture (grain, wheat, canned foods, and vegetable oil) and the wholesale and retail trade. Informal carriers even monopolize the transport of goods over short and medium distances (less than 200 kilometers, or 124 miles).

Over 80 percent of the establishments in the food, wholesale trade, and retail trade sectors claim openly that they make regular use of informal carriers. Fifty-two percent cited the availability and the quality of the informal carriers' service, 30 percent emphasized cost and provisions for payment, and 18 percent revealed that informal transport allows them to avoid investing in their own fleets and to save handling costs.

For these enterprises the recourse to informal carriers is the only solution to their transport problems. Even though the average size of their loads is greater than 40 metric tons, these enterprises are unable to acquire special vehicles (for example, dump trucks weighing more than 15 metric tons, or refrigerator trucks). Moreover, they can neither use the ONT (unavailable), nor buy their own fleet (forbidden by legislation), nor obtain a permit for circulation (because of the administrative difficulties). Thus, they are forced to use informal carriers and their small trucks instead of heavier, more appropriate vehicles for loads of great size.

The attitude of the state toward informal transport is deliberately ambiguous. At times, the local authorities help themselves to what is available in the parking areas. They seize the driver's license of illegal carriers; confiscate their vehicles, which then cannot be recovered without payment of a fine; or put the highway patrol on their trails. The highway patrol then drains truckers' profits by imposing fines and impounding trucks.

At times, there is a lull in the hostilities. The informal carriers make their way about without restrictions and crisscross the country without trouble. Truckers have adapted to this contradictory situation and seem to hold no grudges. During periods of respite, they go about their work without thinking of the problems that may come the next day. When the authorities wage their assaults, the truckers do not allow themselves to be surprised. When police checkpoints are spotted, signals—such as honks of the horn, flashing headlights, and messages left in cafés along the road—are passed on by the first drivers intercepted.

For their part, the authorities are conscious of the positive role that these carriers play in the distribution of goods. Thus, they have never waged a full-scale offensive against informal carriers. Moreover, they never resort to systematic, continual repression. Indeed, during the peak seasons for some agricultural products, public enterprises even call on their services, not the least the ONT itself, which gives informal carriers temporary one-day permits. For example, the convoy of marchers and goods during the "Green March" for the liberation of the Western Sahara was made possible by the effects of so-called clandestine carriers.

Thus, on the whole, the usefulness of the informal carriers cannot be denied, and the existing transport regulations, which date from the 1930s, cannot be applied in the current context without substantial modification. There is, therefore, an urgent need to update the legal framework to reflect the changes that have taken place in the transport sector. Such a process might begin by facilitating the granting of permits for circulation to transporters with suitable vehicles. Why limit the right to use suitable vehicles for the private transport of goods? Why not legalize informal carriers and grant transport licenses upon demand, thereby allowing the use of trucks that can carry payloads of more than 8 metric tons, especially since 75 percent of informal carriers already have capacities of greater than 15 metric tons?

Informal Construction

Morocco has a housing shortage of over 1 million units. Officially, about 50,000 units must be completed annually, although, in reality, 200,000 units need to be completed annually to close the gap.

To remedy this paucity of low-income "popular" housing, the Moroccan government has taken several important steps, but they remain insufficient to meet the needs caused by explosive urbanization. Nonetheless, clandestine informal construction has produced happy and unexpected outcomes. This construction is based on the sale of parcels of land (around 100 square meters or 1,076 square feet) lacking basic infrastructure (water, electricity, and sewage) to individuals who build permanent homes on them. But such real estate transactions are illegal, because legislation forbids the sale of lots judged not fit for the construction of dwellings.

The proliferation of clandestine housing can be explained by several factors:

- A disequilibrium between the supply of and demand for land in the urban zones where construction is legally authorized.

- Real estate speculation.

- An absence of documentation for urban planning. Some large urban zones are not yet covered by development plans. When plans do exist, they are either outdated or out of harmony with realities in the cities.

- Legal constraints affecting the supply of land and preventing immediate transactions. Laws governing land belonging to tribal groups (collective lands) or to social or religious organizations that is legally inalienable (habous lands) are examples. The inalienable nature of these different categories of land, often located on the edges of cities and covering more than 80,000 hectares (almost 20,000 square miles), makes their transfer an extremely long, complex process.

- Lack of requirements for construction permits or subdivision permits during the sale registration.

The construction of so-called clandestine housing is not really clandestine at all. The term should be used with caution because it tends to imply underground activities unaffected by all forms of regulation or organization. In fact, no one is ignorant of these mushrooming dwellings, which are built with astonishing speed in plain view of everyone. Nor is the occupation of these dwellings spontaneous; they are permanent homes, even though they do not happen to conform to certain regulations for urban planning. They are bought from subdividers, or real estate agents, on the unofficial market for land by workers in search of low-cost housing ready for occupancy. Indeed, on the whole, the informal low-income housing sector could be characterized as illegal for both construction and occupancy.

It is also an area of almost daily confrontation between public authorities and people of modest means who want those authorities to recognize another manner of building and living. To gain shelter and secure the right to property, these social actors present the authorities with a *fait accompli*, attempting to alter official regulations and to upset the urban regulatory process, whose aims are to incorporate disparate groups. In effect, the urban regulatory system subscribes to a rigid notion of how housing should function and grow, and this notion corresponds with so-called formal housing and a certain model of consumption. All opposition to this model is attacked.

But the flame of resistance carried by the producers of unregulated housing is not easily extinguished. The number of illegal low-income dwellings is growing, and the Ministry of the Interior estimates reveal that they house nearly 1 million people in Morocco, in cities with more than 30,000 inhabitants. In the city of Fez (with 500,000 residents and a population growth rate of 35 percent), for example, clandestine dwellings housed 5 percent of the urban population in 1971 and now house 30 percent of the population. Located to the north of the *medina* (Ain Haroun, Dhar Richa), to the west (Zouagha, Ben Souda), to the south (Aouinat Hajjaj, Mont Fleuri), and to the east (Ain Nokbi, Sidi Boukida, and Jnanates), clandestine dwellings are spread around the edges of the city of Fez. Ain Nokbi has more than 5,000 residents, and the population of Shrij Gnaoua was 2,500 in 1976 and more than 3,200 in 1989. In the southwest, in Zouagha, the proliferation of unregulated dwellings near the water table, which feeds the Fez River, is putting the population at serious risk of consuming contaminated water. Several demolition campaigns have been waged against these dwellings by the authorities, without great success.

Because of its location and the size of its population, the district of Jnanates offers the best examples of clandestine housing. Located in the northeastern part of the city, a short walk from some of the major gates to the *medina* (Bab Khoukha, Bab Sidi Boujida, Bab Ftouh, and Bab El Guissa), Jnanates is crossed by principal routes from Taza to the east of the city, from Taounate and Quazzane to the north, and from the center of the city to the south. Because Jnanates lies between the city and the nearby northeast region, close to the Hyayna tribes and the Rif Mountains, it attracts thousands of peasants from the countryside, who are looking for work and a roof over their heads at a reasonable price, even though it may mean constructing their homes on agricultural lands.

As its name indicates (*jnanates* is the plural of *jnane*, which means garden), the district of Jnanates in the past supplied city residents with flowers, vegetables, and fruits. It was also a place of relaxation and fun for the urban population during the spring. Today, the district preserves only the names of the past owners of the gardens. Because it is situated on a slope, it is almost inaccessible to vehicles, which endangers the district in the event of accident or fire. Travel on foot is not easy, and the roads' steep slopes and lack of pavement are a nuisance for pedestrians and make walking unbearable when it rains. Finally, the unusual and even bizarre appearance of the buildings reflects the lack of respect for the law evident in their construction.

The population of the Jnanates district has been estimated at more than 70,000, or more than 10 percent of the total population of Fez. This disorderly district, which seems to be blossoming, offers an exceptional portrait of dynamic, busy teams of workers bargaining and building day and night. They confront even the administrative authorities and officials who are well informed about the reality of clandestine dwellings in the sector with a *fait accompli*.

The Jnanates district has the added advantage of being virgin territory for a university investigation, in the form of interviews with different protagonists in a climate of trust.

We met these individuals through ten of our students who had lived in the area for a long time. This allowed us to observe firsthand the entire housing production process and to speak at any time with the local population of subdividers, small-scale construction entrepreneurs, workers, and residents. It is a population whose existence the well-to-do world prefers to ignore.

The subdividers. The subdividers are the first to interact with one another during the division of lots. This first struggle, pitting the landholder against the municipal authorities, often gives birth to unauthorized housing.

Real estate in Morocco is governed by legal texts from 1952 and 1953 and by different financial laws determining taxes on profits from real estate. The division and sale of lots, however, is not subject to administrative regulation. The state thus is unable to rigorously control the full extent of real estate transactions.

A notarized deed is the sole requirement for a registration number for the land. After receiving such a number, a landowner may devote himself to profitable real estate speculation, to the point that today the price of the land represents up to 40 percent of the price of a completed home. The subdivider decides on the size of the lots (which rarely exceed 100 square meters, or 1,076 square feet), depending upon their location and demand. The price per square meter of a parcel of land without electricity, water, or sewage has continued to rise. Today in Jnanates the price of such land is between 1,000 dirham (US$125) and 1,500 dirham (US$187) per square meter. During some periods, the price can reach as high as 2,500 dirham (US$312) per square meter, surpassing even the real estate prices in the regulated urban sector.

This intense speculative activity is carefully carried out by clandestine subdividers. Officially, five real estate agencies exist in Jnanates, but this figure is misleading and does not reveal the full extent of the brokerage business. Informal brokers also operate, without official premises or the authorization required to officially ply their trade. The street, rural markets, and corner cafés are their universe. It is there that they develop a clientele, carry out numerous transactions, and finalize contracts. Some intermediaries even go to Europe and sell land (without, of course, electricity, water, or sewage) or, with keys in hand, houses to Moroccan immigrant workers. Paradoxically, the banks, notably those geared to a working-class clientele, finance land and houses in the unregulated zones of Jnanates through third-party traders representing immigrant workers.

In summary, there exists an entire clandestine organization composed of a variety of actors. Not even the authorities are spared from involvement. When they do not directly participate in the sale of parcels of land, the *mokadem* (elected governor of the district) and the *chioukh* (government-appointed administrator of several quarters of the district) remain silent in exchange for some form of remuneration. This type of payment occurs at every step of the housing production process.

The guarantee of legal possession of the land by the buyer, an important goal, is accomplished by the payment of real estate taxes. Subdividers believe themselves to be protected by the payment to the tax office of the sums due on their real estate transactions. The tax office does not concern itself with the unauthorized nature of the transaction. The receipts for payment of taxes are then shown to the authorities each time the subdivider is challenged and upon each new sale.

The authorities are well informed of the real intentions of the subdividers, but the danger of challenging political alliances forces them to tolerate these practices. The great number and remarkable heterogeneity of subdividers and speculators also explain the state's lax attitude toward control of the real estate market.

Our investigation identified fifty-six real estate salesmen and speculators in the Jnanates district. This number does not include the large number of retail dealers, but is large enough to reveal the social composition of this category of subdividers and speculators (see Table 2.1). These individuals carry out all the administrative operations necessary to divide parcels of land into minuscule lots of between 80 and 125 square meters, and they seek out clients with money.

TABLE 2.1   "Other" Professions of Property Salesmen in Jnanates, Fez

Socioprofessional category	Number	Percentage
Low-level government employee	21	37
Medium-scale merchant and artisan	13	23
Small-scale entrepreneur	6	10
Wealthy farmer	4	8
Miscellaneous (such as grocer, baker, café owner)	5	9
Otherwise not employed	7	13
Total	56	100

SOURCE: Author.

Although low-level government employees and medium-scale merchants (60 percent), small-scale entrepreneurs (10 percent), and farmers (8 percent) dominate the informal subdivider/speculator sector in Jnanates, the importance of grocers, café owners, and bakers in the district is not negligible. Profiting from their established place in the community, members of these groups do not hesitate to become property salesmen when an occasion to supplement their meager incomes presents itself. Often the official jobs of clandestine brokers and real estate salesmen are only a cover. Their workplaces serve as meeting places where they can follow the evolution of the real estate market, negotiate, and use the telephones and office materials as much as possible.

Most of these property salesmen are in their mid-thirties and have been plying their trade since the 1970s. Forty-seven, or 82 percent, of the fifty-six interviewees attended primary or koranic school and secondary school. Ten, or 17.8 percent, received no formal education, and none had sought advanced studies.

The builders. While property salesmen are discreet and work in the shadows, the small-scale builders who take over after them work even more silently. They do not build two or three buildings for all to see without taking care to choose opportune moments for their work.

Because building homes on illegal property is an open challenge to the administrative authorities, the identification of these construction workers was a difficult task.

In Jnanates, small-scale clandestine builders, always busy, take on all types of work, from repairing houses to building homes. The *tâcherons*, the entrepreneurs who organize and head the construction crews, serve as the project managers in the building of unauthorized dwellings. They seem to have a good deal of experience in construction and also in the arbitration required among the different protagonists involved in this microsector.

Young men, mostly from the Sahara, many of these builders have been driven from arid lands or rejected by the industrial sector. But they maintain close ties with their places of origin. Of the forty-two builders interviewed in Jnanates, thirty-seven (88 percent) were from rural areas, and only 12 percent were born in the city. Of those from rural areas, thirty-two were from the Sahara region and five were from other regions. All those from urban areas, except one, were from Fez.

The great number of Saharan small-scale builders who come to the city seeking their fortunes is striking but understandable. Little rain ever falls in the Saharan region (Errachidia, Quarrazate, and Figuig), but the extreme drought in recent years certainly has been the primary cause of an exodus to Fez. Moreover, this migratory process has not been gradual. For 85 percent of Saharans, the migration has been direct from the Sahara to Fez.

Several reasons were cited to justify their migration. The youngest hoped to obtain training, eventually go to school, and find work. The older ones explained their migration in terms of revenue—for example, because of adverse conditions, such as the drought, work at home was less remunerative than work in the city. All, however, came to live with a relation who worked in Fez in construction. Although they maintain close but irregular ties with their families in the countryside or

Small-scale builders wait in the street for a job.

in the Sahara, these newcomers do not wish to return there. Seventy-five percent said they will stay in the city (only 22 percent of these are Saharans), and 20 percent intended to return to the countryside only if they were to gain possession of land there. Thus, the move to the city seems to be definitive and a categorical rejection of rural life.

Most small-scale builders learned their profession on the job through a long apprenticeship with an employer. A minority received their apprenticeship as paid workers in large construction companies, moving from one post to another doing different jobs. A smaller number (4 percent) received professional training in a public institution. This microsector trains its own competition. The length of an apprenticeship can vary between six and fifteen years. Those who are close to their employer and receive greater attention complete their training within an average of eight years. Masonry is an obligatory part of learning the profession. The traditional, but in no way unique, path followed by small-scale builders is from laborer to mason to *tâcheron*.

Division of labor. Even though he is the employer and is fully knowledgeable about the profession, the *tâcheron* participates in the building and is even the principal artisan. He organizes the work plan, recruits the laborers, and supervises all work relating to the crew and the site (equipment, primary materials, and finding a buyer). In periods of intense activity or his prolonged absence, a semiskilled worker helps the *tâcheron* supervise the production process.

The number of laborers varies appreciably from one crew to another, but remains low in most cases. Only 21 percent of the forty-two crews surveyed employed more than eight people; the remaining 79 percent hired five or six laborers. Generally, crews are composed of two semiskilled workers and four unskilled workers. The exception is when cement work is being done or during times of intense activity.

The recruitment of unskilled laborers follows specific laws and depends on economic and other considerations. The *tâcherons* inquire among workers and masons they know well and attempt to reconcile competence, physical capacity, and ethnic background. The relations established are ones of trust and can in no way be reduced purely to economics. Moreover, negotiations between the parties are based on mutual agreement and do not pass through an impersonal employment office.

Salary and work conditions. Salaries differ from one employer to another and depend on family connections and clientele. They are, nonetheless, a function of the type of work to be done and the worker's skill level. A skilled mason must be capable of carrying out all necessary tasks at an appropriate pace with his own tools. The manual laborer, who possesses no specific skills, prepares and transports materials and assists the *tâcherons* and the masons. The manual laborer also does the work requiring great physical exertion. The difference in the average salaries paid to workers and to masons is relatively large and can exceed 20 dirham (US$2.50) a day. This difference in salary is also explained by the fact that, besides his specialized skill, the mason provides his own tools (notably, a trowel, chisel, scissors, plumb line, and level, used to build walls, measure, cut iron, break stone, and place bricks).

Age has an obvious effect on salary level as well. It is accepted that young workers, even if they do the same work as their elders, receive a slightly lower salary.

The salary of the small-scale *tâcheron* often exceeds 100 dirham (US$12.50) a day. This salary is greatly superior to the guaranteed minimum industrial wage and slightly exceeds salaries paid in the formal sector. But it is not enough to permit significant savings for investment in new machines or the hiring of additional workers. The small-scale builder also must survive on this revenue during periods of inactivity and must use it to repair and replace materials and work tools. In short, his objective is survival and only rarely saving and expansion. Nonetheless, he manages to offer low and competitive prices for construction work, thanks to savings on primary materials used in building.

Disregard for norms is also a source of profit; the small-scale entrepreneur is better informed than others about the specific legalities and illegalities of the system of construction in unregulated areas. Upon the slightest suspicion of unwelcome attention, flashlights and candles are extinguished, work tools hidden and the crew converted into a friendly gathering of card players, their laughter fooling even those who are most aware of the area's realities. Swift construction, always at night, is essential.

Once a completed building is occupied, the balance of power shifts in favor of its residents. The residents themselves must make a serious effort to find builders who operate outside of the official system and far from normal market considerations. Generally, the builder can be found at his home, in a café, or at the home of an unofficial broker. He has no sign or distinguishing mark on his door, no specific office, and, as a consequence, no taxes to pay.

Construction agreements. Anonymity is a logical consequence of illegal urbanization. It would be difficult for it to be otherwise, because the customer has neither a plan, nor a construction permit, nor any administrative authorization. Exposing his intentions to an official enterprise would be risky. The terms of the agreement between the customer and builder reveal the complex but flexible social relations linking them.

The first negotiations focus on a choice between a price per meter or a price for the entire job. If payment by price per meter is chosen, an agreement is made on the price per meter for each kind of task (stairs, walls, columns) to be performed by the *tâcheron*. Acquisition of the materials (cement, sand, iron, plaster, etc.) is the responsibility of the customer. The entrepreneur recruits the workers, gathers the work tools, and organizes the production process. The customer advances the money needed at each stage of the work. Once the house has been built, the extent of the different kinds of tasks is measured to determine the remaining sum to be paid to the entrepreneur. This method of payment is very convenient because it permits the land-holder to build according to his financial means, to choose the most appropriate materials, and to stop the work at any stage.

Payment for the job requires an agreed-upon price for all of the work to be carried out. In this case, the entrepreneur organizes the work plan and buys the necessary materials. This agreement also includes a payment schedule. Moroccans living overseas willingly use this formula because they are unable to follow and supervise the con-struction process and often are unable to designate a member of their family to do so.

For this reason and others, payment by the job is generally more common than payment by the meter. Still, the advances paid by the customer under the per-meter arrangement to the builder constitute a means of exerting considerable pressure on the builder and control-ling the construction process. The advances even create a dependence relationship between the small-scale builder and the customer. The customer may even on occasion go so far as to require the dismissal of a worker or mason whom he judges unsatisfactory. This type of social relationship between the builder and customer highlights the vulnerable status of the builders, even though their numbers have increased since 1980 suggesting that business is good.

In spite of their problems, the small-scale builders seem to be making life difficult for large construction companies. The companies complain bitterly about the disloyal competition of these intruders, or "price breakers," who are, they say, intervening more and more in the official market (such as by building villas and chic houses and constructing less costly housing). Indeed, they have urged the authorities to suppress these small-scale builders, who, they claim, lower the quality of construction and disturb the building trade. The threat can even extend to the price of primary materials. Large suppliers, under the pressure from large-scale builders, play an important role here. Not only do they not extend credit to the small-scale builder, but they also do not hesitate to send them low-quality material and to charge them excessive prices.

This carpenter makes furniture in his own shop.

Yet, despite these barriers, small-scale building artisans are multiplying and asserting their authority in zones with unregulated housing. Moreover, it is difficult for the large-scale builders to fight against these discount builders, because of their inexpensive labor, construction prices that do not follow norms, flexibility in the management of lower-quality materials, and the great risk of nonpayment by the customers that they accept.

The pace of informal construction is often very slow, however. This is a function not just of the number of stories to be built but also of the financial status of the customer and the degree of laxness on the part of the administrative and municipal authorities. Nonetheless, for large-scale builders, competing with these small-case artisans is a losing proposition.

The cost of constructing an unauthorized home fluctuates according to demand, which is itself subordinate to the attitudes of the authorities. In periods of state laxness, the customers impose their views and their prices. But when the authorities pose a threat, the entrepreneurs, who take the risk of having their materials confiscated, of being mistreated, and even of being put in prison, demand higher prices. The customers are forced to pay the price for illegal construction, but that price is always less than one-tenth the price of authorized housing.

The occupants. Identification of the occupants of the unauthorized homes in the Jnanates district is easier—everyone knows everyone else. Through the *mokadem*, ten residents of the district, and a few grocers, we were able to establish a relatively representative social classification of the dominant socioprofessional categories, confirmed by the testimonies collected.

Those seeking access to this type of habitat are diverse socially, but they are characterized by a low economic standing. The professional categories they belong to are significant in this respect. They are confined to artisans, workers, low-level bureaucrats, shopkeepers, small-scale builders, and immigrant laborers. The members of this group are not impoverished, but they lack the means to gain access to property in the regulated urban sector because they are highly dependent on the economic climate (traders and artisans) or immigration policies of the industrialized nations (immigrants), or on the government's economic policy on salaries (bureaucrats). The economic fluctuations these people are subject to undoubtedly have a strong effect on activity in this illegal microsector. They stand together against the authorities, struggling to make themselves known. The payment of property taxes is welcome, however; it is certainly only on this occasion that people are disposed to carry out their fiscal duties with a smile, because a receipt from the collection agents is considered a guarantee and recognition by the state. Indeed, it elicits joy and hope. Carefully placed in a chest for important papers, it is exhibited at each questioning or quarrel with agents of the administration.

The state: liberalism, confusion, and firmness. How can the state deal with this complex situation, which features subdividers, small-scale builders, and occupants in quest of a niche that will allow them to survive and will satisfy their different aspirations? Is it necessary to systematically destroy these unhealthy shelters and violently suppress every effort to sell land, build homes, and occupy them in unregulated areas, all because the evasion of state control is unacceptable? This type of reaction on the part of the administrative authorities has proven ineffective. For example, a short time after the demolition in 1981, 1983, and 1985 of clandestine settlements at Ain Nokbi, Jnanates, and Zouagha, those expelled reappeared in the same or other places. The Ministry of the Interior appears willing to deal with unauthorized housing through closer supervision and with a firm hand, but experience has shown that such energetic measures will not bring about a solution to this problem.

Indeed, neither repression nor a *coup d'éclat* can stop this spreading symptom of industrialization. Thus, should a policy of *laissez-faire*, entailing as little intervention as possible, be adopted? Such a policy would include placing trust in the dynamism of the sector and supporting its specific manner of functioning by facilitating training and access to credit and introducing appropriate technology. The authorities, however, alternate between intervention and leaving the sector to itself. This ambiguous behavior is not irrational, even if it leaves the well-informed observer confused. On the one hand, the authorities act with vigor, demolishing illegal buildings, imprisoning those responsible, and announcing that the state will never permit such intolerable anarchy. On the other hand, they complacently watch the daily multiplication of unauthorized buildings, and from time to time officially "regularize" some offenders and install electricity, water, and sewer systems in one or two blocks in the area (Table 2.2).

This attitude of the authorities is not the result of some abstract calculation. Instead, it is a political effort to control pockets of resistance. Economically, it saves considerable investment in infrastructure and services, investment that then can be devoted to the more well-off and more certain supporters of existing power. Jnanates, for example, does not, for the most part, have potable water or electric service. The residents use batteries, candles, and gas lamps as sources of energy and light and get their water from wells and public fountains. Moreover, the Boukherareb River functions as a sewer system, carrying away used water and wastes and giving off a nauseating odor that aggravates the poor sanitary conditions in these settlements. Finally, the residents also are poorly served by the available transport. The district has no official bus station. When they are not already full, the two buses that follow the principal route between Bab Ftouh and Bab Boujloud are used by the residents. Taxis avoid taking passengers

TABLE 2.2   Regularization of Dwellings in Jnanates, 1979–1989

Year	Number of dwellings
1979	26
1980	227
1981	559
1982	1,220
1983	1,068
1984	718
1985	275
1986	283
1987	802
1988	753
1989	392

SOURCE: Services for Architecture and Urbanism, Municipality of Fez.

to the district, and when they do go there, they demand high set prices because the unpaved road is difficult to navigate.

The refusal of the local authorities to comply with requests for housing and service by the social stratum residing in Jnanates has led some observers to believe in the existence of a "division of labor," in which the administration attends to the needs of the middle class and the wealthy, and the informal producers take charge of the development of low-cost, popular housing. This belief in a division of labor is disproven, however, by the government's behavior. By maintaining a kind of equilibrium between liberal and interventionist policies, the state, in addition to benefiting from its avoidance of the obligation to develop costly infrastructure and services for entire districts, keeps entire pockets of an impoverished and refractory population in a precarious state and under the threat of expulsion.

This approach by the authorities weakens the power of housing builders, and at every opportunity the authorities hint that regularization is possible in exchange for total allegiance.

The unofficial producers in turn resort to equally clever practices. The payment of bribes to local elected officials and official agents (*mokadems, chioukhs,* etc.) with the goal of involving them in the system of unauthorized housing is common practice.

Some subdividers even go as far as improving such social services as koranic schools, public ovens and baths, mosques, and infirmaries. Others create cultural associations for those who want to escape from administrative harassment and the repeated complaints of the *mokadem.*

On the whole, the government's policy consists of conciliatory accommodation of the interests of the different protagonists. The construction of unauthorized housing plays an important role in social regulation in the economic system. Through the quantity and quality of the houses built, the small-scale, clandestine producers of housing respond to the needs of a heterogeneous population having a small amount of savings and simultaneously employ an excess of manual labor at a low price. With remarkable flexibility, this microsector, a highly structured social organization, responds to an evolving and changing situation. For this reason, it is better to speak of legal, visible activities and not of an illegal, clandestine sector.

This unofficial sector does not contribute to productivity, however, because the conditions and organization of labor are simple and embryonic. The technology used is unsophisticated, and the administrative impediments are numerous. From this perspective, this sector is not an accumulator of capital, although it could be.

In the end, the artisanal production of housing only partially escapes from state control, and plays a very positive role. Besides serving as a laboratory for social innovation, these informal activities cushion the impact of the housing crisis and render it less acute, if not less explosive. More precisely, housing produced by the informal sector without the knowledge or goodwill of the local authorities has come to the aid of the social and economic system. It allows the construction of housing at moderate prices, reduces the unemployed labor force at a low cost, and serves as a safety valve for urban society. It is time to recognize this reality and take positive steps related to this type of low-income housing. It is also time to examine why so many from this modest social stratum are forced to place themselves outside the regulations and the law to find a home.

Conclusion

The informal sector is an important refuge from all types of administrative impediments, and it is an indicator of the good health of an economy. Thus, it should be viewed as a positive factor and the reasons for its growth examined. In this way, we can discover the gaps in the official mode of development and better respond to the needs of this class of popular entrepreneurs.

In the end, the clandestine and informal nature of work and production reveal the failure of state control of the economy. Is it not often impossible for the small-scale entrepreneur to develop and establish a business legally and within the bounds of accepted forms? Does not the administration have a tendency toward procedural, outdated regulations and endless red tape, all of which prevent the development of ideas and discourage positive, useful accomplishments?

The study of the informal sector in Morocco permits us to not only emphasize the extent to which entrepreneurial energy is profoundly rooted in a society and culture, but also identify the stumbling blocks involved in official modes of economic development. If Morocco faces economic difficulties, it is not because of cultural limitations, or because the country is not ready for development, or because of an insufficient number of entrepreneurs or a lack of entrepreneurial spirit. It is because many laws and regulations have not been adapted to current realities. There is a great discrepancy between state legal norms and popular practices. Many laws are outdated and practically demand violation. This does not mean, however, that the informal sector is equivalent to anarchy. On the contrary, the informal sector is governed by its own logic of functioning and obeys flexible and effective laws that should serve as the inspiration for the development of new regulations. We should not anticipate being overwhelmed by problems, but instead should study the social transformations taking place and develop different legal solutions for the variety of scenarios that may result from these transformations. As soon as it becomes clear which scenario corresponds to reality, the process of approving the appropriate legislation should start.

Law is not a fixed instrument applicable to all time periods. It is a product of politics and culture, which should be viewed in terms of its uses—and not from a bureaucratic perspective. Certainly, the royal letter of August 1989, aimed at accelerating as much as possible the processing of foreign investment proposals, was an important and substantive step forward, which struck a blow against the slowness of the bureaucracy (all proposals not answered after two months are to be viewed as accepted by the administration; in cases of rejection, the administration's decisions must be duly justified). It also revealed the existence of the political will in Morocco to commit the country to a coherent, dynamic, liberal system. The current socioeconomic environment, however, remains governed by outdated legislation, and many obstacles hinder the creation of enterprises and constrain popular entrepreneurial spirit.

Moreover, informality and illegality, although often intelligent and practical, have their negative sides. Informal workers and housing residents often face significant management problems, since they are prevented from forming associations to improve productivity and defend their interests, and they lack access to the official credit system, to modern accounting systems, to the different services offered by the state, and to social and technical assistance. Informal activities also often produce goods and services of mediocre quality. Thus, these realities greatly reduce their contribution to economic and social development.

It is essential to provide assistance to these informal entrepreneurs in the areas of primary materials, management, and credit, so that they can strengthen their businesses. The simplification of administrative practices and the development of a single form summarizing all the necessary information, which could then be delivered to a single office, would certainly be of great value.

It is time to move toward these important reforms of the country's productive system and to discover the informal sector's considerable potential in terms of employment, training, business, and the generation of revenue. To do this, a redistribution of revenue is required, not through taxation or subsidization but through an economy that favors the freedom to start up activities, the liberation of the creativity of the individual, social mobility, and property rights—in short, through the elimination of regulatory constraints and the democratization of access to markets.

The Informal Sector in the Philippines

Although economic informality is a way of life for the majority of the population in most developing countries, public authorities often have a schizophrenic attitude toward the informal sector. On the one hand, they ignore the informal enterprises or view them as a "necessary evil," prone to violate the laws of the land and likely to cause trouble, which should be regulated if not eradicated. On the other hand, these same authorities offer welfare, shelter, and other social programs to help ease the plight of informal entrepreneurs and workers. In either case, the informal economy often ends up with the shorter end of the bargain.

In the Philippines, the public's consciousness of the existence of the informal sector increased during the economic crisis of the early 1980s. As heavily protected industries in the formal sector collapsed, workers laid off from their jobs sought refuge in informal self-employment that could not offer the same security as their former jobs, but nevertheless provided them a means of economic support. Those who were lucky enough to keep their jobs (mainly those employed by the government) found their real income eroded by double-digit inflation (the Philippines has no official wage-indexing policy) and often had to resort to informal activities.

The author wishes to thank Ruben C. Alonzo for the illuminating discussions on the transport industry and Danilo Baudilla and Isagani Inovero for clarification on tricycle operations.

All forms of media, particularly television, were quick to pick up on the trend. In the interest of drama, the media used the term "underground economy" as they featured the plight of illegal sidewalk vendors playing hide-and-seek with policemen (but only when higher authorities ordered a shakedown, for most of the vendors pay protection money); of public school teachers and government employees selling all kinds of items, including prepared food, clothing, and small appliances, to their officemates during work hours; of street children forced by poverty into hawking, begging, and even prostitution. The informal workers continue to make good copy for the media, but all the publicity has not alleviated their plight.

Why do huge numbers of people remain informal? The slow growth of the formal economy, with its failure to create adequate employment, is certainly an important factor. Economists tend to agree on the forces that stunt the formal sector (often used to mean the industrial sector) in most developing countries. The most common explanations are: an overvalued currency that inhibits the growth of the export sector and leads to balance-of-payments problems; a highly protected domestic production sector that rewards inefficiency; a biased fiscal structure that promotes capital intensity; a repressed financial system that rations credit away from small enterprises; and over-expanded and inefficient public enterprises that drain the government budget. Economists have also begun to look at the role of the government itself, through its entangled bureaucracy, in inhibiting informal enterprises from becoming formal.

The solutions offered—a liberal trade and flexible exchange-rate policy, a neutral fiscal system, financial liberalization, privatization, decentralization, deregulation—invariably appear on the prescription list of multilateral and bilateral donor agencies as conditions attached to inflows of funds to developing countries. As Hernando de Soto has pointed out, however, while these conditions are well intended and technically correct in most cases, anything imposed from outside is likely to be abandoned or set aside once the donors' "watchdogs" are no longer watching.

A case in point is the 1981 Philippine trade-liberalization program, which was shelved as the economy ran out of foreign exchange during the crisis years 1983–1985 and later revived by President Corazon Aquino's new government in 1986. A high official of the Aquino government was quoted in the media as saying that he would introduce bureaucratic red tape in customs offices to limit importation of deregulated products.

The imposition of donor conditionalities also offers a convenient excuse for governments when they fail to achieve substantial economic progress. In the Philippines, as in most other developing countries, the World Bank and the International Monetary Fund (IMF) are always held to blame for what is happening to the economy; vested interests likely to get hurt by any reform program seek to rally the people against the dictates of "foreign interests."

Policy reform tends to be more lasting when pressure for it comes from the people themselves, for only then does government see the popular will clearly. Institutions imposed from above are likely to die a natural death; the ones that last are those born of the people's own initiative.

This study rejects the conventional view that the informal enterprise is poor in physical and human capital, is incapable of coping with a hostile environment, and should therefore be the recipient of strong affirmative action programs. Following de Soto (1989), informality is defined more broadly as an activity with universally accepted objectives, carried out illegally or extralegally. The informal sector participant, as the evidence will show, behaves like any other rational economic agent, responding to the environment he faces, weighing the costs and benefits of his position, and deciding what is best for him. The economic environment in many developing countries, however, is conditioned by a host of government regulations and other external factors that make informality the better option for an individual who lacks the resources to overcome those barriers. Reforms that would allow him to afford to become formal would improve not only his situation but also the overall efficiency of the economy.

The methodology used in this chapter follows that of the Instituto Libertad y Democracia (ILD) in its research on the different dimensions of informality in Peru. This involves talking to key participants in the informal economy, to find out what informality means from their perspective and to explore institutional issues that are often missed in cross-section socioeconomic surveys. The scale of this effort, of course, does not reach the same proportions as that of the ILD; nevertheless, we hope that this study will shed some light on the nature and consequences of informality in the Philippines.

The section that follows reviews the magnitude of the informal sector in the Philippines, as analyzed in recent studies using various approaches, and looks at the informal economy's characteristics. The second section examines what it takes to set up a legal business, following existing Philippine laws, and shows how costly and difficult it is to become formal. The third section focuses on the transport sector, one that is commonly expected to be formal in nature, but is in fact a prime example of how informality and institutions supporting it develop. The peculiarities in two other sectors—trade and housing— are briefly explored in the fourth section. The study ends with a summary and a discussion of how, in the Philippine setting, the "rules of the game" are defined and modified, with the purpose of suggesting venues by which social change can be effected so that the informal sector can benefit from the same protection under the law that the formal economy enjoys.

Dimensions of Informality in the Philippines

The magnitude of the informal sector. How extensive is the informal sector in the Philippines? Interest in the underground economy following the 1983–1985 economic crisis spawned several studies along the lines of the "illegal money" approach, where the ratio of currency to money is taken as an indication of the extent by which the economy goes underground to evade taxes (Tanzi 1982). The model posits that transactions within the underground economy are conducted mainly in the form of currency to avoid detection by tax authorities, and that an increase in the proportion of money held as currency would therefore indicate growth in underground activities.

The most recent of these studies (Suarez and Agustin 1989) estimates the relative size of the underground economy at 23–44 percent of measured gross national product (GNP) in 1984 and 31–70 percent in 1985, declining to 26–62 percent in 1986 and 26–49 percent in 1987, as the economy began to recover. The informal economy is estimated to have constituted only 12–24 percent of GNP in 1967. The low value in those ranges attributes illegal money to the rise in tax revenues collected over their lowest level for the period 1967 to 1987; the high value attributes illegal money to the existence of taxes per se.

Another popular way of assessing the magnitude of the informal economy is through the "residual" approach. An estimate of the employed labor force from household surveys is used as the base, from which are deducted estimates of employment in large enterprises (in the Philippines, those with ten or more workers) as gleaned from the Census of Establishments. The informal sector in the Philippines was estimated, according to this approach, to account for 73 percent of non-agricultural employment in 1983 (see Table 3.1), with the trade sector having the highest proportion of informal employment (93 percent), followed by transport (86 percent) and construction (78 percent). In terms of absolute numbers, the services sector accounted for 33 percent of nonagricultural informal employment, despite its including the huge number of workers in government, the single largest formal employer in the country. Employment in the informal services sector comprises mainly domestic household help.

Sectoral estimates for the 1960s and the 1970s show a smaller informal sector (the "unorganized" sector, in the terminology of earlier

TABLE 3.1   Estimates of Employment, Value Added, and Productivity in the Informal Sector in the Philippines, 1983

		Census firms		Informal sector firms		% of total	
	Total	Large	Small	IS(a)	IS(b)	IS(a)	IS(b)
Employment (in thousands)							
All sectors	18,898	2,569	1,022	15,307	16,329	81	86
Nonagricultural							
sector	9,142	2,507	1,020	5,615	6,635	61	73
Manufacturing	1,857	701	187	969	1,156	52	62
Utilities	71	46	0	25	25	35	35
Construction	676	149	2	525	527	78	78
Trade	2,158	157	577	1,424	2,001	66	93
Transport	844	121	12	711	723	84	86
Services	3,536	1,333	242	1,961	2,203	55	62
Value added (in millions of pesos)							
All sectors	214,330	119,305	12,195	82,830	95,025	39	44
Nonagricultural							
sector	176,628	111,999	12,174	52,455	64,629	30	37
Manufacturing	57,144	50,001	1,325	5,818	7,143	10	13
Utilities	6,740	6,590	0	150	150	2	2
Construction	10,946	5,622	43	5,281	5,324	48	49
Trade	39,595	16,901	8,369	14,325	22,694	36	57
Transport	12,246	4,860	233	7,153	7,386	58	60
Services	49,957	28,025	2,204	19,728	21,932	39	44
Value added per worker (in pesos)							
All sectors	11,341	46,440	11,932	5,411	5,819	48	51
Nonagricultural							
sector	19,320	44,675	11,935	9,342	9,741	48	50
Manufacturing	30,772	71,328	7,086	6,004	6,179	20	20
Utilities	94,930	143,261	0	6,000	6,000	6	6
Construction	16,192	37,732	21,500	10,059	10,102	62	62
Trade	18,348	107,650	14,504	10,060	11,341	55	62
Transport	14,509	40,165	19,417	10,060	10,216	69	70
Services	14,128	21,024	9,107	10,060	9,956	71	70

NOTE: Small establishments are defined as those with fewer than ten workers and average monthly sales of less than 1 million pesos. IS(b) includes them as "informal," IS(a) excludes them.

SOURCE: National Statistics Office, *Integrated Survey of Households*, 1983, and *Census of Establishments*, 1983, as reported in Arboleda (1989).

studies). The 1973 Comprehensive Employment Mission to the Philippines sponsored by the International Labor Organization came up with 85 percent informal employment in trade in 1961, 79 percent in 1965, and 81 percent in 1971 (ILO 1974). For transport, the respective figures showed an increasing trend at 62 percent, 74 percent, and 78 percent. The services sector showed an opposite pattern of 49 percent, 48 percent, and 44 percent as government employment more than doubled over the decade of the 1960s. Another study (Bautista 1973) similarly came up with a declining trend for manufacturing, from 55 percent in 1956 to 51 percent in 1966.

In terms of value added, informal activities assessed by the residual approach accounted for 37 percent of total value added in nonagriculture. The value-added rankings differ from those based on employment, with informality highest in transport (60 percent), followed by trade (57 percent) and construction (49 percent).

Labor productivity (measured as value added per worker) differs significantly between the formal and informal sectors, reflecting differences in the use of capital relative to labor. For nonagriculture, output per worker in the formal sector is more than 4 times higher than that in the informal sector. It is 11.5 times higher in manufacturing and 9.5 times higher in trade. For manufacturing, this gap represents about the same magnitude estimated by Bautista (1973) for the latter half of the 1950s, which rose to about 25 times in the mid-1960s.

Who works in the informal sector? How do small informal enterprises operate, and who are their participants? A survey conducted in 1988 in three areas in Metro Manila offers some interesting insights on the nature and characteristics of household-based business operations, their owners, and their workers (Alonzo and Abrera-Mangahas 1990). Most of the enterprises operate as single proprietorships. None are incorporated, and partnerships are few. Family orientation is pervasive; 90 percent of these partnerships are among family members, while 10 percent are among friends. Most enterprises are housed in the residence of the owner or owners; fewer than 25 percent have their own shops devoted exclusively to the business.

People usually start an enterprise to supplement their family income or to create employment for themselves. The exceptions are in repair services and personal services such as beauty parlors and videotape rentals, where the desire for independence and the attraction of profitability dominate. Personal saving constitutes the main source of start-up capital, augmented by loans from relatives and friends. Although borrowing from other sources is minimal, people borrow more from professional moneylenders than from formal institutions. The many livelihood programs of government hardly reach the small household enterprise. Growth takes place nevertheless, as enterprises augment their meager assets over time. This is particularly true for repair services and personal services.

Capital intensity is low, even for the small manufacturing enterprise, which has an average of only 9,640 pesos per worker. This average, however, does not compare all that badly with the bigger enterprises (those employing ten to ninety-nine workers); garment manufacturers in this category have an average of only 14,900 pesos per worker (Tecson, Valcarcel, and Nuñez 1989). The scarcity of capital available to the enterprise is reflected in the way it uses the little that it has: by keeping long hours and operating seven days a week.

In most enterprises, the owner is the primary skilled worker; for extra help, the owner usually hires a young apprentice, not another skilled worker. The apprentice is likely to be a family relation or a friend. Only manufacturing enterprises tend to hire on the basis of job experience. Fewer than half of informal workers receive a fixed salary; many workers get allowances or are paid a piece rate, especially in manufacturing. While certain groups, such as organized labor, condemn these practices as exploitative, they may be the only means of survival for both the small enterprise and the worker.

Direct linkages between the small informal enterprises and the formal sector are very weak. Raw materials, locally made, are bought in small shops within the locality and paid for in cash. The output is sold retail to poor and middle-income households within the same community, and an enterprise's major competitors are small units like itself. Large firms are not considered a threat.

The net income that an enterprise generates is often not sufficient to take care of the owner's family's needs. Fewer than 30 percent of informal enterprises earn more than 5,000 pesos per month, the official poverty threshold for a family of six in Metro Manila. As an enterprise alone usually cannot provide fully for the owner's family, other sources of income must be tapped by the majority.

Lack of capital and credit is the main problem encountered by a small informal enterprise, both in its start-up and in its operation; the smallness of the market and the cost of raw materials are other, far less severe, difficulties. Government is not perceived as a hindrance, as it is in the case of the small or medium formal enterprise with from ten to ninety-nine workers, where official regulations are nearly as problematic as lack of capital (Tecson, Valcarcel, and Nuñez 1989).

But neither does the small enterprise receive any form of assistance from government. In fact, almost half of the enterprise representatives questioned do not think that government programs can be of help. Those who do cite loans as the best form of assistance the government can extend. Training ranks very low; if it is desired at all, on-the-job training is the preferred mode, provided that the enterprise is not made to bear the financial cost.

TABLE 3.2   Characteristics of Informal Household Enterprise Heads and Workers
(percentage of respondents)

Characteristics	Head	Worker
25 years or older	96	49
Female	62	47
Born in Metro Manila	49	37
Business/job as family's main income source	52	30
Nature of previous job		
None	18	34
Self-employed	17	11
Employed by:	65	55
Household enterprise	8	14
Small enterprise	15	19
Large enterprise	42	22
Full-time in previous job	68	24
Job preference		
Stay in present job	60	32
Work in large company	29	15
Put up new enterprise	11	53

SOURCE: Alonzo and Abrera-Mangahas (1990).

The typical owner of a household enterprise is much older than the typical worker; she is likely to be female, to have been previously employed full-time in a relatively large enterprise, and to be happy to stay in her present line of work. The typical worker, on the other hand, is a young, single male from outside the city, not earning enough to support a family, equally likely to be a first-time employee or to have worked part-time before in a small enterprise, and eager to move out of his present job and start his own enterprise, emulating his boss. These differences (see Table 3.2) are wide indeed, and suggest that programs for the informal sector should consider the two groups separately.

Starting and Running a Legitimate Business

The de Soto (1989) study of the informal sector in Peru, documenting the travails of becoming formal (it takes 289 days to register a business formally), has begun to raise the level of awareness of concerned reformists in many developing countries about the way the laws themselves inhibit the growth of small enterprises and exclude the majority of the population from enjoying the protection and the benefits of the legal system. How does the situation in the Philippines compare with that in Peru?

To start a business within the legal framework, entrepreneurs must go through a circuitous and exhausting process. First, they must secure a *barangay* clearance signed by the *barangay* chairman.[1] There is no fixed fee for this clearance, but applicants are asked to donate as much as they can afford to the *barangay* treasury. The chairman sizes up the prospective businesses to determine the affordability level of the applicants.[2] This transaction, however, is transparent, as the *barangay* issues a receipt. If the business is to be established in a residential area, the written consent of the adjacent neighbors is also needed before the *barangay* clearance is issued.

Entrepreneurs then apply for a mayor's permit. If they own their building, proof of payment of the realty tax is required; if they do not own the building, the registration number of the building owner or landlord has to be submitted. If they intend to make improvements or build a new structure, it is an altogether different matter: they must get a building or construction permit from the Office of the Building Official, located at the city or municipal hall, which requires seven copies of the building plan corresponding to the required signatures from seven departments (land use and zoning; line and grade; architectural; structural; sanitary; electrical; and mechanical). The fees for the building permit may run into several thousand pesos, depending on the value of the structure to be put up, and getting all the signatures usually takes at least a week.

Applying for a water connection with the waterworks company (a government corporation) in Metro Manila is also an agonizing procedure. Upon filing the application for a new connection (to which must be attached the building permit), entrepreneurs must wait for an inspector to view the site and figure out where the connection may be tapped; this may take several days, as there are only a few inspectors. Applicants must then check regularly with the waterworks office to see if the inspector has submitted his report ("grease money" will, of course, hasten this process). They then pay the connection fees and wait for a private contractor commissioned by the waterworks company to install the connection. The contractor usually visits applicants and says that, with his busy schedule, the connection may take weeks, but that a facilitation fee (500 pesos in our experience) would move the applicant up in the queue, allowing work to begin on the connection in a few days.

For single proprietorships, entrepreneurs can proceed directly to the Bureau of Domestic Trade (BDT), a national agency that has only one office in Metro Manila, serving a population of 8 million. The function of this office is to register the business name (to ensure that no one else has the same name). The queue at this office, however, is not all that long, suggesting that only a few comply with its registration requirements. Several signatures are also needed at this office, but procedures have been streamlined so that if applicants submit the application form in the morning, they can get the registration papers in the afternoon. The new procedure was installed only in the mid-1980s; before then this process took at least one week.

For limited partnerships and corporations applicants must register first with the Securities and Exchange Commission (SEC) before registering with the BDT. The documentary requirements are: (1) verification of the corporate name, (2) the articles of incorporation, constitution, and by-laws, (3) an affidavit of paid-up capital, (4) a statement of assets and liabilities, (5) a bank certificate of deposit, (6) an authority to verify with the bank, (7) a written contract to comply with SEC rules, (8) the marital consent of the incorporators' spouses, (9) the incorporators' tax account numbers, (10) personal information sheets completed by the incorporators, (11) an inventory of personal properties signed by the owners or subscribers, (12) income tax returns of the incorporators and subscribers, (13) a certificate of authority, and (14) a written explanation of the modus operandi of the business (Zamora 1990). All these documents have to be notarized. The process takes several months without facilitation; even with the help of lawyers specializing in SEC registration, it may still take a full month for the paperwork to get done.

The final step is registration with the Bureau of Internal Revenue (BIR). Luckily for applicants, the BIR has several offices in Metro Manila. The required steps include: (1) payment of the privilege tax or fixed tax, (2) registration of the business name, (3) presentation of the SEC or BDT Certificate of Registration, tax account numbers, residence certificates, and articles of incorporation, (4) registration of all books of accounts, and (5) filing of an inventory of goods statement. In addition, applicants must secure BIR authority for every job order to print sales or commercial invoices or receipts.

A business that plans to hire more than five workers must register with the Social Security System. If it is a corporation, it must register with the Department of Labor. If it is a food-processing business, it must register with the Food and Drug Administration. (Food processing includes bottling sweets and fruit preserves, canning fish products, and a host of other cottage enterprises.)

When the business is finally running, the paperwork needed to comply with all the government requirements continues. The mayor's permit has to be renewed every year, and every quarter a percentage tax on the business has to be paid to the local government and a value-added tax and a withholding tax on employees have to be paid to the BIR. All the other agencies with which the entrepreneur registered have similar quarterly or annual paper requirements. No matter how small the business, an owner needs an accountant and a lawyer to comply with all of the requirements.

Legality carries with it the benefit of possible tax and tariff duty exemptions from the Board of Investments (BOI). Incentives granted by the BOI consist of: (1) an income tax holiday, (2) an additional deduction for labor expenses, (3) tax and duty exemptions on imported capital equipment, (4) a tax credit on domestic capital equipment, (5) an exemption from the contractor's tax, (6) a tax credit for taxes and duties on raw materials for export products, (7) a tax and duty exemption on imported supplies and spare parts in bonded manufacturing warehouses, (8) an exemption from wharfage dues and export taxes, and (9) a deduction of necessary and major infrastructure and public facilities for income tax purposes.

The incentives can be hefty: the income tax reductions granted to registered businesses alone amounted to 525 million pesos in 1987 (Manasan 1990). Incentives amounted to several billion pesos per year if tariff exemptions are included, and yet only 730 firms were registered in 1984 (see Table 3.3). The reason is that entrepreneurs must go through a maze of paperwork, not only to register but also to continue to benefit from these incentives. The BOI, set up in 1967, had only one office, located in Metro Manila, serving the whole country until 1986, when it established a branch in Cebu City in the south. A firm from the Visayas or Mindanao wishing to apply for incentives would need a representative in Manila to follow up on its application. Registration also requires a decision by the BOI governors; much discretion is placed in the hands of the governors, despite the presence of rules that prescribe which industries fall under the incentive scheme. Obviously, big firms with abundant resources are better placed than smaller ones to take advantage of these incentives.

To support export development, exporting firms, even those not registered with the BOI, are offered relief from customs duties on imported equipment and spare parts through the duty drawback and bonded warehouse system. The conditions are rather stiff: (1) the actual

TABLE 3.3   Size Distribution of Firms Registered with BOI in 1984

Assets (in millions of pesos)	No. of firms	% of registered firms
Less than 0.5	34	4.7
0.5–5	191	26.2
5–20	203	27.8
More than 20	302	41.4

SOURCE: Biggs et al. (1987).

use of the imported materials in the production or manufacture of the exported article must be established, including the quantity, value, and amount of duties paid thereon; (2) the duties refunded or credited must not exceed 100 percent of the duties paid; and (3) the exportation must be made within one year after the importation of materials used, and the claim for refund or tax credit must be filed within six months from the date of exportation. There are at least eighteen documents required (Guevara 1990).

Another fiscal policy that seems to be biased against small enterprises is the value-added tax (VAT). Implemented in 1988, the VAT system was meant to replace a gross sales tax system. The self-enforcing features of the VAT are often highlighted by its proponents: an enterprise is encouraged to demand invoices on its purchases to be able to claim a tax credit or refund.

The VAT system's compliance requirements, however, are so tough that enterprises are discouraged from registering. At least ten documents must be submitted, including photocopies of all VAT invoices and receipts; the enterprise is required to present the original copies of the invoices before the tax credit or refund is issued. Export sales and purchases of capital goods require additional approvals as well. The refunds are handled by the BIR central office in Manila, so that a trader from the provinces will have a long wait for his refund. The law itself states that taxes paid on inputs should be refunded within sixty days from the date an application is filed, but mailings take about a month to remote areas, if they arrive at all. The compliance costs are so high that in public hearings traders said they would prefer a turnover tax on gross income to the VAT's paper requirements.

As a result of these problems, only 97,000 enterprises have registered with the VAT system, and there were only 69,950 paying filers as of June 1990, compared with 125,000 enterprises initially expected to be covered. This is not to suggest that small enterprises do not contribute their fair share of taxes. In fact, by failing to register, they implicitly pay the taxes built into the costs of their inputs, but are unable to claim tax credits for them.

The Bureau of Customs is another government agency that causes nightmares for its clientele. Customs laws and regulations allow excessive discretion to low-level authorities, resulting in the proliferation of "fixers" and "facilitators." The difficulties of getting goods out of customs have even given birth to a door-to-door freight-delivery service industry used by Filipino immigrants in the United States to send gifts to their relatives back home. These companies take care of all the paperwork, together with all formal and informal fees involved.

Official efforts are, of course, being made to address the problems arising from all these requirements. The bureaucratic procedures described in this study are drawn from reports of the Congressional Economic Planning Staff that are meant to aid Congress in formulating laws to streamline government practices (Guevara 1990; Zamora 1990). The BOI reports that 81 percent of the 735 projects it approved for incentives in the first half of 1990 are small- and medium-scale projects, with a more pronounced regional spread than before. The Department of Transportation and Communications, as will be seen in the next section, has been simplifying the procedures for awards of land transportation franchises.

A law was passed in early 1990 simplifying the registration requirements for "countryside *barangay* and business enterprises" (those with a work force of fewer than twenty workers and initial equity of 500,000 pesos or less). Popularly known as *Kalakalan 20*, the law also grants registered enterprises fiscal incentives and exemptions from restrictive government requirements, such as withholding of taxes from employees, minimum wage compliance, and registration with the Department of Labor.

There is no doubt that the influence of ILD research on Peru has crossed the Pacific and has played a significant role in making a growing number of Philippine officials (in both the executive and the legislative branches) more aware of how government itself often serves to inhibit the efforts of informal workers to become formal. Movements toward reform, however, require the active and continuing support of the informal workers themselves, or such efforts will be dissipated. In the public hearings on *Kalakalan 20*, for example, many regulatory agencies threatened with loss of control expressed disagreement with the law; this suggests that implementation of reform may run into difficulties unless the potential beneficiaries constantly maintain their vigilance.

Informal Transport

An overview of the sector. Public transport vehicles are mandated by law to carry a franchise or Certificate of Public Convenience (CPC). The only vehicles exempt from this requirement are pedal-driven tricycles (or pedicabs) and *calesas* (horse-drawn carts, several of which still ply the busy streets of Manila proper); all they need is a permit from the local government offices. Since public transport is considered a public utility, subject to stringent government regulations on entry, pricing, and operations, it may be unclear how an informal subsector could flourish within such a tightly controlled environment. And yet, as noted in the section on the dimensions of informality in the Philippines, "residual" estimates indicate that the share of informal enterprises in the transport sector's employment has grown from 62 percent in 1961 to 86 percent in 1983.

Informality is prevalent in both freight and passenger transport. A study conducted by the Asian Development Bank reports that registered trucking companies own only about 10 percent of the total truck fleet in the Philippines, suggesting that a substantial number of trucks operate informally (ADB 1988). This section, however, will focus on informal passenger transport, as it is more significant in size. It also offers a revealing microcosm of how different patterns have evolved in the relationship of the informal enterprise with the law, how the participants have responded to such an environment, and how the legal environment itself has been reshaped by pressure from the participants, either directly through organized efforts or indirectly through disregard of the law. In particular, the two most prevalent forms of urban passenger transport—the jeepney and the tricycle—are discussed.

Both the jeepney and the tricycle are postwar developments. The jeepney was originally crafted from surplus vehicles (the jeeps made by American Motors) left behind by the U.S. forces after World War II, and was to accommodate six to ten passengers per vehicle. As the urban population grew, jeepney bodies were extended to accommodate fourteen to eighteen passengers, and this is the common type seen in the streets nowadays. The tricycle is of two types: the motor-driven sort that carries up to five passengers, and the pedicab that carries up to three passengers, depending on the physical condition of the operator. Many pedicabs are driven by children or adolescents. The tricycle is a familiar sight in most Asian cities, but the jeepney is unique to the Philippines.

Jeepneys have remained largely informal, while tricycles (particularly the motorized ones), although they might be expected to be more likely to stay informal, actually have a stronger semblance of formality. To see what may have given rise to such developments, the nature and characteristics of two industries are examined in detail.

The jeepney industry.

Entry into the system. The process of applying for a jeepney franchise from the Land Transportation Franchising and Regulatory Board (LTFRB) used to be long and tedious. Applicants had to show proof, through official vehicle registration receipts from the Land Transportation Office (LTO), that they had units ready for operation. This meant that they had to register a vehicle first as "private," and then re-register it as a public utility. A total of twenty-one documents were required to be attached to the application form, including proof of Philippine citizenship, evidence of provision for a garage, proof of good financial standing as shown by a bank account or a transfer certificate of title for real property, income tax returns, and the route's "measured capacity." The application form itself had to be verified by a notary public.

Upon submission of the forms, applicants had to publish their request in two daily newspapers. An initial hearing would then be set to establish the necessity of the service to be provided and to listen to the views of the affected parties (both the general public and existing operators whose lines would be affected). Applicants had to send a notice of hearing to the possible oppositors, with the return card of the registered mail serving as proof. This process could take a year or longer, depending on the opposition of the other operators, and the decision might even be negative. Once the CPC was granted, operators could then apply for the proper public utility license plates from the LTO, paying registration fees anew.

All applications throughout the country were processed by the central office in Manila; the twelve other LTFRB regional offices were simply receiving agents. The centralized system and the heavy paperwork have given rise to an industry of lawyers who help applicants with the franchise applications, charging fees ranging from 500 to 3,000 pesos per unit, depending on the profitability of the route. Even the big franchise holders go through these lawyers.

In March 1990, the Department of Transportation instituted several measures that were meant to simplify the jeepney franchising procedures. The language of the pronouncements suggests that the secretary of transportation himself or his advisers may have been influenced by the efforts of the Instituto Libertad y Democracia in Peru. The documentary requirements have been reduced to only five items. A pro forma invoice of acquisition of the vehicle now suffices in place of the LTO certificate of registration and official receipt, freeing the applicant of the need to pay vehicle-registration fees twice. For applicants with only one or two units already paid for, the presentation of the units is considered proof of good financial standing. Operators who apply personally and without the help of a lawyer are provided application forms free of the usual charge of 310 pesos, and are assigned employees to help them fill out and file the forms. Regional applications for intraregional routes are now processed by the regional offices concerned. The LTFRB also announced that the processing of applications for dropping or substitution of units would be reduced from ninety days to only twelve, and a check with a jeepney operator confirmed that the LTFRB has thus far managed to abide by its announcement. In addition, the agency has been opening new routes for Metro Manila operators.

The reform measures were introduced in response to the growing realization that the real cost of acquiring a franchise is much greater than the filing fee that the LTFRB collects. The bureaucratic procedures had been an ordeal, especially for small enterprises unfamiliar with and afraid of dealing with government agencies. Meanwhile, the enforcement of the legal requirements has been sporadic and inefficient, so that illegal means of entry have developed among enterprising operators. The most visible until recently were the *colorum* vehicles, which did not have any CPC and carried license plates meant for private vehicles. Until the 1960s *colorum* jeepneys and tricycles flourished in the metropolitan area; it was also common for private cars and trucks to operate for hire without the proper permits. The franchising agency, over the course of several transformations (from the Public Service Commission to the Board of Transportation to the present LTFRB), had been unpredictable in the granting of franchises; from 1983 to 1986, only provisional franchises that had to be renewed every year were granted.

Despite the tightness in the awarding of CPCs, the agency responsible for issuing license plates (which also has gone through several reorganizations, from the Land Transportation Commission in the 1970s to the present Land Transportation Office) apparently issued plates even to vehicles without valid franchises. In 1976 the number of jeepney units authorized by the then Board of Transportation was 28,114, while the number of public utility jeepney plates issued by the then Land Transportation Commission was 45,919. For freight trucks, only 4,556 units were authorized in 1976, compared to 11,772 units issued truck-for-hire license plates in 1975 (Alonzo 1980).

Most of the *colorum* units, which have not yet completely disappeared, are owned by small operators, since the owners of large fleets have the economies of scale to apply for an official franchise. The *colorum* vehicles are also usually in queue for the *kabit* system, another major form of illegality in the transport business, which is perhaps even more extensive than the *colorum*, although much less visible.

Kabit means "attached" and refers to the practice by franchise holders of attaching the public utility license plates of some other legally authorized vehicle to an unauthorized one. Since the acquisition of official permits is complicated and the operation of *colorum* units is highly visible and therefore risky, the *kabit* system has evolved, whereby unused permits are rented out illegally by official franchise holders to a small operator, also called a *kabit*. Rentals are usually payable on a monthly basis, with the rates and terms determined by market forces; highly profitable routes (especially the long ones) command premium prices. The rental fees in Metro Manila range from 125 to 150 pesos per month. The permit holder takes care of all the paperwork and government transactions, including the annual vehicle registration and the quarterly payment of the common carriers' tax, although at the vehicle owner's expense. The system is almost impossible to detect, for the vehicle is registered in the name of the franchise holder. The true owner executes a deed of sale for the jeepney to the franchise holder, and for his protection receives a counter-deed of sale in return.

The system is deeply entrenched in jeepney operations, even though the LTFRB allows the outright transfer of the CPCs or operating permits. It is this system that the agency, with its recent liberalization measures, is trying hard to eradicate, for the system is perceived to be working against the interests of the small operator, who is seen to be paying exorbitant fees to the big franchise holder. Thus, although the lease of franchises is technically legal, the LTFRB refuses to accept applications for such leases.

It may be too early to evaluate the consequences of the liberalization measures. They are likely to have only a minor impact in terms of eradicating the *kabit* system, despite good intentions. A closer look at the nature of jeepney operations may shed some light on the issue.

The nature of jeepney operations. The typical jeepney operator owns only one or two vehicles; an operator is likely not to have a franchise but to be instead in the *kabit* system in association with a big franchise holder. Why does the jeepney enterprise remain small? Why does the big franchise holder not operate all his units?

The explanation commonly proposed for small-scale operations is the presence of capital market imperfections, such that the small entrepreneur is prevented from expanding because of lack of access to credit. The cost of an assembled sixteen-passenger jeepney, with a diesel engine and reconditioned parts, is 200,000 pesos, mainly because of high tariffs to protect the local vehicle "manufacturing" industry, which really consists mostly of assembly. This cost is more than fifteen times the average annual per capita income.

Loans for the purchase of vehicles, however, are easily available from finance companies, which are closely allied with vehicle dealers. The terms usually require a downpayment of 30 to 40 percent, with the balance payable over two to three years. The effective interest rate can be substantial, at 5 to 7 percent per month, although this is certainly competitive with the rates of "loan sharks" in the informal credit market, who lend at 10 percent per month with a repayment term of one year. The vehicle itself serves as collateral. The finance companies are not strict in credit investigation; neither business entry nor expansion is thus seriously constrained.

Yet the typical jeepney enterprise remains small. There were many big operators during the jeepney "boom" in the 1950s and 1960s, with some having as many as sixty units in operation, financed mainly through vehicle suppliers' credit or loans from finance companies arranged by the suppliers. Eventually, however, the big operators

The barker for the jeepneys (the man walking) serves several functions: he sees to the proper queuing of the vehicles, barks for passengers, then collects the tong or protection money from the drivers for the policemen in the area. In return he gets a percentage of the daily take.

found themselves losing money. They discontinued operations, but kept their franchises and offered them for illegal lease under the *kabit* system.

The reason smallness is the norm probably lies in the fact that jeepney operations are characterized by diseconomies of scale (Alonzo 1980). The revenue-generating asset is mobile, and it is difficult for the owner to monitor the operations of the enterprise without driving the vehicle. Hiring a conductor to monitor revenues not only adds to costs but also reduces revenue, as the conductor takes up space in the cramped jeepney. Other costs also increase disproportionately with the scale of operations. Garage facilities, for example, can be had at negligible unit cost for the small operator, whose residence can serve as the garage. The owner is assured of the safety of the vehicle there and finds it more convenient to manage the business from home. These advantages easily disappear as the number of vehicles grows beyond the capacity of the home garage.

Meanwhile, the acquisition and maintenance of franchises appear to be subject to significant economies of scale. Several operators own franchises that have hundreds of units, of which only about a dozen are run by the operators themselves, the rest being leased out illegally. One franchise holder we interviewed has thirty-eight units along three routes but does not operate a single vehicle. He says he knows a franchise holder with many more units who is said to be so efficient at operating the *kabit* system that she can give the *kabit* a public utility license plate in a single day.

In the 1970s, the government appeared to have recognized the economies of scale in franchise acquisition and maintenance, but not the diseconomies of scale in actual jeepney operations. It required operators and drivers to form themselves into transport cooperatives, and established a bureau within the Department of Transportation to assist them. The cooperatives were meant to facilitate dealings with various government agencies and to reduce the cost of spare parts through bulk purchases. Few of these cooperatives still exist today, but the bureau survives. Perhaps the main contribution of the policy has been to facilitate the formation of national drivers' unions, which cause the government major headaches with their strikes whenever the price of fuel is adjusted.

The limitation of entrepreneurial capacity imposed by the nature of the enterprise is probably also the reason behind the "boundary system," another illegal institution wherein the jeepney is "leased" daily to the driver, who pays the operator an agreed amount depending on factors such as the hours of vehicle use, passenger capacity, the age of the vehicle, and route profitability. In most cases, the driver pays fuel expenses, while all other maintenance and operating expenses are borne by the operator. The driver pays fines and bribes associated with traffic violations (such as loading and unloading in a prohibited zone, disregarding traffic signals, and not completing the required route), while the operator pays for vehicle-related violations (such as operating against regulations with the operator's knowledge, lack of proper license plates, smoke belching, and traffic obstruction when the vehicle breaks down in the middle of the road). There are usually two alternating drivers during the week for each vehicle because of long operating hours: the vehicle starts the day at five or six o'clock in the morning and retires to the garage at eight or nine o'clock in the evening. Some run on a twenty-four-hour basis, seven days a week. The hectic nature of city driving also takes its toll on the drivers.

The officially recognized mode of compensation in the industry is either a percentage of revenues or a fixed salary, and the government (through the Department of Labor) attempted to enforce this regulation strictly in the 1960s and the early 1970s. Jeepneys then were required to issue tickets to passengers, and revenues were to be the basis of the driver's share under a percentage system. The issuance of tickets did not flourish, for several reasons: conductors, as pointed out earlier, are costly; some drivers would deliberately understate revenues; passengers had no use for the tickets; the jeepney trips are typically short, and issuing the tickets takes time; the system is dangerous, as the drivers tend to issue tickets while the vehicle is moving in order to save time. With a salary system, on the other hand, the jeepney driver has no incentive to generate revenue and may not make the scheduled number of trips. The salary system thus works against the welfare of both the owner, who loses revenue, and the passenger, who finds fewer vehicles on the road. The boundary system seems to offer the ideal matching of interests of driver, owner, and passenger.

It took a long time for the government to recognize the difficulty of enforcing the percentage and fixed-wage systems. Since the early 1980s, the government has turned its back on the issue. The boundary system is still officially illegal, but the authorities do not enforce the requirement to compensate jeepney drivers through the percentage or the fixed-wage systems. In fact, in 1980 the Department of Labor was looking for ways by which the maximum boundary fee, rather than the minimum wage for drivers, could be set (Alonzo 1981).

The costs and benefits of informality: a summary. In summary, there are three major modes of illegality in the jeepney industry: the *colorum*, the *kabit*, and the boundary system. The *colorum* arose because of the length of time it takes to receive a franchise. In Metro Manila, with the LTFRB's recently adopted policy of liberalization in the issuance of franchises, the *colorum* vehicles are declining in number. They still exist, but are mainly "frictional" in nature, consisting of vehicles waiting to get into a *kabit* or perhaps even apply for their own franchise.

The *kabit* system, on the other hand, is still widely practiced, as the jeepney drivers and operators themselves acknowledge. Simplification of franchising procedures may have lowered the cost of entry somewhat; the franchise holder we interviewed complained that one *kabit* with five jeepneys was attracted to the LTFRB program and decided to apply for his own franchise. However, for the smaller operators, the cost of acquiring a franchise remains high relative to their scale of operations.

The benefits of being a *kabit* extend to operations as well. In the *kabit* system, the franchise holder takes care of the quinquennial franchise renewal, the annual vehicle registration for license plates, and the quarterly payment of the Common Carriers' Tax (CCT). The CCT runs high at 3 percent of gross revenues; if paid in full, it may render jeepney operations nonviable. (The small operator may not know, although the franchise holder certainly does, that the Bureau of Internal Revenue actually allows a presumptive level of gross revenues, at 800 pesos per month, so that an operator needs to pay only 72 pesos per quarter.) The franchise holder also handles all transactions with other government agencies. The operator is thus buying a package with the informal lease of the franchise and may not be interested in getting an official franchise. In effect, the franchise holder buys government services wholesale and then retails them to the small operator.

Because the system is illegal, however, the participants incur substantial hidden costs as well. As mentioned earlier, the vehicle is "sold" to the franchise holder by the operator, with a counter-deed of sale to protect the true vehicle owner. The danger to the operator is that the franchise holder may run away with the title. Some franchise holders do this when the operator is heavily in arrears on the monthly lease payments. In one case, a big franchise holder died and his heirs claimed ownership of all the vehicles under their father's name. A long legal battle ensued before the true owners got their vehicles' titles back. Another cost is that operators cannot use their property as collateral for borrowing. Franchise holders, on the other hand, run the risk of being held responsible if a vehicle has a major accident. Or, in the event of a major abuse of the franchise by an operator (such as constant cutting short of routes or operation along unauthorized routes), franchise holders may be threatened with the loss of all their franchises by the LTFRB.

Legalizing the *kabit* system thus appears to be one deregulatory move that would benefit all parties concerned in the public transport industry. After all, sublease of franchises is allowed in other utilities. Small operators would have the security of keeping the title to their vehicles; big franchise holders would not face the risk of assuming the liability of an operator in case of a major vehicular accident. The government would save resources that would otherwise be spent dealing with thousands of counterproductive transactions. If the government were to succeed in its present efforts at convincing all operators to seek their own franchises, the volume of work for the LTFRB would increase five times. Legalization should not, of course, prejudice the applications of those operators who would want to own their own franchises.

The boundary system is perhaps the most prevalent form of illegality in the jeepney industry, covering at least 90 percent of operations. (A few long routes have twenty-passenger jeepneys that can afford to have a conductor and still operate on the percentage basis.) Currently, the system is tolerated by the authorities, who have learned to accept the fact that, given the nature of operations within the industry, it appears to be the most efficient mode of distribution of factor payments. It is now time to make the system officially legal. Otherwise, some bureaucrat in the future may resurrect the issue, leading to the harassment of jeepney operations by unscrupulous law enforcers once again.

The tricycle industry. Tricycles are even more numerous than jeepneys, but they serve much shorter routes and are legally allowed only on secondary roads. Including the sidecar, the motor-driven type costs 40,000 pesos and the pedicab costs 9,000 pesos. As with jeepneys, credit is relatively easy to obtain from the vehicle suppliers or from finance companies, although at high interest rates.

Tricycle operations are similar to jeepney operations. The boundary system is again the dominant mode of factor payment; if it is difficult for the jeepney to maintain a conductor separate from the driver, it is impossible for the tricycle to do so. Operating a tricycle is also subject to decreasing returns to scale, for it involves constant interaction between the driver and the owner, it is difficult to monitor how the driver takes care of the mobile asset, and the cost of garage facilities rises disproportionately with increasing scale of operations. Most operators are therefore small.

If one were to judge illegality on the basis of the disorder that the vehicles create on the road, one would get the impression that these tricycles are totally unregulated. Illegality in the tricycle business, however, appears less prevalent than in the jeepney business, because of the different legal framework covering them.

The local government is the agency mainly responsible for tricycle operations. To secure a franchise, an applicant has to get a *barangay* clearance from the chairman, showing proof of ownership of the tricycle. The clearance is presented to the Tricycle Regulatory Unit of the local government, which issues a permit. The applicant presents the permit to the LTFRB, which automatically issues a franchise. The franchise is then presented to the LTO for the official public utility license plates. Working full time on the papers, an applicant can get a license within a week, as there are no public hearings or publicity involved.

Why is the process so smooth? The procedures were streamlined only in the mid-1970s, when the authority to award franchises was, in effect, decentralized to the local governments; the national government agencies were left with documentation and registration functions, since they had to approve the applications automatically.

The local governments in turn delegated the function of supervision to the *barangays*, which encouraged the formation of associations of tricycle operators and drivers. Each local tricycle operators and drivers association is registered with the Securities and Exchange Commission as a private group; the association conducts hearings on applications for new franchises and facilitates and follows up papers for the applicant. The association does not usually charge a fixed fee for the application, but expects the applicant to contribute to the association's revolving fund. The contribution includes the service of following up the papers for the franchise and the license plates through the local government, LTFRB, and LTO.

Tricycle drivers are also required to be members of the association. The membership fee is usually about 500 pesos, payable in daily installments once the driver starts working. As in the jeepney industry, there are more drivers than operators, and the drivers are often relatives of the operators, on the presumption that relatives will take better care of the vehicle.

Most local chapters of the association limit entry to *barangay* residents. In the more organized communities, there seems to be social pressure as well to limit the number of units owned by any given operator. This may be another reason, aside from diseconomies of scale, for the preponderance of small tricycle enterprises. When congestion appears to be setting in, the association raises the ante for a new applicant's contribution. One association we interviewed has raised it to 10,000 pesos, which is meant to be prohibitive, as the current market value of such a line is only 2,000 pesos.

The association also raises funds through daily collections; a dispatcher collects a daily fee of two pesos from each tricycle, keeps half of the collections as remuneration and turns over the other half to the association. The officers of the association receive no salary; the fees are used for day-to-day expenses such as grease money for the policemen and other public authorities who may trouble members about traffic and other violations.

Not all tricycle routes have an organized association; the associations usually work in residential neighborhoods and in well-defined short routes that do not cross city boundaries. One big village has four associations (one for each of the four main entries to the area) that live harmoniously with each other, despite each group's having several hundred members.

Lessons to be drawn. The review of the jeepney and tricycle industries given above offers an interesting study of the way basically similar operations have developed different institutional arrangements in response to the different legal environments confronting them.

In both industries, diseconomies of scale in operation have led to domination by small enterprises. Both industries are also subject to substantial economies of scale in the acquisition and maintenance of franchises and in meeting the compliance requirements of government agencies. But in the jeepney business the institution that has developed to use such economies is the informal *kabit* system, with the big private franchise holder illegally leasing out CPCs, while in the tricycle business it is the operators' and drivers' association, duly registered with the Securities and Exchange Commission, that rations the permits to the small operators.

The informal *kabit* system is perceived by government as exploitative, whereas the formal association is viewed as fostering equity. Policies to eradicate the *kabit* system, ranging from the encouragement of the formation of jeepney cooperatives to the liberalization of franchising procedures, have come and gone. But the system is likely to endure, for the private benefit-cost calculus of the jeepney operator and franchise holder still makes it the best alternative. Tricycle-type associations in the jeepney industry are difficult to manage, as the experience with the jeepney cooperatives has borne out, and the business of retailing the franchising aspects of jeepney operation is perhaps best left with the private franchise holder. The lease rates, after all, are determined by the market; although they look steep relative to the direct cost of acquiring a franchise, the indirect costs of dealing with the government regulatory agencies are high for the small enterprise, and other services are provided by the franchise holder as well.

The tricycle industry would probably have taken the informal path if not for the devolution of national transport agency functions to the local governments. The associations would probably still have developed, but in an underground manner, and they would therefore have functioned less effectively. But the lessons learned from the tricycle experience are not directly transferable to the jeepneys, and it may be better for government to officially acknowledge and grant legal status to the dominant *kabit* system. The same should be done with the boundary system, which, despite the authorities' looking the other way, remains illegal and unnecessarily subjects both jeepney and tricycle operators to the threat of harassment by law enforcers.

There are, of course, other issues that plague the transport industry. Regulation of the importation of vehicles and spare parts has hurt the industry, especially during the crisis years of 1983–1985, when the number of public utility vehicles declined absolutely. Government attempts to set fares are highly political and usually trigger transport strikes. The official fares are adjusted only intermittently, when the price of fuel fluctuates. With inflation eroding the real value of the fares, drivers and operators are forced to charge passengers at higher rates than the maximum, and problems with the law once again ensue. The protection of the domestic automotive manufacturing program has also led to high prices for vehicles and spare parts, causing a severe shortage of public transport facilities (especially buses and taxicabs). But these are issues that are best left for more detailed scrutiny in a separate study.

Informality in Other Sectors

Informal trade. Among the enterprises recorded in the official *Census of Establishments*, petty retail trade constitutes the largest group. Even the poorest settlements have a *sari-sari* (variety) store every four or five houses. Food stalls called *carinderias* are also very popular. All these establishments are officially required to register with the Bureau of

Domestic Trade, but our 1988 survey of household enterprises in Metro Manila showed that only 22 percent are so licensed; this may even be an overstatement, as it was based on self-declaration (Alonzo and Abrera-Mangahas 1990). More than half, however, are registered with the local government.

The phenomenon of being informal with respect to the national government but formal vis-à-vis the local government also occurs for most of the other small enterprises, as Table 3.4 shows.

The small *sari-sari* stores located in the residences of their owners are often tolerated by the authorities. Vendors who locate elsewhere, however, are constantly at odds with the law. This is especially true of those who sell in the informal mini–public market or *talipapa*. It may be instructive to look more closely into how these *talipapa* vendors cope with various government regulations. The account given below is drawn from interviews conducted by two economics students (Santos and Serrano 1990).

The *talipapa* at the entrance to a large university in Metro Manila started with a few stalls selling prepared food to the jeepney and tricycle drivers who used the area as a terminal while waiting for passengers from the university. In the mid-1970s, two huge government offices with several thousand employees were relocated to the area, and soon stalls offering fish, meat, and vegetables (a "wet market") began cropping up. For their utility requirements, vendors hooked up illegally to the main electricity line and to the university's water line. With the university putting pressure on them to move out, they organized a vendors' association in 1985, contributing set-up fees of 500 pesos per vendor. The association registered with city hall and with the Securities and Exchange Commission as a nonstock, nonprofit organization. It then lobbied the city government and convinced it to intercede for the vendors with the university. The vendors got legal electricity and water connections, and now pay business taxes regularly to the municipal government.

TABLE 3.4   Registration Status of Household Enterprises (percentage of respondents)

Activity	Registered with	
	National agency	Local government
Vending	22	51
Crafts/manufacturing	28	46
Personal services	30	55
Repair services	21	51
Transport	60	88
Construction	9	28

SOURCE: Alonzo and Abrera-Mangahas (1990).

For these vendors, the cost of becoming formal in the eyes of the local government means paying a business tax to city hall of as much as 150 pesos per quarter, depending on their sales declaration. In addition, they pay a daily hawkers' fee that varies according to the nature of the commodity sold: 2 pesos for fruits and vegetables, 5 pesos for rice and other cereals, 6 pesos for fish and meat. The association retails electricity at 2 pesos per day for a fluorescent light for three hours' use (from six to nine o'clock in the evening). The bigger stalls have their own water meters and sell water to the smaller stalls at 0.50 peso per pail. The association also collects a daily fee of 3 pesos per vendor for garbage disposal and for the cost of meetings.

A voluntary credit cooperative has also been formed. Each member contributes 10 pesos per day up to 1,000 pesos. A member whose contributions reach 100 pesos is already eligible to secure a loan. The maximum amount that a member can borrow is 1,000 pesos, payable in fifty-five days at a 10 percent interest rate over that period. An officer of the association collects the daily amortization of 20 pesos. Nonmembers who borrow from other informal sources pay 20 percent interest within sixty days.

Another group of vendors in a mini–public market near a major suburban intersection recently formed an association and call themselves the *Talipapang Gala* ("itinerant market"). Because they do not have the proper permits, they have been moved from place to place

Informal workers often display their wares on light, cheap structures like these wood-frame boxes so that they can easily get away if the patrolman on the beat decides to clamp down.

by local authorities. They have organized to lobby more effectively for a secure location, and the *barangay* council is helping them with their application for registration with city hall. But perhaps because the association is not yet well established, the city treasurer's office is assessing them 300 pesos per quarter for the business tax, compared with the 150 pesos per quarter for the older *talipapa* discussed earlier. The vendors are willing to pay only 100 pesos per quarter. City hall suggested by way of compromise that they form into groups of three, which the vendors do not want.

In a third case, a *talipapa* in front of a huge shopping complex, the vendors' association, which has long been registered with the SEC, is having problems recruiting members. Only forty of the seventy vendors in the area have joined the association; the others are afraid that they might be relocated by the city government. The business taxes that this *talipapa*'s vendors are charged are much steeper than those for other *talipapas*; it is not clear whether this is meant to discourage the vendors from operating in their current location or whether the "presumptive income" applied by the local authorities to businesses in the area is high. It is also possible that the municipal authorities are taking advantage of the relative weakness of the association, which has failed to attract all local vendors into becoming members.

These accounts illustrate how informal entrepreneurs engaged in retail trade respond to the different requirements of the law. The main recourse is the formation of an organization that will lobby for their interests. But association has its costs, with the vendors contributing fees that can amount to as much as what the government directly draws from them. Needless to say, at least part of these costs are eventually passed on to the vendors' consumers, most of whom belong to the poorer segments of society. A legal environment that would do away with this need to organize for the protection of the right to engage in legitimate business would certainly be in the interest of all concerned.

Informal housing. De Soto's study has shown how people in the informal sector of Peru make substantial investments in housing, in magnitudes that far outweigh what the government has achieved with its shelter program (de Soto 1989). But because the Peruvian informal households lack secure tenure and titles to their property, they find themselves unwilling to increase their investments, as they are unable to capitalize on them. They cannot use their most precious assets as collateral for securing loans. Does a similar pattern exist in the Philippines?

A survey conducted by the National Housing Authority in 1984 showed that, at the time, 26 percent of the Metro Manila population were squatters. More recent estimates by the Metro Manila Authority

show the squatter population to have grown to one-third of the metropolitan population.

Another study, focusing on two slum communities, concludes that security of tenure adds significantly to the investments people make in housing, a common finding in developing countries (Licayan and Sagun 1984). One area, lying within the campus of a large university, is populated by squatters who have no legal right to the land. The other area, some three kilometers away, used to be a squatter colony but was included in the government's Zonal Improvement Program, and the residents were granted tenure in the late 1970s.

Comparisons of the value of housing in the two communities are telling. In the squatter area, where average incomes were higher (the heads of households worked mainly at the university), the average value of housing structures was 11,600 pesos. In the tenured slum community the average value of the structures was 16,600 pesos or 44 percent higher. On a per-square-meter basis, the difference in value was even higher, at 76 percent. The study further showed that residents in the tenured slum area added improvements to their residences valued at 5 percent per year, while there were no appreciable improvements in the squatter community.

In late 1988, a group of squatter families in Taguig, Metro Manila, formed an association and negotiated with the landowner for the purchase of the property. A government housing finance agency provided a low-interest loan to the association, and some of the loan proceeds were used to purchase materials for the concrete steps (opposite) and the drainage ditch (above) seen in the photos. The dwellings have not yet been improved, perhaps because the reconstitution of the master title into individual titles for the parcels is still being processed as of early 1991. This type of amicable settlement of land disputes between squatters and landowners is unfortunately very rare.

Squatters in Metro Manila, however, face a problem somewhat different from those confronting the squatters in Lima. Whereas most of Lima's "invaders" apparently appropriate government property, a substantial proportion of invaded land in Manila is titled to private individuals. Out of the city's 3,000 hectares, only 625 hectares are public property.

The Philippine National Housing Authority has in the past relocated squatters on public land to resettlement areas outside the metropolis, giving them their own piece of property to amortize at very low cost. The settlers, however, often found the new areas too far from their places of work, and many eventually sold their rights and returned to the city. Recent relocation sites are closer to the metropolis.

In cases of invasion of private property, it is left to the owners to go to court. The courts do respect the pleas of property owners with a clear right to their land; eviction notices are swiftly granted and served by the sheriff's office. If the squatter colony is large, however, the residents have usually organized and eviction may not be feasible. In some cases, the landowner asks the local government or the National Housing Authority to buy the property for resale to the squatters. In other cases, nongovernment organizations mediate between owner and squatters to negotiate the sale of the property.

Institutions are thus in place to address the squatter problem. But given the magnitude of the situation, the government resources allocated to the "social housing" program are insufficient, and the subsidized loans offered to squatters may even attract more squatting. Meanwhile, private efforts, through the voluntary sale of squatted land, are hampered by the slow process of reconstitution of titles, which can drag on for years. Even the housing agencies of the government find it difficult to deal with the office of the Register of Deeds.

Toward an Agenda for Institutional Reforms

This study set out to examine informality in the Philippines from the standpoint of the informal participant's relationship with the law, following the framework and methodology of the ILD's research on Peru. It has shown that the fixed costs of starting a business and complying with all the legal requirements are a serious strain on the meager resources of the small entrepreneur. The costs of staying in business, imposed by various government rules and regulations, similarly impose a heavy burden. While the financial and fiscal incentives offered to formal enterprises are substantial and, on paper, nondiscriminatory, they are often outside the reach of the small businesses, because of the high cost of complying with the documentation requirements.

This chapter has examined informality in the Philippines, particularly in the transport sector, but also in trade and housing, using interviews with key participants. The two transport subsectors considered here—jeepney and tricycle operations—have developed different forms of institutions in response to different legal treatment (although both sets of institutions basically sought to minimize the costs imposed by government regulations). The laws will have to change for the informal transport workers to have a realistic chance to gain formal status. In the informal trade and housing sectors, associations were formed, not only to lobby for official recognition, but also to take care of the members' needs, such as sanitation maintenance and credit among vendors. These activities are normally handled by the state in the more developed countries.

The general conclusion of this chapter is that government rules are overly strict. In certain cases, regulation is necessary, for chaos would prevail if jeepneys and tricycles were allowed to ply any route and vendors could locate anywhere they chose. Enforcement, however, generally has been lax and sporadic. As a result, the informal sector has grown large, often with the complicity of the law enforcers themselves, who are paid to look the other way. But the threat of prosecution remains, keeping the informals from expanding their operations.

The pursuit of institutional reforms will, of course, depend on how the rules are made. In the Philippines, for almost fifteen years before 1986, almost every law was issued by presidential decree or executive order. The Parliament served merely as a rubber stamp for the president. Initially, this system was lauded by many as providing "dynamic flexibility" and a quick response mechanism for any situation. Only much later did people realize that this also meant bad laws could be passed as easily as good ones.

The 1987 Constitution reintroduced the system prevailing before martial law, wherein an independent bicameral legislature coexists with the executive and judiciary branches. The revival of Congress has been met with mixed reactions; while there are those who hail it as establishing more governmental accountability, others bewail the fact (or perception) that the government is so concerned with politics that it accomplishes little. Both views are probably partly correct, but the net effect of the new institutions appears to be positive. The experience of 1986 has made people more aware that they need to be consulted on major issues, and public hearings are conducted before the passage of important laws. Sometimes, however, the public hearings are railroaded; invitations to known opponents may arrive only after the hearing, but the records will nevertheless falsely reflect their having attended.

People's organizations and cause-oriented groups are very active in putting pressure on the legislature to enact certain laws and on government agencies to pursue certain administrative reforms. The debate is often carried out not only among political commentators in the various media but also in costly newspaper advertisements. When divergent interests clash, there is the appearance of chaos and nothing seems to move. Rightist elements are quick to exploit the situation with claims of paralysis in the present government and the need for a stronger executive. But these are the costs of democratic processes.

Some significant policy reforms have been instituted under the new political framework. This study has discussed several of them, such as the *Kalakalan* 20, which would simplify business-registration procedures for small enterprises, and the administrative reforms being implemented by the Department of Transportation with respect to public transport. The local autonomy code, which would devolve more powers to the local government, is still being debated in the legislature, however, with the congressmen apparently afraid of losing political power to their rival local executives.

Certainly, all is not well with the nation's economy and polity. The new institutions have yet to establish roots. The causes espoused by many organized interest groups may be parochial and even harmful to other segments of society. A prime example is the strong lobbying by organized producers for the domestic market against the implementation of a recently passed executive order restructuring tariffs, which led to the order's postponement. Meanwhile, the consumers being hurt by excessive protection are diffused and unorganized.

Grass-roots organizations, such as those of the informal entrepreneurs, also need to be more informed about macroeconomic policy issues and their long-term consequences. The country cannot afford a jeepney strike every time oil prices are adjusted to reflect world market developments. The government, especially Congress, too often reacts to popular sentiments by accommodating them and postponing the necessary adjustments that, although they might hurt consumers in the short run, would put the economy on a firmer footing in the long run.

The Informal Sector in Sri Lanka: Dynamism and Resilience

Informal economic activities are an integral part of the Sri Lankan economy. Informal enterprises dominate the rural economy, are extensive in towns, play a vital role in cities, and are indispensable in the metropolis, Colombo. Their activities cover the whole range of goods and services. They provide the basic needs of food, shelter, and clothing; they play an important role in transport; they produce manufactures for local use and export; they offer indispensable services to the business community; and they are significant providers of financial services. Indeed, without the informal sector, the wheels of commerce would turn slowly. Food supplies would diminish to famine levels. Transport would be hopelessly inefficient. Moreover, food, clothing, and basic services would become too expensive for the majority of Sri Lankans.

Informal enterprises are so extensive and pervasive that they are taken for granted, and the largest group of Sri Lanka's informal

I am very grateful to my collaborators for the assistance given to me in different ways in the preparation of this chapter. They include P. M. D. Fernando, Gunapala Gamage, Dayasiri de Mel, V. J. Inbaraj, Raj Kotwala, and Amal Sanderatne. I am also thankful to Dharshanie Alles and Asuntha Paul for painstakingly composing several drafts of the chapter on the word processor, and to Nanda Abeysekera for carefully checking the manuscript.

71

actors—farmers—are overlooked, while those engaged in illicit and illegal occupations—bootleggers, bookies, prostitutes, and drug peddlers—are generally recognized as informal. If the entire range and array of informal activities could be accurately accounted, it might be shown that they contribute a larger share of gross domestic product (GDP) than does the formal sector. Though a precise estimate is impossible to make, the observations that most agricultural produce comes from informal small farms; that most mining and quarrying, construction, nonfactory industry, and retail trading is informal; that a significant proportion of transport and related services are provided by informals; and that informal financial sources are important in town and country alike support the estimate that informal sector activities are equal to about 50 percent of GDP.

Sri Lanka permits the existence and operation of the informal economy, except for illicit activities that fall outside the pale of the law. Informal enterprises are an integral part of the social fabric of the country, and many of their activities have deep social roots. Informal entrepreneurs often have support in high places, and when they transgress the law, influential persons intervene to extricate them. As part of its policy of eradicating poverty and unemployment, the government fosters development of informal self-employment ventures among youth, even to the extent of persuading banks to extend them credit. There is a growing official recognition that self-employment projects help to alleviate unemployment and contribute significantly to the economy of the country. The promotion of informal enterprises is accepted as an economically rational strategy for development.

The law in Sri Lanka allows a person to carry on a business under his or her full, true name without any additional requirements. Therefore, an informal enterprise need not go through the process of registration, though this process is simple, extremely cheap (five rupees or twelve U.S. cents), and more or less automatic, taking only about two weeks. Local government bodies may levy an additional fee, but they do not require much time or paperwork.

There are several reasons why Sri Lanka's informal firms remain informal. Registration, compliance with administrative rules, maintenance of proper accounts, strict observance of labor laws, and payment of taxes and other fees would add a great deal of complexity and cost to many simple operations, resulting in a loss of comparative advantage for informal firms. In addition, bureaucratic procedures and formalities are an incomprehensible burden to many informal entrepreneurs. Tax avoidance is a less important consideration for very small informal enterprises, but more prosperous informal entrepreneurs do not relish having to pay municipal taxes, business turnover taxes, and income taxes. When compelled to become formal, they avoid taxes, often with the help of accountants and tax advisers. Finally, most informal actors perceive the supposed advantages of the formal sector, such as access to banking facilities and credit, as unavailable to them even if they were to enter the formal economy. "Banks," they say, "won't give us money in any case."

The informal-formal nexus is often a symbiotic relationship: the two economies coexist rather than compete; they complement rather than supplement; they are interdependent and often vertically integrated, though without formal links. Informal enterprises often provide a less expensive, acceptable alternative, and where formal and informal firms provide the same product or service, their marketing is different, and the price and quality of the product distinguishable. Their clientele may be differentiated by economic or social class, though the vast majority of Sri Lankans do, to a greater or lesser degree, patronize the informal economy. Formal firms often subcontract with informal ones for partly or nearly finished products, inputs for manufactures, and a multiplicity of services. Many informal enterprises are by-products of the formal sector or offshoots of it. Far from overwhelming the informal economy, the recent growth of Sri Lanka's formal sector has generated a new impetus, provided new opportunities, expanded markets, and created new needs for informal activity.

What, then, are the disadvantages of being informal? Some businesses and government departments do not, or legally cannot, contract with individuals or unregistered enterprises. To get orders, a firm needs printed letterhead, a telephone, a recognized reputation, and previous fulfilled contracts. An unregistered business enterprise cannot open a bank account, which is a serious disadvantage, as payments are usually made by check. Formal bank credit is difficult to obtain without a banking relationship, audited accounts, and proof of tax payments, so the informal firms opt for informal finance, which is easier to get and has more flexible terms, but is decisively more costly. Certain concessions in duties on imported raw materials for manufactures are available only to registered firms, and so informal enterprises pay higher import prices.

Informal businesses, by the nature of their activity and location, often transgress health and hygiene laws, traffic rules, and zoning and construction regulations. Such transgressions often provide officials and police opportunities to harass informal entrepreneurs and obtain bribes and benefits. Transgressions are often allowed to continue, with the bribery adding to the cost of the informal enterprise.

No doubt there are costs and disadvantages that accrue to society and the economy as a result of informal businesses' not being formally registered. Many informal entrepreneurs might expand their activities if their resource bases could be augmented either through bank credit or equity participation. Some informal enterprises that began as home-based industries have grown to be big businesses with the help of bank finance, especially with special credit schemes designed to finance small industries at low rates of interest. Informal businesses, by remaining informal, may be producing less than their attainable levels. Apart from creating a lower output, informal firms also deny the government tax revenues.

The Informal Economy: Scenes and Human Faces

Sri Lankans interact with the informal sector early in life. Children leaving their school gate will come upon the familiar figure of a woman selling local olives boiled in brine, or sliced raw mango, served with powdered chili and salt, or mustard and vinegar. As adults, Sri Lankans turn to the informal economy for food, clothing, shelter, transport, education, and financial services, as well as many other goods and services.

A survey of informal sector activities.

Food. Vendors of vegetables and fruits, selling from kiosks, wheelbarrows, or stands set up for the day, or even from gunnysacks spread out by the road, are a common sight in Sri Lanka. The produce they sell is either procured from suburban areas and moved into the city for sale or purchased from an urban wholesale market. In some cases the vendor makes the purchases directly; in others, a middleman does the procuring and collects a commission on the sales. When possible, the vendor purchases fruit by offering a price for the entire crop of a given tree; the fruit is picked and sold by the vendor as it matures. Alternatively, a middleman, generally one who has access to transport, obtains fruit from a wholesale market at a discounted price and supplies vendors with their needs. Itinerant vendors of vegetables and fruits coexist with produce merchants in the various municipal markets in the city. Generally there is no friction between the two groups.

Informal fish selling is a similar operation. Vendors carry their fish in baskets from house to house on foot or by bicycle, or set them down for sale on the roadside. Fish are either purchased directly from fishermen by the vendor, or, more likely, by a middleman, who purchases part or all of a catch on the beach as the net comes in, and who distributes the fish to vendors. The fisherman, dealing as he does with a perishable commodity, is unable to devote his time to sales, and therefore depends totally on the middleman, another informal entrepreneur.

Most vegetable and fish vendors do not have enough capital to purchase their daily stock. They therefore borrow the sum from an informal lender and repay the loan at the end of the day with interest, reborrowing the capital the next day. This interest, converted to an annual rate, is astronomical. Suranganee, a fish seller, borrows 500 rupees each day. On a good day she sells her stock for 700 rupees, pays "madam," an informal lender, 50 rupees, and is able to retain about 100 rupees after expenses for transport and meals. On a bad day she manages to pay back just the capital and interest, and on some days not even the interest. On such days "madam is very good," for she allows Suranganee to repay on the next day, or in two days. Despite thirty years of selling fish, Suranganee has been unable to generate her own capital. Instead, she pays an interest rate of 3,650 percent per year!

Cooked and processed food is an important informal industry, featuring a linkup between the informal and the formal economies. The sale, through grocery stores, of homemade cakes, rolls, pastries, and fudges has grown in recent years. Housewives wishing to earn a little money prepare these foods and provide them to a grocery store for sale on a regular basis. Production of these goods is in the informal economy; their sale is through a formally registered grocery store. There are also confectioner's shops whose supplies are produced by independent bakers in their own home kitchens. On the other hand, many products of the formal economy, like bottled beverages and tobacco, are often sold by informal vendors.

Rosie, who lost her husband in a car accident a few years ago, has a paltry income of 1,500 rupees a month from the interest on her husband's pension fund. This was barely adequate to support Rosie's two small children and mother. She began baking cakes and pastries at home. When this became too strenuous, she shifted to catering for parties and now earns an added income of about 3,000 rupees a month.

At one time, city workers would have their lunch prepared at home and delivered to the office, for a relatively small payment, by lunch carriers on bicycles. Today, the lunch carriers have disappeared. What has emerged in their place are suppliers of lunch parcels. Cooked lunches are made (rice and curries, with a choice of fish, meat, or vegetables), packed in thin plastic wrapping, and then parceled in sheets of newspaper and sold throughout the city and its suburbs. These lunch parcels are produced either by eateries or in the home kitchens of individuals, but they are almost invariably sold through formal establishments (luncheonettes, grocery stores, and even laundries!). Here again, a symbiotic relationship exists between the informal and the formal sectors. The informal sector does much of the production, but the marketing is left to outlets in the formal sector, which have the capacity and the means to sell products efficiently. It must be said, though, that there are also informal eateries that sell lunch parcels, along with other items, including food, drink, and tobacco.

Typical of a small-scale entrepreneur in the lunch-parcel business is Noeline, who lived for a time in Australia but returned to Sri Lanka to look after her aged grandaunt. Noeline saw in the lunch-parcel trade a means of steady income. Today she makes thirty parcels a day and sells them at the standard price of 15 rupees each. Her profit is around 2,500 rupees per month. Noeline's clients know her, and they prefer to buy her parcels, owing to their dependably hygienic quality. Noeline's informal economic activities also encompass other catering, interior decorating, and house cleaning.

Shelter. Housing construction is, by and large, an informal enterprise. Informal bricklayers, carpenters, masons, plumbers, and construction workers operate individually or in groups. They are skilled in the construction of housing units and business premises, except for high rises and large buildings, which are generally erected by construction firms.

An individual building his own house in Sri Lanka may engage an architect to design the house, but beyond this he will likely entrust the job to a *baas*, or head of an informal group of construction workers. A *baas* and his gang will charge considerably less than a construction firm or a contractor. Most simple construction is done in this way.

Word passed around a neighborhood, particularly in the hardware stores, will produce an informal plumber, mason, or carpenter to do home repairs. Some of these workmen have regular jobs, but take on private jobs outside working hours or on holidays, or will absent themselves from their regular jobs.

Repair services. Import liberalization and money sent home by Sri Lankan workers in the Middle East have allowed a proliferation, among a wide segment of the population, of electrical goods, including televisions, videocassette recorders, stereo sets, tape players, and electrical appliances. This situation leads naturally to a demand for a service and repair sector. There are several types of such businesses. At the most formal level, there is the agent for the manufacturer of the appliance concerned. There are also smaller repair shops that undertake the repair of any appliance, regardless of its brand name. These shops may or may not be in the formal sector. Some of them employ their own technicians, while others obtain the after-hours services of electricians working for formal enterprises. Finally, there are repair workers who operate purely on an individual basis.

A similar pattern exists for businesses that repair motor vehicles. Individual informal mechanics are responsible for a significant volume of motor repairs and are often preferred to large garages as offering greater expertise and integrity, as well as more flexible hours of work.

Clothing. A revolution has overtaken informal clothing manufacture in Sri Lanka. At one time, only a few ladies conducted dressmaking schools in the country's major cities, catering to "genteel" young ladies from middle-class urban and suburban houses who learned dressmaking as a personal accomplishment, like music and cooking.

The picture is dramatically different today. Sri Lanka is full of modern household sewing machines purchased with the earnings of workers employed abroad. As a result, dressmaking classes have now multiplied and been transformed into more egalitarian sewing schools. Because of the growth of the formal textile and garment industries, a wide variety of textiles has become available, and garment workers have been exposed to new styles made for markets in developed countries. The influence of the garment industry on informal clothing manufacture is significant.

Themis is a *mudalali,* or entrepreneur, who earns a fortune purchasing fabric remnants in bulk from the garment factories in the suburbs south of Colombo. Themis has contacts in each of these factories who ensure that he will succeed in the bidding to buy such throwaways. Themis takes the remnants to a large house, where young girls and boys sort the pieces by fabric, size and color. The smaller pieces are packaged as cleaning cloths and sold to shops for five rupees per package. The shops sell these packages to customers for seven and a half rupees each.

The bigger and better pieces are bought by informal garment manufacturers. Matilda is one manufacturer who obtains her supplies from Themis. Her five female sewing machine operators make clothes, using both fabric remnants and textiles bought in the local market. The operators earn from seventy to eighty rupees a day, depending on the number of items sewn. Mary, a recent widow, has a more limited operation. She obtains fabric pieces directly from a garment factory and makes only underwear. She sells her output to a distributor who supplies all the pavement hawkers in one populous town. The secret of Mary's success is that her prices are lower than the prices of similar products in the wholesale marketplace.

The garments produced by these informal manufacturers include underwear, children's dresses, and even men's shirts and women's skirts and blouses. Equally varied is the manner of their sale; one can find them for sale at sidewalk stands or in more formal shops.

The informal clothing industry illustrates how spinoffs from the formal economy (fabrics from the garment industry, remittances from workers in the Middle East) have stimulated the growth of the informal sector. The informal and formal clothing industries coexist, with no clash between them.

Another informal clothing business dates back to far earlier times. Hidden away in the heart of Colombo is a thriving industry that recycles clothes by making "reconditioned" garments. Old trousers and shirts, bought by agents calling at private homes, are cut into smaller pieces and made into children's garments. A pair of recycled blue shorts, the standard uniform of school boys, is sold at a wholesale rate of five rupees per pair; a new pair costs as much as seventy-five rupees. Recycled clothes, cleverly made from old materials, are often sold by street vendors as new. In any case, the price difference is so large that recycled clothes are the only affordable type for a large number of poor people.

One of the chief informal industries in Sri Lanka is the batik cloth-printing industry, which, though found all over the island, is concentrated in areas frequented by tourists. Shirts, blouses, wall-hangings, and long dresses are among the many batik items produced in these informal enterprises. Generally, an owner of a "batik factory" employs a designer and a few girls to do the printing by hand. Most of these enterprises are situated in homes, though some factories producing batiks on a larger scale are formal enterprises.

An informal industry that has developed recently is the manufacture of soft toys. This, too, is a spinoff from the garment industry, as these toys are made out of remnants from clothing factories. The soft toy industry has grown to such proportions that it has achieved vertical integration, with some places specializing in producing particular parts, such as eyes, ears, eyelashes, and so on.

Subcontracting in manufacturing. The informal sector in manufacturing has grown considerably, owing to an expansion of the practice of subcontracting. Although subcontracting has long been a mode of industrial production, its real growth has occurred since the economic reforms of 1977, which liberalized the economy and promoted private production of export goods. Informal enterprises have therefore been linked to export markets, by virtue of their subcontractual relationship to large industrial ventures. Among the areas of such subcontracting are the manufacture of artificial flowers, joss sticks, garments, footwear, electrical components, and umbrellas. In most of these enterprises, informal production is done either at home or in small units informally organized by an entrepreneur. Most such informal workers are women, partly because many of these activities are believed to be more suited to female abilities, but perhaps more because lower wages can be paid to women working part-time or at home (Centre for Women's Research Sri Lanka 1989).

Transport. Transport is an important informal activity. Informal firms transport goods by nearly all means—from trucks to human carriers. The Pettah, which was the mercantile center of Colombo in colonial Sri Lanka, has, today, fallen from its earlier eminence, but it remains a significant trading area for all manner of goods. A common sight is the human figure either carrying loads on its back or trundling goods in a trolley. There was a time when these porters were registered, each one with a distinctive number, which placed them in the formal economy. Today, however, they are very much part of the informal economy, hiring out their services to whoever needs them, whether from the formal or the informal sector. A typical carrier is Cassim, who has been transporting goods on a trolley for the past twenty-two years. He rents the trolley from a "merchant" who has about 150 of them for hire, at 17 rupees each for the day. On an average day Cassim takes in about 100 rupees and takes home about 70 rupees after paying for the trolley and for his meals and tea. On days when he is unable to earn enough money, he pays the trolley hire fee on a subsequent day. The owner gives him a maximum of three days' grace. Cassim complains he has less and less work. "The bazaar is not very busy now," he says. When it is suggested that business may be slow because there are too many trolleys, he says no.

Razak is one among an estimated 1,500 to 2,000 carriers of goods in baskets in Colombo. He hires a basket each day for 7 rupees, and says he takes in between 50 and 60 rupees per day. Although a basket costs between 350 and 500 rupees, Razak and his fellow carriers have not bought their own, though the savings would repay the purchase price in about three months. They do not think that a bank would lend them the money to buy a basket.

Porters like Cassim and Razak are known as *natamis*. So is Dason, who loads and unloads trucks that bring and take merchandise from a glass shop in the Pettah. There are five other *natamis* like Dason near the glass shop. Dason has been working for eighteen years for the same shop. He considers himself such a specialist that he would not condescend to work in any other task, unless as a favor to someone known to him. On days when he has little or no work, he ignores opportunities for other work, preferring to spend his time smoking and chewing betel.

Natamis are found throughout the Pettah, outside the wholesale shops, waiting to be summoned to their task. The day's work done, the *natami* leaves his trolley or basket with the shop owner, from whom he is sure of obtaining work the next day, and spends the evening drinking, gambling, and perhaps smoking cannabis. Sufficient unto the day is the evil thereof!

The *natamis* are specialized in their work, are thoroughly honest and dependable, and are knowledgeable about businessmen in the Pettah. They require few instructions, if any. They provide a completely dependable courier service, quick in delivery, and the only practical means of delivery through the Pettah's narrow streets, congested with parked vehicles and teeming crowds.

There is no informal sector in the bus services that ply in the country because both state-owned and private services must conform to routes laid down and formally allotted by the government. However, in other areas of passenger transport, the formal and the informal exist side by side and sometimes even interact with each other.

There are three categories of transport vehicles used for carrying persons—the trishaw (motorized tricycle), the car, and the van or bus. Even though these vehicles are registered to collect fares, they do not necessarily belong to taxi companies or persons registered as fleet operators. They often belong to individuals who drive them for hire themselves or who rent them out to drivers; the day's takings are divided between the owner and the driver on a pre-arranged basis, or the owner receives a fixed sum of money at the end of the day.

This is particularly the case with tricycles. John owns his trishaw, which he bought two years ago for 63,000 rupees. He bought it from savings by working in Germany as a seaman. He says he earns about 350 rupees on an average day and 500 rupees on a very good day. He also says his overhead expenditure is around 100 rupees for gasoline and refreshments. He works as long as he can on weekdays, but, being a Christian, he doesn't work on Sunday. Many Sri Lankans returning from the Middle East have invested in a trishaw and either operate it themselves or hire it out for an income. A new trishaw now costs about 90,000 rupees (US$2,250).

Unlike John, Dasa rents his trishaw from a *mudalali* who owns six such vehicles. On an average day Dasa earns about 300 rupees, from which he has to pay 150 rupees in rent and meet fuel costs (the rent on newer trishaws is about 200 rupees). He says he gets only about 75 rupees for his labor except on a very good day.

Trishaw fares are flexible and are arrived at through bargaining with the driver before the vehicle is engaged. Though established taxicab companies exist, the bulk of city passenger transportation is in trishaws, which can be easily hailed on the roads—unlike taxis, which are much fewer. Taxi services with radio cabs in the formal sector appear none the worse for competition with the informal sector.

Passenger vehicles are also available for hire, although they are registered for private, personal use. These vehicles are, in fact, privately owned and used for private transport, but are also operated for hire for certain limited purposes. There are cars among them, but the majority of them are passenger vans, which are cheaper to operate, carrying a larger number of passengers than cars, yet with similar running costs.

It is common in Sri Lankan urban areas to find children transported to and from school by passenger vans. The vans may then either be

The trishaw, a popular mode of transport for people, is also used to transport goods, such as bananas.

driven away on other work or stay parked by the school premises to take the same children home at the end of the day. These vans also often take the children of the owner to school, and not infrequently the owner drives the vehicle himself. There are vans transporting children to schools from distances of as much as 20 miles. These vans do not regularly operate for hire but do only specific, limited jobs. Similar private van transport arrangements are available for travel to and from office areas at rush hours. Vans are also available for hire for trips to the airport or by groups going out on picnics, pilgrimages, or pleasure trips. All arrangements are, naturally, made informally, and one does not go through the telephone directory to find them. It is not that they operate surreptitiously, but merely that these informal entrepreneurs rely on word-of-mouth advertising rather than promotional campaigns.

Education. Sri Lanka is renowned for its high literacy rate (87 percent), its free education system extending from primary school through university, and its network of more than ten thousand schools. Given this institutional context, education until recently was not only almost entirely in the formal sector but was mostly a government activity. Informal educational services consisted mainly of limited private tutoring for public examinations—and then mainly in mathematics and science subjects, and among the affluent.

The situation has changed dramatically in the past few years; informal educational services have multiplied many times over. The reasons for this are several. The severe erosion of teachers' salaries by inflation has left them with no alternative but to find additional sources of income. What began as tutoring for a trickle of more affluent children who were backward in certain subjects has been contrived by the teachers themselves into a huge program of essential teaching for vast numbers of students. Extracurricular teaching has been made essential by teachers deliberately neglecting their teaching at school, by their favoring students who are tutored by them, and by their making it quite clear that the syllabus will not be completed in school alone. This informalization of educational services got a boost when, in 1989, for months on end, schools were closed because of insurgent activities.

Another reason for the increased informalization of education is the high demand for certain employable skills, including knowledge of English (which is inadequately taught in most schools), computer programming, and accountancy. In the fields of computer programming and accountancy most teaching is in tutorials, which, although registered and therefore officially in the formal sector, are often very small enterprises with only one or two teachers. Alongside these tutorials are individuals who teach these subjects in their homes, often in an outer room or a garage converted for the purpose. Some teachers visit their pupils' homes for a higher fee and teach the individual pupil, or a group of his or her classmates or neighbors.

This situation has now reached such proportions that it is generally admitted that if a student is to make good, private tutoring is a *sine qua non*. Informal educational services and the private tutorial have virtually taken over quality education in Sri Lanka, though of course most children, particularly in rural areas, are denied such informal education because of its expense.

Financial services. Financial services are an important informal activity. Informal lenders in urban areas are a source of financing for a wide range of economic activities, from petty trading to the large investments of unincorporated firms. Such borrowings are used by retail vendors to purchase the produce they sell, by proprietary enterprises to purchase capital items, and by traders for financing their stocks. In urban areas the high rates obtainable in informal lending have led to the development of a significant informal credit market. Some of the funds for this market are personal funds from entrepreneurs, and others come from institutionalized sources. The informal credit market has been a boon to many small formal enterprises that have increased their incomes by lending from their liquid funds.

In rural areas, informal moneylenders predominate. Professional moneylenders and others who combine lending with trading and marketing fill most rural financial needs. Informal credit societies and rotating credit groups also operate. Considering the fact that institutional lending serves fewer than 4 percent of farmers growing rice and other food crops, there can be little doubt that informal sources provide most funds in the rural economy (Sanderatne 1989b).

Brokering. Informal brokering is a feature of business in the Pettah. Brokers, who are a storehouse of information on the Pettah's business climate, its imports, and the movements of its goods, are relied on by many wholesalers to determine when to sell their products, in what quantities, and at what prices. They move among the business houses, mingling and chatting with the proprietors and arranging deals for them. They appear to earn commissions ranging from 2,000 to 10,000 rupees per month.

Another conspicuous informal enterprise is the unofficial market in duty-free goods. Sri Lanka has a duty-free complex in which visiting foreigners and Sri Lankans returning from abroad are allowed to purchase goods, up to a prescribed limit. Many Sri Lankan workers returning from the Middle East do not use their entire duty-free allowance. Informal traders have developed a secondary market in duty-free goods by purchasing duty-free allowances for a fee and then selling the goods to others, at a price that is still considerably cheaper than that in the regular market. Goods traded in this manner include refrigerators, television sets, videocassette recorders, stereo sets, and other household electrical items. The turnover of these items is sufficiently large that, with a small margin of profit per item (200–300 rupees each), the informal traders are able to make handsome incomes. Returnees, for their part, obtain a few thousand rupees more for their currency, since those who sell their duty-free allowance are given a higher rate of exchange on the informal market.

Other informal enterprises. Although this description has attempted to capture the flavor of the extensive informal sector, several areas of informal activities still have not been touched upon. These include the very important area of prospecting for precious and semiprecious stones, and the trade in these stones, which lies largely outside the formal activity. Traditionally, the gem trade conducts its business without records, on absolute trust and conforming to a number of superstitions. The high value of gems and the traders' desire to avoid taxation are also important reasons for remaining informal.

Small-time informal carpenters hawk their furniture—including beds—on the streets and deliver the furniture to homes.

Another area of considerable importance in the informal sector is the manufacture of pottery, brassware, silverware, and wooden handicrafts. These activities have increased in importance, owing to an expansion of markets created through tourism and exports. There are also a number of commodities processed from Sri Lanka's coconut crop. These include brown and white coir fiber, carpets, brushes, and brooms. Finally, informal production of furniture for household use is an extensive enterprise. Though large furniture firms operate in this trade, they often subcontract with small informal carpenters, who produce most household furniture; the furniture is then marketed through formal and informal channels.

Such then is the vast expanse of the informal sector.

Profile of an informal entrepreneur. The story of Pala, an informal entrepreneur turned formal, illustrates the difficulties, exploitation, and harassment faced by most informal actors, as well as the resilience, skills, and innovativeness of some of them.

Pala came to live at the suburban home of the Heraths when he was only four years old with his widowed mother, who became the domestic servant in the household. When he was six, his mother remarried and left the Heraths. She left behind little Pala, who was to work as a servant while he attended school. He studied at the nearby government school until seventh grade, then at a charity school and a tutorial, in an attempt to pass the O-level examination. Within the Herath household, he learned English, helped now and then by Mrs. Herath.

At nineteen Pala worked in the pantry of a small hotel, then for one year as an apprentice with an electrician who took pains to ensure that he did not learn wiring. Instead, Pala was taught how to break walls, and how to plaster them after the wiring was done. Both jobs left him with no savings, and no real skills except perhaps the skill of survival. Pala then worked as a clerk in an engineering firm for two years.

Still dissatisfied with his lot, Pala met by chance his old school friend Shan, who suggested a possibly profitable business enterprise— that of making medicated bandage strips, whose import had been banned. They bought large bandage rolls, cut these into strips, attached a piece of gauze dipped in flavin, and sold the strips in packets of 25 to shops. This enterprise, which was a success at first, gradually became unprofitable after a change of economic regime brought back imports of bandage strips.

Then, with his friend Shan, he attempted to sell pharmaceuticals to retail outlets. The wholesale distributor required him to purchase the pharmaceuticals, which he was then to deliver to the various outlets. Since he required 500 rupees and had only 100 rupees of his own funds, he borrowed 300 rupees from the Heraths' son, who had recently returned from working abroad. Shan chipped in with another 100 rupees, and so began their enterprise of distributing pharmaceuticals. They soon encountered cash problems caused by delays in collection, which left them short of money to purchase from the distributor. They changed their system to one of delivering on the basis of orders only, but this brought them inadequate income, and ultimately they lost their original capital. Pala was long unable to pay his patron the money he had borrowed.

Pala next helped supervise the construction of a friend's house, which led him to informal work in construction, including wiring and house repairs. He soon obtained contracts for construction work, assembled workers, and supervised them.

While he was in this line of work, he came across an advertisement for repairing the air-conditioning system of a very important building in Colombo. He had no experience in this field, but the engineer overseeing the plant promised to help him.

Pala faced two serious problems. First, in order to tender a bid he required letterhead and a business address, which he did not have. Second, he did not know how to tender bids in an appropriate way. So he went to an accountant he knew, who agreed to help him in return for a partnership in the enterprise, got in touch with the engineer, and determined a price for the contract of 17,500 rupees. Pala had found that the cost of getting the work done, excluding his own labor, would be 7,000 rupees. The accountant suggested that the remaining 10,500 rupees be divided equally between the engineer, without whose assistance the tender would not be accepted, and the two of them. Pala hurriedly printed twenty-five sheets of a letterhead, included the telephone number of the accountant, and gave as his business address the address of a Buddhist temple in Colombo whose priest he knew. While the letterhead was being printed, he rushed to the Registrar of Companies, filled out the registration form, and paid the fee of 5 rupees. He obtained the registration number immediately, as the accountant had conferred in advance with an appropriate bureaucrat. The registration document was promised in two weeks' time, and it arrived as expected. The order was obtained and the contract executed.

To cash the payment check for 17,500 rupees, Pala required a bank account in the name of his business. Pala decided to open the account in a bank where the accountant's brother was the manager, although the bank was about thirty miles away. Pala called at the bank, met the accountant's brother, filled out the forms, made an initial cash deposit of 100 rupees, and later cashed the check. The accountant now suggested that the profit be divided differently from the original agreement and that Pala give him, the accountant, 5,000 rupees, that he give the engineer 3,000 rupees, and that Pala keep 2,500 rupees. For Pala, this was more income than he had received ever in his life. He was happy and grateful to the engineer and the accountant.

The accountant and Pala continued to operate the firm, which remained in Pala's sole name. The accountant was to receive a two-thirds share of each contract, while one-third went to Pala. They registered with Public Corporations to do contract work for the government of less than 25,000 rupees. The type of work varied according to demand, and generally consisted of contracts to provide furniture, partitioning, and plumbing.

At this time severe restrictions on imports were in place, and certain types of bolts and nuts were not available in the country. The accountant began to manufacture these items in a fairly primitive and labor-intensive manner. Pala became the salesman for these items. This was done in addition to Pala's contract work, as such work was uncertain and periodic. The demand for these nuts and bolts was initially so heavy that they could obtain advances of payment against orders. But with the liberalization of economic policy in 1977 and the establishment of large factories to turn out these products, they lost the market.

The accountant and Pala decided now to establish their contract work on a firmer footing. One of the difficulties he had faced earlier was the temple address. Customers would call at the temple and, finding no business, take their orders elsewhere. Pala also often lacked suitable tools. The accountant and Pala rented a small office, obtained a phone, and arranged to borrow tools from the company in which the accountant was employed. Since the office required a permanent staff, the accountant employed a woman to be in charge of the office. Work progressed well for about three years, but difficulties arose once the woman became romantically involved with the accountant. About this time they also began to find it difficult to obtain skilled plumbers and masons, as there had been an exodus of labor to the Middle East. Pala had financial difficulties and so quit the enterprise.

Pala began another phase of contracting by himself. This time, Sam, a gentleman who was involved in a firm that required various construction jobs to be done, assisted him in various ways. Pala completed several projects to the satisfaction of the firm. Since payment for orders was normally made after completion of work, Sam assisted Pala by agreeing to pay half the cost in advance and to pay the remainder in stages as various parts of the work were completed. At this time Sam's firm decided to move into the field of selling gems. For this purpose they required display windows and jewelry boxes. Sam suggested that Pala execute this order, but Pala had no experience in this type of work. So Pala went about visiting jewelry shops and places making these products, pretending to be seeking to buy, and obtained prices. He then went to a neighborhood specializing in the manufacture of these items and made contact with Guruge, who had worked in this business for over twenty years and had recently lost his job. Pala employed Guruge to give him information on the machines and implements required, all of which, in fact, cost only 500 rupees. Pala had no difficulty in finding the money for these items, as he had saved money from his previous year's earnings.

He made a few sample boxes and took them over to Sam's company, where they were refused as not being good enough. Pala offered to provide new, better, samples, and said he would guarantee that the final products would conform to those samples. He also sought a firm order from the company and asked that 50 percent of the value of the order be paid in advance. The firm agreed and placed a first order for 10,000 rupees.

Again Pala needed to register as a business enterprise in order to open an account to cash his checks. He had no difficulties registering, paying five rupees as before. He met with officers of one of the two state banks in the vicinity after he received his business registration and opened an account on his second visit with a small sum of money. The bank placed its seal on the business registration. Subsequently, the bank account was closed because Pala assisted his old friend Shan by writing him some checks, which Shan promised he would not cash until equivalent deposits were made. Shan did not keep his word and the bank closed Pala's account.

Pala required a bank account to continue his business, but he realized he could not open an account with the same registration without disclosing that the first bank, whose seal was on his registration, had closed his account. He therefore went to the Registrar of Companies and registered his business anew with the same name, but a new address.

Meanwhile a new development had occurred. Mr. and Mrs. Herath, who brought him up, invited him to occupy the garage in their house and manufacture his jewelry cases there. The Heraths had grown old and feeble, and Pala's presence was, for them, a form of security. To Pala this was a godsend, as he was having difficulties at his own house with thugs who sought protection money.

Pala has since progressed continuously, gaining a strong reputation for his jewelry boxes. An indication of the quality of his product is that the president of Sri Lanka sent his wedding gift to Prince Charles in a box made by Pala. He now employs six laborers. His two brothers, employed in government enterprises, work for him part-time, and his third brother is one of his employees.

With a decline in tourism since 1983, owing to security problems in the country, the demand for jewelry boxes declined. Pala therefore diversified his products and now makes steel and aluminum display racks and cupboards. He also designs machinery for the manufacture of jewelry boxes. He now owns more advanced machinery, and instead of using imported velvet cloth he does the flocking with a machine he has bought, and imports raw materials for it. He also obtains remnants from the garment industry for use as cloth for his boxes. He has no cash savings, but has bought a house in which his mother and brothers live.

Pala's transition from informal to formal exemplifies the constraints and difficulties imposed on the expansion of an informal entrepreneur's activities. He had no option but to commence informally, acquire skills and know-how in a most tedious and time-consuming manner, and transfer his skills from one enterprise to another. His ability to obtain work was constrained without the trappings of formality—premises, registration as a business enterprise, letterhead, bank account, and telephone. Without these he would have been denied access to clients and markets in the formal sector.

Conforming to minimal formal requirements, Pala now has carved out for himself an enterprise that is formal in status and informal in its functional behavior, like many small enterprises in Sri Lanka. Operating as a full-fledged formal enterprise would render him uncompetitive and rob him of a very personalized and distinctive enterprise.

The Analysis

Contribution to GDP. The narrative and description of the informal actors in the previous section indicated their presence in every sector of the economy, albeit mainly as small enterprises. Despite their pervasiveness, the nature of informal enterprises precludes a proper accounting of their activities in national accounts, except insofar as they are included in the output of formal enterprises or are included through indirect calculations of gross domestic product. Therefore, Sri Lanka's GDP, estimated at 203.5 billion rupees, or US$6.4 billion, in 1988, is itself an underestimate.[1]

One way to arrive at an estimate of informal output is to discuss the significance of informal enterprise in each sector of the economy. Sri Lanka's agricultural sector contributes 25 percent of GDP. Informal output of agriculture is largely included, since GDP estimates of agriculture are arrived at through production statistics, export volumes, and per capita consumption estimates. Except for the plantation crops, tea and rubber, and about 10 percent of coconuts, which are produced in the formal sector by wage labor, the bulk of agricultural output comes from very small holdings in the informal sector. A detailed analysis on the basis of the size of units discloses that the informal sector in agriculture contributes about 15 percent of GDP.

In mining and quarrying, which contributes about 3 percent of GDP, the informal sector is significant. Its contribution is inadequately accounted for, however, since a significant proportion of quarrying, excavation of sand for construction, and mining of precious and semi-precious stones is not included in government figures. Considering the value of these items, it may not be an exaggeration to propose that an additional 3 percent of GDP comes from informal mining. About 1 percent of GDP included in the official figures is from informal mining.

Of the manufacturing sector (including export processing), which contributes about 16 percent of GDP, export processing and factory industry account for nearly 90 percent. Therefore, the informal manufacturing sector's contribution to the already accounted GDP is as small as 5 percent of manufacturing, or less than 1 percent of total GDP. A considerable amount of small-scale manufacture is not included, however. Considering the fact that there were, in 1983, 88,000 manufacturing establishments employing fewer than five persons, the informal contribution in this sector cannot be inconsequential (Sri Lanka 1983). A somewhat dated estimate places the informal sector's contribution to manufacturing at 44 percent of value added (World Bank 1978), while a more recent estimate places it at 15 percent of manufacturing, or 2.1 percent of GDP (ILO/ARTEP 1986). It appears that 1 percent of presently calculated GDP, and an additional 2 percent of actual GDP, is a reasonable estimate of the informal sector contribution to manufacturing.

The construction sector contributes about 7 percent of GDP. Except for large-scale projects, the construction of most housing and small business units is done by the informal sector. Therefore, about 4 percent of GDP could be considered informal sector output.

The other main contribution of the informal sector is in services, including financial services. In this sector most informal services are not included in the official estimate of GDP. Personal services and financial services together contribute about 8 percent of GDP: it would not be an exaggeration to add an additional 8 percent as being from the informal sector. Wholesale and retail trade contributes a substantial 20 percent of GDP. This is another sector in which the informals contribute significantly: about 7 percent of GDP could be estimated as being from informals.

A reestimate of GDP, including both what has been accounted for in present estimates and what has been excluded, shows that the informal sector contributes between 40 and 60 percent of Sri Lanka's GDP.

Rationale for informality. In the Sri Lankan context, the reasons for remaining informal do not include the difficulties of registering a business as a formal enterprise. Registration is a relatively simple procedure, its costs are inconsequential, and the delay is not material. An individual can register as carrying on a business in other than his own name by merely filling in a form and paying only a very small fee. Similarly, he may register a business as a sole proprietorship or a partnership with ease, paying the same tiny fee. The fee for registering a limited liability company varies with the share capital, but the maximum fee is 5,000 rupees (US$125). There are additional costs of registering a larger business organization in the form of a limited liability company, because such registration requires a formal memorandum of association, which has to be drafted and printed. These documents, however, are available from lawyers and law firms. The standard memorandum covers the full gamut of activities applicable to all companies, regardless of specific business activity and, if necessary, can be made to include the specific activity of the proposed company. This could cost anything up to 10,000 rupees (US$250), which would include the costs of printing. Those enterprises that seek to be organized in such a manner can easily afford such a cost. There is no delay encountered in registering such a business. When it is important to register a business in less than two weeks, it is possible to obtain quick registrations through a personal contact or by special request.

Informal enterprises exist for a variety of more important reasons. As the description of Sri Lanka's informal activities illustrated, there are a number of enterprises in which informal activity is the type most suitable: mainly those activities in which labor comprises the main resource. For participants in such informal activities, even the thought of entering the formal sector, as other than a paid employee, does not arise. In fact, to be a *natami*, an informal carrier of goods, once required registration and a uniform, but no longer. In the case of several other informal enterprises, such as those preparing lunch parcels, catering food, and sewing at home, operations are often part-time, involving only the resources of a single family. Conversion of such enterprises into formal ones is probably not even conceived of by the informal actors, who wish to operate in the same familiar, flexible manner they are used to.

Beyond the "home" level, there are small garment-sewing establishments, small manufacturers, and small trading operations that, even if they have a more complex structure, share the same simple nature, with a relatively unsophisticated organizational setup and a simple accounting mechanism. Here too, informal operation is the preferred mode of activity, the concern being that formalization would increase costs, run down profits, and reduce competitiveness.

The genesis and continuance of many informal enterprises can be attributed to their ability to produce goods and services more cheaply than could a formal organization. They are able to effect economies in the use of capital, their overhead costs are minimal, and their labor productivity is higher. As a study by the Marga Institute (1979:108) observed:

The informal key cutter is more convenient, quicker, and cheaper than the large shops.

Economies are manifested in the use of capital, the use of intermediate
materials and the use of labor. . . . Investment on buildings is
minimal. The capital equipment in reconditioned second-hand form
and other various types of ingenious improvisation are put to good
use. Waste and scrap material, equipment in disuse and disrepair
and other capital equipment which has been in use beyond what is
regarded as its economic life have been put to use or kept in service
in tolerably serviceable condition.

The economies effected in this manner enable informal enterprises
to market their products at a lower price. When their products are
qualitatively comparable, they have a competitive advantage. This indeed
is the economic rationale for the persistence of many informal enterprises.

There are many informal enterprises that produce somewhat
inferior commodities and cater to a distinguishably different market,
whose concern is utility and low price rather than the final finish, the
packaging, the trademark, or any guarantee of quality. Sri Lanka's
economic development is at a stage where a large proportion of its
population have diverse new needs, but income levels that do not allow
the purchase of high-priced products manufactured by formal enterprises. As the Marga study (1979:108) pointed out:

> Therefore the informal sector as a mode of production of a certain
> range of goods and services in the urban economy and meeting certain
> types of demand performs an important function at the present stage
> of urban development.

Several informal entrepreneurs disclosed in interviews that they
wish to remain outside the formal sector in order to avoid conforming
to official requirements of completing forms, submitting tax returns,
having their accounts audited, paying Employment Provident Fund
contributions, and paying the 1 percent Business Turnover Tax (BTT).
Any registered enterprise with a turnover of over 300 rupees per day
attracts the BTT. Informal entrepreneurs point out that an enterprise
must have a daily turnover of 1,000 rupees even to meet the basic living
expenses of a single owner. This they wish to avoid, as even 1 percent
of their turnover would be a significant drain on their profits. The
manner of levying the BTT, however, is such that the informal
enterprises that maintain no audited accounts and give no formal
receipts are able to avoid paying it. Income tax liability is similar. The
aversion of the informal entrepreneur to tax situations is as much a
result of a lack of ability and means to maintain necessary records
as of an uncertainty that tax requirements might wipe him out. The
informal entrepreneur would likely not be able to afford accountants
or tax consultants who could advise on how tax liabilities could
be minimized.

As the profile of the informal entrepreneur Pala indicates, there are limits placed on the expansion of informal enterprises. For instance, informal businesses are unable to claim those concessions that the Ministry of Industries grants only to registered enterprises. They cannot contract with large organizations, government departments, or public corporations, nor can they open bank accounts as businesses. Without business bank accounts they are unable to receive payments by check. It is mainly these conditions that persuade some informals, those who wish to expand, to register their enterprises. Some of these enterprises could develop into larger, formal enterprises if their resource bases could be expanded, if the market for their products could be increased, and if their organizational abilities were able to cope with more complex challenges. Not many enterprises have made this transition, but many of those that have, have grown to be very large organizations. For instance, one large confectioner began by selling homemade sweets to his office mates in a private firm. He gradually increased his sales in an informal manner, and then expanded to a small formal enterprise. He obtained bank credit, organized his firm into a larger complex with his sons, and is today a manufacturer of a wide range of very popular sweets, which sell throughout the country. Similarly, an enterprise that currently owns and runs a hospital offering traditional medical remedies began as a home-based enterprise for manufacturing a single balm. One large group of companies that today manufactures and trades in hardware, electronics, textiles, and engineering services developed from an itinerant vendor of empty bottles and scrap materials.

Not all informal entrepreneurs either desire or are able to expand beyond a certain level, however. Some have limited aims and targets, and are satisfied if these are reached. Others are unable to cope with the complex organizational structures that would result from expanding. Others are constrained by the limitations of the market for their product, and the difficulty of catering to a more sophisticated market.

It should also be mentioned that a fundamental reason for the existence of a large informal sector is the inability of the organized employers to hire the large numbers entering the labor force annually. Those unable to find employment elsewhere turn to whatever enterprise can bring an income, and they often find ingenious and innovative means of selling a product or service. This is undoubtedly the greatest underlying reason for the large informal sector in Sri Lanka at this stage of its economic development.

Paradoxically, the process of development itself has led to an expansion of informal enterprises. Apart from the demand for cheap, inferior substitutes, the availability of cast-off materials, exposure to technologies, expansion of subcontractors for industrial products, and urbanization have all contributed to the growth of informal enterprises.

Credit. One of the biggest disadvantages that informal businesses have in common with very small formal enterprises is their inability to get bank credit. Low social status, lack of collateral, ignorance of bank procedures, and lack of sophistication have left many informal entrepreneurs alienated from the formal sources of finance. They are therefore compelled to borrow at very high interest costs. Vendors often borrow daily at 10 percent per day, while other informal enterprises borrow at rates ranging between 5 and 20 percent per month. The implications of this are twofold: the earnings of informal entrepreneurs are eroded by interest payments, and so they continue to live at subsistence levels. This in turn implies an inability to accumulate capital.

Although one of the biggest disadvantages of being informal is inaccessibility to bank credit, many informals believe that their status in this regard would not change by their becoming formal. They continue to resort to informal finance, which is itself a very extensive informal enterprise in the economy, as a more flexible and convenient, albeit expensive, option. Consequently many informal entrepreneurs remain tied inextricably to informal lenders and continue at a meager level of operation without improvement or development.

While commercial banks provide reasonable facilities to large enterprises, small enterprises find it difficult to obtain such credit even under special schemes such as the Small and Medium Industries (SMI) credit scheme. Part of the difficulty is the need to fill in complex forms and provide feasibility reports. Even where such reports can be provided, there are additional needs: collateral, documentation of earlier business performance, tax certificates, business turnover records, and so on. All this indicates the difficulties informal businesses face in obtaining credit. Recently there has, however, been a new thrust in banking policy to provide easier credit facilities, particularly for small enterprises. Some of these are described in the next section.

Infrastructure. Many deficiencies in the infrastructure of the country and in government services make it difficult and costly to operate any business. Foremost among these are problems of communication. While the postal service is well developed, speedy, and reliable, the telephone system leaves much to be desired. Very often telephones are out of order, and consequently telephone communication is unreliable. Over one-half of the country's telephones are in metropolitan Colombo. Telephone facilities outside of the metropolis and out of the main towns are very inadequate. The extension of direct dialing throughout most of the country has effected considerable improvement, however. Today's national total of over 100,000 telephones compares with fewer than 50,000 in 1978. Nevertheless, obtaining a new telephone connection is a very difficult proposition and takes considerable time. Mere payment of the fee with an application does not ensure the telephone connection. The official cost of installing a telephone for business use is 1,000 rupees; if the connection is required within a month there is an additional fee of 15,000 rupees, and a further additional fee for a priority connection of 5,500 rupees. Even the payment of these fees does not necessarily assure one of obtaining a telephone on time. Until recently it took between two and three years to obtain a telephone, unless one used influence to obtain the connection. Large business organizations are able to pay the additional costs of expediting a telephone connection, but such costs are exorbitant and beyond the reach of small enterprises.

Persistence and growth of informals. The preceding discussion has adduced a wide range of reasons for informal entrepreneurs' remaining informal. The conventional logic, that informal actors would become formal if the costs of conversions were less than the benefits, is a truism. Yet it misses the dynamics of and rationale for informal enterprises. Many enterprises would likely remain informal in any case, as they are a more suitable mode of operation in a number of services and in the production of a wide range of goods.

As has been brought out in this discussion, there is no doubt that many informal entrepreneurs consider the costs and burdens of paying additional taxes, conforming to institutional procedures, keeping accounts, abiding by labor regulations, and submitting tax returns and statistical information not worth the benefits they perceive they could gain by becoming formal.

The two types of informal entrepreneurs who tend to turn formal are those who find their market restricted by informality and those who wish to expand into much larger units of production. Small informal enterprises that are unable to sell their products or services to certain institutional clients convert themselves to formal enterprises through registration, though the character of these enterprises may change very little. Many Sri Lankan microenterprises, employing only a few persons, are informal operations turned formal, continuing to function in an informal manner and conforming to the fewest possible formal procedures. The second category is a small number of informals who have chosen to be formal in order to expand their enterprises. Some of these enterprises have since become medium or large companies and have expanded their range of economic activities; they are formal enterprises in name and in character.

A vast majority of informal enterprises remain such, as informality is an efficient structure for certain economic activities. In many types of economic activity an informal mode of production is less costly and more convenient for the consumer. Many products and services of informal firms are comparable to or better than those produced by formal enterprises and are cheaper. Handicrafts, home-cooked food, and many personal and household services are some activities of which this is likely to be true.

There is also a large, less sophisticated clientele desiring cheaper substitutes for a wide range of products of the formal market. This sort of demand has expanded with increased urbanization and consumerism and is more adequately catered to by informals, who produce inferior substitutes cheaply.

Even when it is economically rational and not necessarily costly to convert to a formal and larger enterprise, informal entrepreneurs may still prefer to remain informal, if a more complex organization is beyond the personal managerial control and capability of the informal entrepreneur, if the required financial resources are unavailable, or if the risks are too daunting.

Helping the Informal Enterprises

Informal economic enterprises, with the exception of illegal and illicit activities, are accepted as essential components of the Sri Lankan economy. Some of these informal activities have deep social roots and are essential to the life of the community; many are vertically or horizontally linked to, and have a symbiotic relationship with, the formal sector. What is more, informal activity, though continuously changing in character, has grown rather than diminished with the country's increasing development and has become an essential means of meeting the community's economic and social needs.

Recently, there has been a distinct political recognition of the role of informal enterprises in the Sri Lankan economy and a growing realization that the encouragement and stimulation of informal economic enterprise is essential as an economic strategy to increase employment, alleviate poverty, and raise the income of a considerable section of the community. Active encouragement of informal enterprise has been therefore a priority of government policy in Sri Lanka since 1988. President Premadasa's *janasaviya* program to alleviate poverty; the provision by banks of credit facilities for self-employment schemes and small enterprises; the distribution of about one million acres of land to the landless; and the Praja Naya Niyamaka scheme, to link the formal banking system to informal lenders, are specific expressions of this new thrust in policy.

One fairly conventional approach that has been adopted at various times to help promising informal enterprises consists of attempting to improve their facilities. The logic is that if informal enterprises with limited resources have been successful, then with "better" facilities and conditions they will be still more successful. Examples of this approach will illustrate the lessons of the experience.

The first example is the spontaneously developed roadside marketing of cashew nuts and king coconuts, which has been conducted for decades, if not over a century. Young women, attractively clad in the traditional cloth and jacket, sold cashews and king coconut water to travelers at Bataliya on the Colombo-Kandy road. Both these items cost slightly more than they did in market towns, but many a traveler wished to bargain with the pretty girls. The roadside stands were tourist attractions, and many tourists took photographs. Many of the vendors earned a good living and were able to save adequately for their dowries.

The government decided to help this enterprise, by improving the "primitive" sales points by developing an improved infrastructure. A new "village," appropriately called Kadjugama (cashew village), with better stalls and parking facilities for cars and buses, was developed. But Kadjugama of necessity had to be tucked away from the highway. Most travelers bypassed these stalls and a thriving trade became less profitable.

This young woman prepares bundles of boiled cashew while she waits for customers for her fried cashew nuts and king coconut water.

The second instance is from a suburban city where a thriving Sunday fair had existed in the town hall premises for many decades. The authorities decided to move the informal traders to a newly constructed set of stalls. These proved too expensive for the traders, who moved to other points, such as sidewalks, elsewhere in the town. The authorities, finding the stalls unoccupied, put pressure on the traders by preventing them from selling on the sidewalks (an illegality to which the authorities had hitherto turned a blind eye). Even these pressures failed and the fair continues on the congested roadside. Several similar efforts have been made to provide informal traders with modern structures in the form of supermarkets. In nearly all cases informal traders have been uprooted from their traditional places, but have refused to occupy these modern structures, owing to the additional rental costs and the fact that their clientele prefers to shop at other informal outlets rather than in the supermarket stalls. Supermarkets have of course developed, but they are run by different businessmen and exist side by side with the informal traders outside.

These two illustrations demonstrate that intervention in informal enterprises without due regard to the needs of the informal economy or its individual entrepreneurs can be disastrous. Many informal entrepreneurs have fashioned their enterprises to suit the conditions of a given environment and the particular needs of certain categories of customers.

Another set of interventions in informal marketing has been successful. Colombo's sidewalk hawkers have been provided with new stalls and located in new bazaars. Similarly, a large area in Colombo has been reserved for informal traders, government marketing outlets, and private companies. This Jathika Pola (national bazaar), which began as a weekly market, became a weekend bazaar and now operates daily. Intervention here was geared to the needs of traders and customers and was therefore productive in expanding informal enterprise.

Another successful form of assistance has been the establishment of shops to sell handicraft products. A state corporation, Laksala, was established some years ago as a sales point for local crafts. Brassware, silverware, jewelry, batik materials, coir products, and a wide range of handicrafts were sold through this outlet, at first in Colombo, and later in a few other cities. At first it catered mainly to tourists and the export market, but now a domestic demand as well has been created for these products. The success of Laksala has led to the development of several similar shops by the private sector and other government agencies. Here the state assisted informal traders merely by providing them access to markets which they would not have been able to reach on their own.

Sri Lanka's small informal craftsmen have faced difficulties in obtaining inputs such as brass and silver. The Ministry of Rural Industries has sponsored a credit program for craftsmen with a state bank and set up a channel to supply small quantities of raw materials to them. This has reduced the capital needs of informal craftsmen and has also provided them market access.

One of the biggest problems faced by informal entrepreneurs is the inaccessibility of institutional credit, which keeps informal enterprises dependent on informal sources of finance. The recognition that institutional lending has many limitations has led to several efforts to aid the small borrower through adaptations in institutional lending. The first experiment was the establishment of Cooperative Rural Banks (CRBs) in 1964 under the auspices of the People's Bank. These are not true banks, but departments of cooperatives, which mobilize savings and lend funds for limited purposes. They are small in size, less intimidating than full-fledged banks, and established within rural cooperatives, which are familiar institutions in the villages. They are also a means of extending limited banking facilities to areas where economic conditions would not justify the establishment of a branch bank. CRBs also operate at hours more convenient for the local clientele, and are able to be more flexible in the provision of credit, owing to their personal knowledge of borrowers (Kahagalle and Sanderatne 1977). One thousand such rural banks have been established throughout the country. They have been very successful in mobilizing savings, which have amounted to over 2 billion rupees. Their lending, however, has been less than half their deposits, and has served only limited purposes (Sanderatne 1988:15–17).

The other more recent innovation was the establishment of Regional Rural Development Banks (RRDBs) in 1985. These unit banks are expected to provide the credit that other commercial banks do not, and that is currently provided only by informal lenders. In order to perform this function, RRDBs were given guidelines ensuring that they not compete with existing financial institutions, but supplement them by providing credit to small farmers, rural artisans, petty traders, and small entrepreneurs not adequately serviced by banks. The area of operation of each bank was also limited to make these objectives effective. Eleven RRDBs, with 80 branches, have been established. Unlike CRBs, they have lent more than their deposits. About 45 percent of their loans have gone for agriculture, 15 percent for small industry, and 23 percent for trade and business. There is evidence that they have lent for a wide variety of purposes and that many informal enterprises have obtained funds from them (Sanderatne 1989a).

In October 1988, a novel scheme was inaugurated, whereby the two state banks are to attempt to link with the informal sector by lending to individuals who will in turn lend in an informal manner to small borrowers. Under this scheme, known as the Praja Naya Niyamaka (PNN), the banks lend to persons of proven creditworthiness

(PNNs), often on the basis of collateral, at an interest rate of 1.5 percent per month (18 percent per annum), and expect the PNNs to lend at an interest rate not exceeding 2.5 percent per month (30 percent per annum). The banks give the PNNs guidelines on how to lend but do not require them to provide documentation or other proof of their lending. Since this scheme is meant to assist the small borrower, loans are not expected to exceed 5,000 rupees.[2]

Under this scheme the financial resources of the banks are expected to supplement the resources of the informal sector to meet the small borrower's credit needs. The increased supply of funds from the PNNs and the consequent increased competition among informal lenders are expected to bring down the cost of borrowing and improve the conditions of borrowing. The banks are expected eventually to appoint about 14,000 PNNs throughout the country. Flexibility and convenience in lending, which banks as institutions were not able to provide, can be provided by the PNNs, with the resources of the banks. In the first two years of implementing this scheme, the two state banks appointed about 7,000 PNNs and lent about 400 million rupees to them. PNNs have lent for a wide spectrum of purposes, including very small loans for self-employment, petty trade, and various service businesses. However, some of the PNNs have tended to concentrate on larger lending and have not lent to very small enterprises as required under the scheme.

Among the scheme's difficulties, which the PNNs have themselves pointed out, is that the upper limit of credit given them by the banks (200,000 rupees), or the limit imposed within this maximum depending on the creditworthiness of the individual PNN, is inadequate. They contend that they are unable to explain to borrowers that they have exhausted their resources, since they have been appointed as "agents" by the banks. Many PNNs consider the margin of 1 percent per month inadequate, as they must bear the entire credit risk; the total income derived by PNNs from loans totaling 100,000 rupees is only 1,000 rupees per month. The maximum individual loan limit of 5,000 rupees is also considered inadequate, and PNNs have, in fact, often lent higher amounts.

The PNN scheme is undoubtedly a useful experiment in linking the informal lender with the institutional system. The banks should continue to lend to creditworthy PNNs and should give PNNs more freedom to operate as they see fit to ensure that informal lending continues unfettered. The link with the banks should not result in the introduction of formal procedures. Since the PNN bears the risk and the money he lends is "his" money, the PNN should be free to lend in any manner he likes. Banks should use only "moral suasion" to achieve the objectives of the scheme; otherwise the formal-informal linkage could become a "kiss of death."

Apart from the PNN scheme, several other attempts have been made to link formal and informal finance. One model, used by banks even prior to the appointment of PNNs, is that of lending to nongovernment organizations (NGOs), which in turn lend to groups and individuals on their own terms. The NGO takes the responsibility for monitoring the loans and ensuring their recovery. The two state banks have recently made special efforts to expand this model as part of the government's program for poverty alleviation. Such lending through intermediaries has assisted a larger number of informal enterprises than would otherwise have been the case.

In October 1989, the president of Sri Lanka appointed a task force to identify 1 million acres of underutilized land for distribution among the landless. During the first six months of the task force's operation, 600,000 acres were identified, 180,418 acres blocked out, and 75,749 acres handed over to landless persons. Although the program was expected to be completed by October 1990, it is still being implemented. This policy further illustrates the government's policy of assisting those without resources and encouraging self-employment and informal activities.

Since the informal sector has been recognized as an integral part of the Sri Lankan economy and society, there have been various efforts to assist informal enterprises. Such assistance has sought to provide infrastructural facilities, new markets for informal products, credit schemes to assist informal businesses, and financial assistance for the self-employed and informal economic enterprises. Despite the intention of the government to encourage and facilitate informal enterprises, however, rules, regulations, and bureaucratic procedures and delays continue to be a severe restriction on informal activity.

One needed policy intervention is the minimization of rules and regulations that hamper economic activities. These rules and regulations affect both formal and informal enterprises, but informal businesses more adversely, for three reasons. First, informal enterprises may not have the ability to apply for resources, concessions, or exemptions as they are not formal organizations and cannot provide needed documentary evidence. Second, coping with regulations is costly and the unit costs of meeting requirements are greater for small enterprises. Third, conforming to regulations, procedures, and red tape is not only time-consuming but could also be almost insuperable for the small businessperson. Large institutions have contact with higher officials and can use such contacts to assist themselves, but informal entrepreneurs have to use brokers and intermediaries and thus incur additional costs. Controls and regulations, which often achieve little of their intended result, are costly for informal enterprises and may be discouraging potential informal enterprises.

The bylaws and regulations that have been formulated in the interest of sanitation, health, a clean environment, orderly and rational zoning, and road safety are problematic and conflicting. These apply to both formal and informal enterprises alike, but informal businesses tend to violate them more. They cannot be exempted from compliance, as the objective of these laws is ostensibly the protection of the public. Yet these regulations are often an excuse for prosecuting officers to harass and extract fees from informal enterprises that operate in contravention of the laws and regulations.

Conclusions

Informal economic activities operate throughout the economy of Sri Lanka and account for a substantial proportion of its GDP. Informal economic activities are an accepted form of enterprise; except for those informal actors who operate outside the law, such as bookies, prostitutes, drug peddlers, illegal foreign-currency exchangers, and the like, other informal enterprises are permitted. Such informal enterprises, if they wish, could become formal enterprises without difficulty. Sri Lanka's law and required procedures are not time-consuming or costly. The registration of a business enterprise does not present insuperable problems. Therefore the formality of an enterprise is mostly determined by the entrepreneur's own choice.

The choice to remain informal arises for many reasons, varying according to the nature of the enterprise, its market, the type of product, and mode of its production. Many informal entrepreneurs find it less costly to operate as an informal enterprise and believe that conversion to a formal enterprise would not confer many advantages. Such conversion, on the contrary, would entail compliance with a host of rules and regulations, accounting procedures, and payment of additional taxes, all of which are time-consuming and costly, and require a different form of business organization. Only those informal entrepreneurs who wish to expand their operations, and therefore require additional bank financing and concessions from government organizations, are prepared to formalize their businesses.

This does not imply that remaining informal is without costs. Informal financial services are much costlier than bank credit, and certain segments of the market are not accessible to informal enterprises. The full potential of some informal enterprises therefore remains unexploited.

Recently the state has recognized the informal sector as a means of expanding production and increasing employment. The government is therefore implementing programs to provide more land to the landless and is designing credit schemes for craftsmen, small enterprises, and self-employment projects. It has persuaded the state banks to link with informal lenders to increase the supply of credit to small enterprises in an informal manner. While these policies are of recent origin, there have been other attempts to help informal entrepreneurs in previous decades. Some of these interventionist policies, such as the provision of marketing facilities and development of infrastructure to assist informals, have been a success. Others have been failures, owing to a government misperception of the informal entrepreneurs' needs. With the growing recognition that informal economic enterprises can contribute substantially to economic growth, it is likely that there will be further attempts to assist this sector in the future.

An overall perspective that emerges from this discussion is that interventionist policies designed to help informal enterprises should be espoused with caution, as inappropriate and overregulatory policies that are detrimental to those enterprises may result. The best ways to encourage and assist informal businesses would be to improve the efficiency of government organizations, by minimizing bureaucratic regulations and controls; to improve economic infrastructure; to provide training in skills that could be useful for informal enterprises; to improve marketing facilities; and to facilitate access to resources. These policies would not necessarily have to be aimed at informal enterprises, but such enterprises would be benefited most. Policies and institutional devices to provide credit to informal enterprises would be particularly useful, and Sri Lankans' recent experiments to provide such credit, especially by channelling bank resources through informal lenders, may have a significant impact in increasing informal economic activity. Nongovernment organizations can also assist in improving the efficiency of informal enterprises.

The Informal Sector in Thailand

In the past the informal sector has been associated with hawkers, shoe-shine boys, beggars, street vendors, and the like. This characterization, however, is now obsolete. The informal sector is composed of people from all occupations. Some are government officials, some are merchants, and some are students. The informal entrepreneur can be either a poor street vendor or a rich garment trader. In Thailand, at least 50 percent of the urban labor force works in the informal sector. Although the size of the sector has gradually declined over time because of rapid economic growth and government policy, the number of informal actors in certain industries, such as motorcycle transport and street vending, has increased.

Informal workers remain outside the formal economy for various reasons. Perhaps the most important are the legal prohibition of certain economic activities and the failure of the law to recognize informal enterprises. In recent years, the number of informal workers in the motorcycle transport and vending industries has increased in response to the government's positive attitude toward them. As democracy in Thailand has gradually grown stronger, there have been attempts to deregulate the economy, to simplify bureaucratic procedures, and to reform laws that obstruct economic activity.[1] In some areas, however, such as motorcycle transport and vending, legal reforms have not yet been passed. Another reason workers remain informal is that they are not subject to regulations and thus can provide flexible and convenient services at low cost. This is the case for informal moneylenders. In addition, informal entrepreneurs avoid paying duties and taxes and complying with labor-protection laws. The desire to exploit cheap labor, however, is not an important motivation for informality. Most informal workers are self-employed and do not hire any employees.

Staying outside the formal economy can have high costs. Informal enterprises not only have to pay monthly bribes to government officials, but are also subject to various biases against informality in government policies. As a result, they pay higher capital costs and are at a disadvantage in competing with large-scale enterprises. Nevertheless, they manage to survive and to provide useful services to society. This chapter will attempt to explain the role and problems of the informal sector, as well as to outline a long-term solution to its problems.

The Composition of the Informal Sector

Most studies of the informal sector in Thailand survey informal enterprises by using a structured questionnaire. Very few studies have employed an ethnographic (that is, empirical) method.[2] This is why it is so difficult to get a personal, "human" picture of the informal actor. I have therefore chosen to conduct personal interviews to serve as the basis of this study.

Table 5.1 shows various characteristics of the informal actor, depending upon the set sampled in four difficult studies. Prachoom (1984) studied the informal sector in the Bangkok slums; Teilhet-Waldorf and Waldorf (1983) and Pasuk and Pradith (1988) both surveyed skilled and unskilled informal workers and entrepreneurs; Larsson (1980) examined only owners of informal shops and other enterprises. Most of these studies found that almost half (45–49 percent) of sample workers were female.[3] Women predominate in the service and trade sectors. One study found that 80 percent of all vendors of processed food were women (Malee 1989). All studies but one found that the largest single generational grouping of informal actors is composed of those between twenty-five and thirty-four years of age.

Most of the workers in three of the studies had only a primary-level education. This means that they usually acquired their skills from their work experiences. The studies tended to confirm that most informal workers are rural migrants who have come to the city in search of better jobs and higher incomes.

Most informal actors are in trade, which is easy to enter. They acquire trading skills either by on-the-job experience or by apprenticeship to

TABLE 5.1   Characteristics of Informal Actors in Thailand

Characteristics	Study			
	Larsson (1980)	Teilhet-Waldorf and Waldorf (1983)	Prachoom (1984)	Pasuk and Pradith (1988)
Sex				
Female (%)	59	47	49	45
Age	43% aged 25–34	52% aged 30–34	Averaged 32 years of age	66% aged over 50
Education				
No education (%)	n.a.		9	
Primary (%)	23	83.6[a]	79	63[a]
Higher education (%)	77	16.4	12	37
Status				
Migrant (%)	34	76	60	57
Father's occupation				
Salesman (%)	27	n.a.	n.a.	n.a.
Service (%)	14	n.a.	n.a.	n.a.
Farmer (%)	10	n.a.	n.a.	n.a.
Administrator (%)	10	n.a.	n.a.	n.a.
Average monthly income	B14,800	B1,470–3,270	B1,597	B5,867

n.a. = not available.

a. Percentage includes those who have no education and those who have a primary education.

SOURCE: Larsson (1980); Teilhet-Waldorf and Waldorf (1983); Prachoom (1984); Pasuk and Pradith (1988); and ILO (1988).

parents who are merchants. Thus, informal studies tend to observe that many informal workers have fathers who are salesmen.

Studies of the informal sector show that the informal actors' incomes vary widely, depending upon the composition of the sample.

The informal entrepreneur: three examples.

Manop, a garment seller. In front of Thammasat University in Bangkok, students can buy cheap shirts and blouses from a van that parks near the university gate. The owner of the van is a young man, thirty-two years old. He has two vans—one is used as a garment shop, and the other is used to transport stock. His monthly gross intake is at least 65,000 baht, providing a net profit of 20,000 baht. His sale volume is about twenty shirts per day.

Manop is a son of a policeman and Chinese woman. After graduation from a vocational college, Manop worked as an accountant with a large retail garment chain for almost eight years. He started his first business, selling blue jeans and T-shirts, a few years after he became an accountant, with an investment of only 10,000 baht from his own savings. He would sell clothing after he returned from his regular job and work until 10 P.M. Manop finally resigned to pursue his garment-sale business full time. He began selling used clothing, earning a gross profit margin of 300 percent. Although vendors in his area were often arrested by the police, he established a relationship with a soldier who usually protected him from crackdowns. He was arrested a few times, nevertheless, and had to pay a fine of 500 baht each time.

When he moved to a new location, Manop decided to buy two used vans with his savings of 300,000 baht. To park in the new location all the time, he had to pay the informal marketplace leader 200 baht a month, and more recently 300 baht. Finally, Manop began buying cloth and subcontracting with tailors to make blouses of his own design.

Although Manop is an innovative and determined young man, his self-proclaimed weakness is that when his subcontractors provide him with low-quality products, he neither complains nor rejects the garments. He says that if he had been more choosy about the quality of his merchandise, he would already have been a millionaire.

Surasith, an owner of motorcycle routes. Now in his late forties, Surasith was born in Ratchburi, about eighty-five kilometers west of Bangkok. After leaving home, he found work as a ticket collector on a minibus. He moved to Bangkok when he was twenty-five and worked first as a bus driver and ticket supervisor, then as the manager of a small private bus line in Thonburi.

Seven years ago, someone set up a motorcycle route along Surasith's bus route. The number of motorcycle drivers multiplied rapidly, hurting the bus company's business. Finally, Surasith quit the bus company and joined the motorcycle fleet as chief driver. After a few years, he came to own most of the motorcycles on the route. He began to set up a few other routes, because he had good connections with the police. Today he owns five motorcycle routes with about 300 motorcycle uniforms,[4] worth at least 6 million baht. His motorcycle business is so successful that he has recently entered the trucking industry as well.

Lek, a Chinese moneylender. Lek, a fifty-three-year-old man, lives in Nakorn Ratchasima, a province in the northeastern region of Thailand. He was born in a province in the central region. In his teenage years, he had extensive experience as an employee in a gold shop, an itinerant merchant, and a native doctor. Although he never went to the formal school, he learned how to read and write from another employee at the gold shop. Now, although he owns a grocery store, his major occupation is moneylending.

His trading activities, especially grain trading, helped him become acquainted with the local farmers. When he began to lend money, he already possessed the necessary knowledge of his customers' ability to repay and their spending habits.

Besides grain trading and lending to the farmers, Lek also lends money to the civil servants in the city. Every year, he makes loans totaling 700–800 thousand baht to about seventy-five clients—of whom more than 70 percent are farmers.

Lek will lend only to people he knows he can trust or to people who are introduced by his friends. His clients must own collateral land. Before lending, he will always assess the value of the land, as well as seek information about his client's ability to repay.

In extending a loan, he will write a contract that ensures repayment of interest and principal. If borrowers default, Lek will try to compromise with them, asking them to renew their loan contracts and pay the interest. If this does not work, he will hire the police to enforce the contracts. Legal enforcement is used only as a last resort.

The Size of the Informal Sector

Substantial variation in the estimates of the size of the informal sector is caused by differences in definition. There are at least five methods of defining the informal sector. The first approach is to designate all service activities as informal. This method is very crude and is also unsatisfactory as it leaves some important components of the informal sector designated as formal, and vice versa. A more subtle definition is to characterize the informal sector in terms of economic features, such as competitive behavior and labor-market conditions. The main difficulty is that these features are difficult to quantify for purposes of empirical research. In the third definition, the informal sector is said to consist of itinerant workers without a fixed workplace. This view is outdated, as it includes only a narrow stratum, consisting of street hawkers, peddlers, beggars, and the like. The fourth definition, which is adopted in most empirical research, is based on either worker characteristics or establishment size, or on a mixture of both. The worker-characteristics method suffers from many defects, which can be remedied by combining it with an establishment-size criterion. There has been some disagreement over the size qualification of enterprises, however.

Realizing the weakness of each definition, the International Labor Organization has proposed that the informal sector has the following characteristics (ILO 1972): ease of entry, reliance on natural resources, family ownership of enterprises, small scale of operation, labor-intensive and adapted technology, skills acquired outside the formal school system, and unregulated and competitive markets. Although the ILO's definition is the most realistic one, it is impossible to apply using available official statistics alone.

Most of the studies undertaken in Thailand have adopted the fourth definition—that is, the method of using either firm size or worker characteristics (see Table 5.2)—because it is the most convenient empirical approach. Other studies have used different definitions, focusing, for example, on itinerant workers and also employing parts of the ILO's definition. In addition, one study has used a macroeconomic technique to identify the size of the underground economy.[5] Only studies that defined the informal sector according to worker characteristics, the ILO's concept, or legal status will be discussed here.

Three studies found that in Thailand, small- and medium-scale enterprises constituted 63–77 percent of all enterprises and employed about 10–15 percent of all paid employees. But this figure appears to be underestimated, for two reasons. First, a different study, which used a combination of factors to define the informal sector, found that informal employees represented about 40 percent of all employees in urban areas (Chalongphob 1987). Second, paid employees are not the largest group of workers in the urban employment structure. The most significant groups were self-employed persons and unpaid family workers, who together constituted about 33 percent of the urban labor force in 1987 (see Table 5.3). Professional workers, however, are also included in the self-employed category. In fact, these workers belong

TABLE 5.2 Definition and Size of the Informal Sector in Thailand

Definition	Study	Size	Year
Firm size			
Ten workers or fewer	Somsak and Chesada (1983)	63.0%[a]; 9.8%[b]	1980
	Kuroda and Kasajima (1987)	64.0%[a]; 10.7%[b]	1984
	Department of Labor (1988)	77.4%[a]; 15.0%[b]	1988
Ten workers or fewer; unpaid-family and	Pawadee (1982)	67.1%[c]	1980
self-employed workers	NESDB (1986)	50.0%[d]	1984
Ten workers or fewer; wage determination	Chalongphob (1987)	40.0%[e]	1984
Ten workers or fewer; minimum-wage, self-employed, and temporary workers	Prachoom (1984)	87.0%[f]	1980
Worker characteristics			
Self-employed workers	Larsson (1980)	n.a.	n.a.
	ILO (1988)	n.a.	n.a.
Unpaid-family and self-employed workers	NSO (1971–1987)	43%[g]	1971
		33%[g]	1987
Itinerant workers	Prachoom (1980)	8,777[h]	1979
	Thienchai (1982)	8,167[i]	1981
	NESDB (1986)	20.247[j]	1989

(continued)

TABLE 5.2   Definition and Size of the Informal Sector in Thailand (continued)

Definition	Study	Size	Year
Legal status	Duangmanee and Suchada (1985)	10–51%[k]	1980
	Nipon (1987), Nipon and Prayong (1989)	40–50%[l]	1960–1985
	Nipon (1990)	26–33%[m]	1990
Underground economy	Sorayuth and Tanai (1988)	25–40%[n]	1961–1984

n.a. = not available.
a. Percentage of all enterprises.
b. Percentage of total employment.
c. Percentage of sample female migrants.
d. Percentage of employed workers in Bangkok.
e. Percentage of employed workers in municipal area.
f. Percentage of sample workers in Bangkok slum. Out of these, 44 percent worked in enterprises with fewer than 10 employees, 22 percent were self-employed, 21.8 percent earned less than the legal minimum wage, and 12.2 percent worked temporarily. Note that categories are not mutually exclusive.
g. Percentage of all employed workers.
h. Number of hawkers.
i. Number of hawkers and vendors.
j. Number of hawkers and vendors.
k. Percentage of total net financial assets.
l. Percentage of total loans.
m. Percentage of public transport (measured by passengers per day).
n. Percentage of GDP.

TABLE 5.3   Estimate of the Informal Sector in Urban Areas in Thailand,
1971 and 1987 (percentage of total employment)

Status	Bangkok		Whole kingdom	
	1971	1987	1971	1987
Self-employed	20.1	17.6	25.6	20.8
Unpaid family workers	12.0	9.6	17.7	12.6
Total	32.1	27.2	43.3	33.4

SOURCE: National Statistical Office, *Report of the Labor Force Survey*, Round 2 (July–September 1971) and Round 3 (August 1987).

to the formal sector. When the informal sector is defined as consisting of workers in firms with fewer than ten workers, unpaid family and self-employed workers, but excluding professional workers, its size is at least 50 percent of total employment (National Economic and Social Development Board 1986).

Another group of studies employed legal status to separate formal from informal credit markets. They found that urban and rural informal credit markets provided as much as 45–50 percent of total credit in 1980–1987.

In conclusion, if the informal sector is measured by looking at the number of employees of enterprises, in combination with worker characteristics, it includes 50 percent of total employment, although this percentage is declining. The informal credit market's role in meeting the credit needs of rural people is also declining. The number of informal participants in some occupations, however, has been increasing rapidly over recent decades. The number of hawkers and vendors in Bangkok increased by 130.7 percent during the 1979–1989 period, because of the high rate of return in trading activities that do not have to pay land rent.[6]

Although the size of the informal sector can be estimated from previous studies, the estimate may not provide an accurate picture of the informal sector. A path-breaking study by Hernando de Soto redefined the informal economy as "the people's spontaneous and creative response to the state's incapacity to satisfy the basic needs of the impoverished masses. When legality is a privilege available only to those with political and economic power, those excluded—the poor—have no alternative but illegality" (de Soto 1989:xiv).

Following de Soto's approach, the study undertaken for this chapter found that, in 1989, informal transport operators provided from 26 to 33 percent of all public transport in Bangkok. The number of motorcycle operators, moreover, has rapidly increased in recent years. A case study of motorcycles for hire in Bangkok may shed some light on the development and problems of the informal sector.

Informal Motorcycle Transport: A Case Study

Thailand's National Economic and Social Development Board reported that in 1984, on an average weekday, about 6.3 million passengers used public transport in Bangkok (NESDB 1986). Sixty-eight percent of them used public buses operated by the Bangkok Metropolitan Transport Authority (BMTA); 22 percent relied upon privately owned, legalized minibuses; and 10 percent used taxis and motorized tricycles (called *samlors*). Obviously, the NESDB neglected the role of some informal means of transport, namely, small minibuses (called *silorleks*) and hired motorcycles, which provide transport for people who live far away from the main streets. In the past two decades, these informal means of transport have played an increasing role in Bangkok. The number of illegal minibuses has increased, from 2,075 vehicles in 1976 to 10,627 in 1989, while the number of hired motorcycles jumped drastically, from fewer than 100 in 1976 to 16,021 in 1987—an increase of 160 times (see Table 5.4). Based on my survey, I believe that in 1988 the *silorlek* and hired motorcycle operators provided transport service for 1.5 million and 1.4 million passengers per day, respectively.[7] These two modes together account for about 26–33 percent of total public transport service in Bangkok.

The hired motorcycle serves several purposes. Its most important service is to transport millions of people who live along side streets that cannot be traveled by public bus. Second, it provides rapid transportation during rush hours. Third, it provides messenger service and other services, such as delivering lunches to office workers. In spite of its increasing role, however, motorcycle transport services have still not been legalized.

The purpose of this section is to explain and analyze the rapid growth of informal motorcycle services in Bangkok. It also seeks to account for the evolution of motorcycle services, and the manner in which informal operators have successfully organized their industry. Finally, this section will assess the performance of the industry. Perhaps the most interesting question is how informal transport operators can successfully establish routes without any legal recognition.

Development of the informal transport service. After three decades of urban-biased development, the population of Bangkok has grown rapidly, from 1.5 million in 1961, to 2.5 million in 1970, and 8.2 million

TABLE 5.4 Number of Private and Public Transport Vehicles in Bangkok, 1978–1988

Type of vehicle	1978	1980	1982	1984	1986	1988
Private						
Passenger car (fewer than 7 persons)	189,695[a]	221,275[a]	268,758[a]	392,359	437,659	570,000
Passenger car (more than 7 persons)	59,152	77,877	106,810	124,056	155,846	219,343
Private truck	65,058	55,377	85,032	65,495	79,649	122,101
Motorcycle[b]	129,078	172,008	338,846	435,516	589,671	775,538
Public						
Silorlek (small minibus)	2,075[c]	n.a.	n.a.	n.a.	6,542	7,874
Taxi	n.a.	n.a.	n.a.	13,500	13,500	13,493
Interprovince service vehicle	13,606	14,736	14,468	n.a.	n.a.	n.a.
Passenger car	n.a.	n.a.	n.a.	408	408	n.a.
Samlor (tricycle)	n.a.	n.a.	n.a.	7,406	7,406	7,406
Bus	4,740	n.a.	n.a.	n.a.	n.a.	4,865[d]
Legalized minibus	n.a.	n.a.	n.a.	n.a.	n.a.	2,194
Hired motorcycle[e]	n.a.	n.a.	n.a.	n.a.	n.a.	16,021[f]

n.a. = not available.
a. Including diplomatic cars.
b. Including hired motorcycles.
c. Data for 1976.
d. Data for 1989.
e. Fewer than 100 in 1976.
f. Data for 1987.
SOURCE: World Bank (1978); Department of Land Transport (1982–1988).

in 1988. Meanwhile, public transport has failed to keep pace with rapidly growing needs. Informal transport operators have filled the gap.

Before 1975, private bus companies were the major operators of transport service. Since the bus fare was held artificially low by the central government, however, they were unable to expand service in response to growing demand. As a consequence, operators of illegal minibuses (or two-row buses, called *songthaews*) were induced by market opportunity to expand their businesses. They were able to charge the same fare as the large-scale bus companies and make a profit, since they had much lower overhead costs. There were about one thousand illegal *songthaews* in 1971, when the government decided to legalize them. In return for the legal right to operate on the main streets, *songthaew* operators were required to form three companies, each of which was to provide service in a separate zone (Viboon 1976). A small fee of 1,000 baht was charged for the route license.

The deterioration of the service of the legalized private bus companies was a rationale for some politicians to push the government to nationalize private transport firms. In 1975 the government did so and formed a new state enterprise, the BMTA. Despite the rapid increase in demand for transportation, the BMTA failed to increase the number of buses, owing to financial difficulties. At the same time, the influential taxi and tricycle cooperatives had successfully lobbied the government to limit the number of taxis and tricycles in Bangkok. A severe shortage of public transport service, therefore, stimulated a second uprising of illegal *songthaews*. Then, in 1980, the government decided to legalize the *songthaews*, allowing them to operate on BMTA routes, on two conditions: (1) that they pay a monthly fee of 1,200 baht to the BMTA, and (2) that they change to a new, safer model of minibus.

The *silorleks* were also legalized, but they were given the right to operate only on side streets. For the first time, the Land Transport Department (LTD) was able to keep these *silorleks* off the main streets, because legalization of certain routes allowed illegal routes to be better patrolled. The liberalization resulted in an increased number of *silorleks*, from 577 in 1976 to 7,874 in 1988, as shown in Table 5.4 (Viboon 1976; Metropolitan Police Bureau 1988).

In the late 1970s, there were still few hired motorcycles, but after 1982, the number of hired motorcycles started to increase at an exponential rate. They now outcompete their main rivals, the *songthaews*, *silorleks*, and *samlors*.

As a consequence, in 1988–1989 official estimates show that there were about 16,000–20,000 hired motorcycles while *silorleks* and *songthaews* numbered only 7,874 and 2,753, respectively. The number of formal transport vehicles, which consist of the BMTA's buses,

TABLE 5.5   Number of Public Transport Vehicles in Bangkok and Method of Operation

Mode	Year	Number	Route	Fare
Formal sector				
Public bus	1989	4,865	Fixed	Fixed
Private minibus	1989	2,194	Fixed	Fixed
Taxi	1988	13,493	Nonfixed	Bargain
Samlor	1988	7,406	Nonfixed	Bargain
Silorlek	1988	7,874	Fixed and nonfixed	Fixed and bargain
Songthaew	1989	2,753	Fixed	Fixed
Informal sector				
Motorcycle	1988	16,000	Fixed and nonfixed	Fixed and bargain

SOURCE: Bangkok Mass Transport Authority; Department of Land Transport (1988, 1989); Metropolitan Police Bureau (1988).

legalized private minibuses, taxis, and *samlors*, increased only slightly in the 1980s (see Tables 5.4 and 5.5). The relatively moderate, but increasing, role of informal transport vehicles, therefore, reflects the government's willingness to legalize informal operators.

Evolution of the hired motorcycle service. Motorcycles have been available for hire in rural areas, especially in southern Thailand, for more than two decades. The first motorcycle service in Bangkok was founded in the northern suburb of Don Muang in 1969 (Metropolitan Police Bureau 1988). The first motorcycle route in downtown Bangkok started at Ngarmdooplee Lane, near Lumpini Park, around 1980. The area had a large population that lived in the lanes and narrow roads and needed means of access to the main street. The number of motorcycle routes has increased rapidly since 1982. Twenty-two out of forty-nine routes I surveyed were established between 1982 and 1984. I estimate that the number of hired motorcycles in late 1989 exceeded 25,000 vehicles, compared with the police's estimate of 16,051 in 1988. The fact that this new type of transport service has become so popular without any government intervention means that it is the most efficient form of transport invented by the informal operators. Obviously, the net benefit that certain segments of society receive from such an institution greatly exceeds those from other existing modes of transport. The creation and evolution of this economic institution can be explained by the demand and supply framework. The interesting questions are why motorcycle transport developed and why it became so popular so fast.

Informal motorcycle transport grew quickly in Bangkok because it is more flexible and convenient than other forms of transport.

At least two main factors affect the demand for motorcycle service. The first one is the high land rent caused by rapid urbanization of Bangkok. Metropolitan Bangkok has rapidly expanded into its suburbs and beyond its boundary into the nearby provinces. Such rapid urbanization[8] has drastically affected land prices and land-use patterns in Bangkok. Residential areas have been pushed out of the inner city, and most poor people have been driven out to the fringe of Bangkok. These people cannot afford to own cars and must rely solely on public transport.

The poor also often live far from public bus routes. Lack of planning in the suburban areas has led to a road system that consists of major roads (with four or more lanes) and narrow local roads or lanes, which are generally less than four meters wide and one to three kilometers in length and are developed privately. The Metropolitan Police Bureau (1988) estimated that there were more than ten thousand such lanes in Bangkok in 1987. These lanes cannot accommodate large buses or other large vehicles, and only motorcycles, *samlors*, and *silorleks* can transport those who live there. Since per capita income in Bangkok is almost three times higher than the national average, time costs for Bangkokians are high. People, therefore, are willing to purchase "time," and motorcycle service has expanded to serve them.

Since the early 1980s, motorcycle service has replaced *silorlek*s and *samlor*s in many areas. There are obvious economic reasons for the comparative advantage of the motorcycle service. First, *silorlek*s and *samlor*s have one important weakness in terms of service: they generally will not depart until they have taken on a minimum load of passengers. Thus, each bus may wait ten to forty minutes before leaving the station. In sparsely populated areas, service is so irregular that it is impossible to predict arrival times. A motorcycle, however, serves one passenger and hence can depart immediately. Operators can make a profit by transporting one passenger per trip because of motorcycles' low fuel consumption. Motorcycles also have lower average operating and maintenance costs per kilometer than *silorlek*s. The fare of three baht for the first kilometer can easily cover the average operating cost. Thus, motorcycles can perfectly serve the needs of the people, even if the fare per trip is more expensive than that of *silorlek*s or *samlor*s.[9]

Second, motorcycles are more mobile and flexible on congested roads than other vehicles. Moreover, motorcycles can provide door-to-door service, even for passengers who live in extemely narrow lanes.

The first motorcycle route in Bangkok was not intentionally established as a transport business. After a few sailors in Ngarmdooplee Lane bought motorcycles for commuting purposes, their neighbors asked them to take neighborhood children to school. As demand increased, the sailors formed a group to provide transport service in the mornings and evenings. Finally, when more drivers joined it, the group set up management rules to control the behavior of member drivers. These rules, which were democratically agreed on, included standard fares, departure schedules, safety regulations, orderly parking practices, and prohibitions on drinking and gambling while on duty. Such management practices have resulted in reliable, dependable, and safe service.

The motorcycle service would not have grown so rapidly had the government not given the green light to its existence. Since some of the motorcycle routes overlap with legalized *silorlek* routes and the BMTA's concessionary routes, the issue is whether motorcycle service violates the law. Fortunately, in 1983, the Metropolitan Police Bureau concluded that the use of motorcycles for passenger service did not violate Thailand's Car Act. The director of the Land Transport Department has also ruled that motorcycle transport does not violate either the Car Act or the Land Transportation Act. These rulings, in effect, allow motorcycle operators to freely appropriate routes, to establish new routes to improve service, and to provide more specialized services. And yet, the motorcycle routes have never been completely legalized.

Establishment of routes. A motorcycle route is a line of travel between a starting point in a residential area and the main street, where people can catch public buses or visit business centers. In general, the distance of each motorcycle route is from one to three kilometers.

The process of establishing routes. Commuting needs establish the value of a route. Foreseeing a profit opportunity, transport entrepreneurs appropriate a route as their property. Almost all of the routes in our survey were established by a small group of from three to five motorcycle drivers. The group leaders, who initiate the route, belong to two categories: (1) government officials, especially soldiers and low-ranking policemen, and (2) hooligans and gangsters in the route area.

Gangsters usually have a more limited choice of routes than do government officials. They can only establish a route in their own "territory," because if violence between gangs erupts, the police may intervene and the route may not be allowed. Since government officials can use their connections with higher-ranking bureaucrats, they have more route choices. It should be noted that only one of the routes in our sample was established by a group composed of neither officials nor hooligans. Fortunately, the area they chose was not governed by gangsters.

The process of route selection and route establishment involves economic calculation. In general, a few entrepreneurs determine the route's feasibility and the optimum number of drivers. Most entrepreneurs prefer routes not served by other means of transport, to avoid

This group of motorcycle drivers waits for fares at the parking station for its route.

conflicts. As already explained, motorcycles can outcompete other transport modes. The emergence of a new fleet of hired motorcycles will therefore generally result in a conflict of interest with any existing transport operators. To resolve the conflict, the leader of the motorcycle drivers must negotiate with the existing operators. In all sample cases but one, the negotiation led to some form of compromise. For example, the motorcycle leaders usually offer competing *silorlek* or *samlor* drivers the opportunity to join the motorcycle business. In some cases, *silorlek* and *samlor* drivers who try to maintain their operations are later forced to join the motorcycle drivers, after losing most of their business to their new rivals. In one route, where the owner of the *silorlek* fleet had good connections with the police, the motorcycle drivers agreed to pay a monthly fee for the right to use the *silorlek* route. Violence erupted in only one case, in which the motorcycle leader decided to seize the route by force.

Obtaining police approval. Even after successfully establishing a route, the motorcyclists face one more important task before beginning operation. The motorcycle group leader must seek unofficial approval for the operation from the precinct traffic police chief. While there is no law prohibiting motorcycles from providing transportation service, the police can cite motorcycle drivers for traffic violations. Such authority, if strictly enforced or intentionally abused, can be disastrous to a motorcycle service business. To avoid such clashes, the leader of the motorcycle group must ask for police approval. There are two types of approval costs. First, each motorcycle driver must pay a lump-sum entrance fee ranging from 3,000 to 5,000 baht. Second, many motorcycle enterprises must pay a monthly bribe to the police. The bribe varies between 1,500 and 30,000 baht per month, depending on the number of motorcycles on the route. Such monthly payment, in fact, is a ransom that motorcycle drivers pay in exchange for exemption from traffic violation fines.[10] Some greedy policemen individually solicit extra money and goods (such as liquor) from the motorcycle operators. Each time they may receive from 10 to 100 baht.

Not every motorcycle driver has to pay the entrance fee. At least one group of drivers surveyed did not have to pay bribes. The owner of the route told us that the police chief of the station was honest and knew that people desperately need motorcycle transport service. Another owner said that he merely bought some chairs for the local police station in exchange for the right to operate in one route. Moreover, most of the leaders who are government officials, especially soldiers and policemen, do not have to pay entrance fees. They have enough power to deter the police from demanding them.

In some cases, a motorcycle route crosses into the territory of a second police precinct. If they do not pay bribes to the police in this second precinct, the drivers will have to take off their jackets every time they cross the precinct boundary.[11] The drivers will remain subject to harassment, however, until they pay the bribe.

Besides the monthly bribe, the police have another incentive to monitor the motorcycle service. In order to prevent thieves and petty criminals from operating as motorcycle drivers within their precinct, the police keep on file the name, address, and occupation of all motorcycle drivers in that precinct. Every time motorcycle route owners want to increase the number of motorcycles in their route, they must notify the police chief. And, of course, the monthly fee also increases.

The monthly and lump-sum bribes are, at least in part, payment for the property right over a route. This right enables route owners to operate routes on an exclusive and transferable basis. Owners can exclude drivers who fail to pay for the right to operate, and they can sell their rights freely. These two aspects of property rights are required conditions for efficient resource use. However, the rights are not complete, since they originate in bribery and trespassing on the rights of other transport providers without any legal recognition from the state.

Exclusive and transferable property rights. When a route is initially established, the first group of drivers has the right to operate on the route without paying an entrance fee. They simply pay the owner of the route a daily queue fee, or *win* payment, of from five to twenty baht (see Table 5.6). (*Win* means motorcycle route.) Part of the *win* payment goes to the police.

TABLE 5.6   Entrance Fee, Value of Route, and Fees Paid by Motorcycle Drivers in Bangkok

Type	Value (in baht)
Price of jacket	3,000–40,000
Value of route[a]	40,000–300,000
Entrance fee for each motorcycle (paid to police)	3,000–5,000
Monthly bribe to police (per driver)	100–200
Fees paid by driver	
Daily jacket rental	20–60
Fee for a new driver	200–1,700
Daily *win* (queue) fee	5–20

a. Equivalent to the price of a jacket multiplied by the number of drivers.
SOURCE: Author.

All motorcycle drivers are required to wear special numbered jackets so that they can be identified by the police.

Motorcycle drivers who want to join the route later must pay an entrance fee, by purchasing a jacket from the route owner. Table 5.6 shows that the price of a jacket ranges from 3,000 to 40,000 baht, depending upon the expected profit from the operation. Those who buy jackets usually have their own motorcycles and must make *win* payments to the route owner. Owners of several jackets often rent them out at a daily rate ranging from 20 to 60 baht. If there is a change of drivers, the new tenant driver has to pay an initial fee of 200–1,700 baht to the route owner. On some routes the new tenant drivers also have to pay a brokerage fee of from 100 to 500 baht to the route dispatcher.

Thus, there are two types of property rights associated with motorcycle routes: route rights and jacket-ownership rights. On a few routes, the owners sell jackets to the drivers, on the condition that the jacket can only be resold to the route owner. In most other cases, however, the jacket can be resold to anyone. Therefore, the property right to the jacket is transferable; it is also exclusive, because although the jacket can be rented out, no one without a jacket can join the route.

The route right is also exclusive and transferable. Motorcycle drivers have to pay *win* fees and the entrance fees to the route owner.

The route right is also transferable: my survey found that several routes had been sold to new owners. The selling price ranged from 40,000 to 250,000 baht, depending on the number of the motorcycles in the route and the expected profit.

Incomplete property rights. The property rights associated with motorcycle routes are not complete, however. They are subject to seizure by force or through other illegitimate means. Out of forty-seven routes in this study, four routes had been taken by force from the original owners. In most cases, the original owners were soldiers still in government service. The invaders were hooligans or other influential persons in the area. The soldiers were reluctant to contest the seizure, fearing the incident might cost them their main government jobs. There were also three unsuccessful attempts by ruffians to take over routes, but the route owners in these cases were tough enough to resist. Some owners, who had good relations with the police, asked the police to help them. Since motorcycle transport property rights can change hands by force, it is not surprising that, ultimately, most routes end up in the hands of gangsters or government officers who can use force or authority to protect their property.

In other cases, the local police chief allowed a new fleet of motorcycles to move into an existing route. The new group simply set up a starting point (or terminal) across the road from the existing enterprise or at the other end of the route. In one instance, the new entrant was an influential person in the area. In another, a minibus operator, outcompeted by motorcycles serving the same route, also began operating motorcycles. In yet another case, a second group of motorcycle operators, who set up a station at the other end of the lane, took away half of the route from the first group of operators.

Finally, in one area the police allowed two new groups to operate on routes that had no previous direct service. The new groups took some passengers from a neighboring group already in existence.

Informal motorcycle transport operators, acting in pursuit of their own self-interest, have successfully provided transportation for a large number of people in Bangkok who would otherwise go unserved. Although transport property rights can be established in an informal way, the rights are not complete. They can be taken away by force or can be diminished in value when new competitors are allowed to operate on nearby or overlapping routes. Complete, legal property rights over motorcycle routes must be established to provide incentives for operators to maintain their services.

Structure, conduct, and performance of the motorcycle transport industry. This section will assess the economic efficiency of the motorcycle transport industry.

Structure. There is no exact estimate of the total number of motorcycles and routes in Bangkok. Two surveys conducted in 1988–1989 yielded widely different results. A survey by the Land Transport Department found that there were 10,268 motorcycles and 829 routes in 1988. A Metropolitan Police Bureau survey in early 1989 gave a much higher figure of 16,051 motorcycles, but only 479 routes. Based on our survey in late 1989, we believe that the number of motorcycles reported by the police survey may be more accurate. But the police survey's reported number of routes may be too low, since the Bangkok Police Department did not itself perform the site survey.

Probably the most important reason for a failure to obtain an accurate estimate of the number of motorcycles is the dynamic growth of the motorcycle transport business. As already mentioned, the number of motorcycles has been increasing very rapidly. Many motorcycle drivers work part-time; some drive only at night, and some drive for only a few hours and rent their jackets to other operators. Motorcycle routes also change hands quite often. Based on these considerations and the sample survey, I estimate that there were about 20,000–25,000 motorcycles and about 700–800 routes at the end of 1989.

There are two kinds of motorcycle groups: single-owner and group-owner. Most of the groups (83 percent) have a single owner. The rest have several owner/drivers who jointly established the group. This survey found that group-owner groups generally operate fewer motorcycles and charge a higher entrance fee.[12] The objective of such groups is to maximize the average income of all the owner/drivers. Owner/drivers are therefore reluctant to recruit new colleagues because, as the size of the group increases, the cost of managing it may increase faster than the average income. On the other hand, the owners of single-owner groups want to maximize their income from rent and jacket sales, which increase with the size of the group. As the group size increases, however, the owners' net income per driver declines. This factor places a limit on group size. Moreover, as the group size increases, the sale price and the rental rate of the jacket also decline.

According to the survey, there are three types of parking stations (or motorcycle terminals). Most of the sample routes (thirty-four out of forty-seven routes) had a parking point at the beginning of a lane that transverses a residential area. Eleven routes had parking stations at business or communication centers. Only two routes located their parking station on the main street. It should be noted that thirty-seven of the sample motorcycle routes had a single parking point, and twelve routes had two parking points, one at the beginning of a lane and another at the other end. In the case of a densely populated, dead-end lane, a second station is likely to be located somewhere inside the lane and operated only in the morning rush hour.

Although most lanes are served by only one motorcycle group, there is usually more than one group in densely populated lanes. For example, before the construction of a lane to connect two main roads, there might be only one motorcycle group, parked in a lane that goes part of the way between the two main roads. After the construction, a new group would be established at the other end of the new lane. There were two such cases in the survey. A second type of competition takes place when a new group is set up at the far end of a long lane that connects two main roads. Two routes in the survey had this kind of competition. A third type of competition occurs when there are two groups at opposite ends of a lane that connects two main roads, and along the lane, there are several branch lanes whose population density is high enough that new groups are set up to serve people who live there. One such case was found in the survey.

When groups park in business centers (such as markets) and on main roads, there is usually more than one group serving the same neighborhood.

Entry to the motorcycle transport industry is relatively easy. Although there are costs, including the expense of negotiations with the police, bribes, and a willingness to use violence to protect one's property, total entry costs are low. It is, moreover, not very costly to leave the industry, since there is not much sunk cost. Route owners do not have to incur a fixed investment in a parking station. They usually just park their motorcycles on a public road or rent a parking station from a private landowner. Since route ownership rights can be sold, the owners can recoup most, if not all, of the future value of the route. Finally, motorcycles themselves can be sold, because the used motorcycle market is very active.

It can be tentatively concluded, therefore, that the motorcycle transport market is characterized by a competitive structure, for two reasons. First, more than half of the sample routes had more than one competitor. Motorcycle operators also have to compete with operators of other modes of transport. Second, entry to and exit from the market are relatively easy. Nevertheless, many motorcycle groups enjoy a locational advantage in two respects. In cases of groups that park on main streets or at business centers, the group that first entered the market usually commands the best location. Groups that are the sole operator in a lane also have a monopolistic position.

Conduct. This section will discuss three aspects of conduct: market-sharing agreements, fare pricing, and quality of services.

First, in areas served by more than one motorcycle group, the competitors usually reach some implicit agreement about the boundary of their services. Each group has its own monopolized area, called a prohibited area, where other groups are not allowed to pick up passengers. Outside the prohibited area, there is free competition. A group that parks in a trading center or on a main street usually has no monopolized area, except the area in front of its parking station.

Such implicit agreement resulted from a process of evolution. In the early years of the motorcycle transport trade, there were disagreements and quarrels among competing groups. They usually settled their disputes on a basis of equal-distance market sharing. This pattern of agreement became the norm. The informal transport operators have usually worked out peaceful agreements to share markets so that prohibited or monopolized areas are kept to a minimum.

Second, different motorcycle operators charge the same standard fare for almost every route. Even the fare charged by operators with a monopoly in a certain area is the same as that charged by other operators. For example, a group with a monopoly in a residential area will charge its passengers seven baht for a service from their homes to the bus station. On the way back, these passengers will pay the same fare to another operator whose group is based at the bus station. This phenomenon is called a "contestable market." Although there is only one group in the residential area, because the market can profitably accommodate only one firm, the market is contestable in the sense that, if the group charges too high a price, a new entrant may charge a lower fare and take away its business. It should be noted that there is a maximum fare that motorcycle operators can charge because of competition from other modes of transport.[13]

The fare is higher at night because of the operators' time costs and fewer opportunities to take on passengers. However, this study found that, in business or communication centers where competition is keen, night fares are the same as the day rate.

When passengers want to travel to a destination outside a regular route, the fare is subject to bargaining. There are two competitive forces that dictate the fare. First, the passengers often have a choice among different motorcycle groups. Second, they can usually choose among drivers within a single group. They can bargain with the first driver in the queue; if the first driver demands too high a fare, the second operator may be approached.

Finally, quality of service is an important consideration for motorcycle groups. Transport accidents are few, for accidents can ruin the reputation of a driver and hence the profit of the route owner. Every motorcycle group, therefore, has rigid regulations against improper driving behavior. Motorcycle drivers are not allowed to drink or to gamble while on duty. They must drive carefully, within the proper speed limit, and not attempt to overtake other motorcycles. If they are caught violating the rules or if there are complaints from the passengers, drivers will be suspended for several days. Another measure to ensure proper behavior is making drivers responsible for the cost of accidents. There is no insurance available to motorcycle drivers. This study found very few route owners willing to help pay for the cost of accidents.

Another aspect of the quality of motorcycle service is its regularity. In every group, there is a rule that drivers who cannot work for a day must return their jackets to the chief driver so they can be rented out to other drivers. If drivers fail to return their coats, they must pay the regular *win* fee, which ranges from five baht to twenty baht per day. This rule ensures that there is a stable supply of motorcycle drivers.

Performance. The performance of the motorcycle transport industry can be judged by the growth of the industry, as measured by employment and income growth and by the rate of return to factors of production. As mentioned, the industry has experienced rapid growth since 1982. If total employment in motorcycle transport is 20,000, it represents 1 percent of jobs in Bangkok.

In 1989, the industry generated annual income of about 1.76 billion baht[14]—of which 43.2 percent is net income for motorcycle drivers, 23.5 percent is paid in rental fees for motorcycles, 8.8 percent is paid in rental fees for jackets, and 3.1 percent is paid in *win* fees, which constitute the route owners' income.[15]

The average net income of motorcycle drivers is 127 baht for their eleven-hour workday. If an eight-hour workday is used as the standard, a driver's daily income is 92 baht, which is higher than the 1989 daily legal minimum wage of 78 baht. Motorcycle drivers earn more than unskilled workers, because their jobs are riskier and require some skill. Drivers do not earn higher income than other jobs with similar characteristics, however. Drivers are mostly young people with primary and secondary education, but some are older, and some have college degrees. Many civil servants take a motorcycle transport job as their second occupation.

The main source of income of the route owners is the daily *win* fee. Since the daily *win* fee ranges between 5 and 20 baht, a route owner earns about 12,150 baht per month for a typical route with fifty-four motorcycles.[16] About 2,600 baht will have to go to the local police station. This route owner's net income would be about 9,550 baht per month, which is more than four times higher than the net monthly income of a motorcycle driver who works eight hours a day. Part of this disparity is due to the owners' entrepreneurial ability to control and supervise the operation. Another significant portion of the owners' income is, in a sense, rent, as there is a limit on the number of routes in any particular area. This "rent" is a return for the owners' willingness to engage in an illegal activity and willingness to protect their informal property rights.

The size of the rent obtained by a route owner can be measured by the price the route commands when sold. The price is usually substantial, ranging from 40,000 baht to 300,000 baht.

Some drivers also derive rental income, by owning and renting out jackets. In 1989, jackets sold for an average of 15,000 baht apiece. Since the jacket can be rented at a rate of 26 baht per day, the return to the jacket owner is about 5 percent per month.

Reasons for Informality

There are at least four reasons why a large number of people in Thailand are informal or choose to be informal.

Legal barriers. Perhaps the most important reason is that the law does not allow certain activities, or does not allow them in certain places. For example, free entry, small investment requirements, and an attractive rate of return are factors that draw many to take up vending activities. But the laws prohibiting selling on public streets cause vendors to remain informal.

After the 1986 elections, the new Bangkok governor issued an order temporarily allowing vendors to sell on the sidewalks of some public streets. He had to revoke his order, however, since it was in violation of the Land Traffic Act. If the vendors were to be allowed on the public streets, new laws had to be passed.

As previously mentioned, the motorcycle transport industry is not in violation of the law. And yet, the business is not legally recognized, and, therefore, the government cannot issue route rights. Moreover, since some influential policemen have a vested interest in controlling the motorcycle business, other government agencies have refrained from intervening.

The informal credit market exists because lenders can escape government regulations imposed on financial institutions. There are two major government policies that seek to regulate the financial sector: a limit on the number of financial institutions and interest-rate controls. These two policies have enabled banks to form a legalized cartel that tends to ration credit in favor of large-scale enterprises and businesses of which the banks are part owners. Small-scale enterprises and people who want to borrow to finance such businesses have to rely on informal moneylenders. Although there is a usury law, it has never been effectively enforced. Therefore, the moneylenders can charge high market rates of interest (3 to 10 percent per month).[17] The moneylenders are, nevertheless, essential because they provide loans that can be easily obtained by anyone. Clients can even seek loans on holidays or at nighttime.

Cost of registering a small business. Before 1982, in practice it took at least one month to obtain a commercial business registration permit, and no less than three to four months to get factory permits, for factory owners had to contact several government offices personally. For example, a fireworks factory had to obtain the approval of the Ministry of Defense.

In 1982, in an attempt to promote exports, the government set up a one-stop service center at the National Department of Factories and asked all government offices to simplify permit issuance procedures. As a consequence, the number of days officially required for the issuance of commercial registration permits declined from seven days to one day. The registration fee is now only fifty baht.

The procedures required to obtain permits for partnership firms and corporations are more complicated and take longer. It used to take fifteen days to get a commercial registration permit for a partnership firm. Now, it takes less than seven days, with a registration fee of 1,001 baht for a three-person firm. If applicants hire a law firm to help them get a permit, the commission ranges from 500 to 1,000 baht. A corporation permit requires twelve to fifteen days to acquire, and the registration fee is 5,500 baht for a firm with one million baht of registered capital. The fee will increase by 5,000 baht for each additional one million baht of capital. If the applicants do not have access to all required government papers and documents, it may take as long as five to six months to acquire them. This is why the commission fee charged by law firms for handling a corporation permit application ranges from 4,000 to 6,000 baht.

In order to run a factory, applicants are required to apply for a factory permit and a permit to operate a factory, in addition to the registration permit. It now takes about a month to get these permits, compared with the two to three months required before 1982. The legal commission fee ranges from 6,000 to 8,000 baht. For factories that may create a nuisance in the surrounding neighborhood, the permit application procedures are more complicated. The applicant has to solicit letters from prospective neighbors stating that they will not be disturbed by the new factory. As a result, it takes about two months and a legal commission fee of 20,000 baht to get such a permit. Sometimes, the law firms must bribe government officials; in such cases, the commission fee will, of course, be higher.

In conclusion, although there are certain procedures that have to be met, it does not appear that the cost of registration for a small-scale enterprise is excessive. The government policy of rationalizing bureaucratic procedures obviously has helped reduce the cost of registering a business. This explains why, for example, there were as many as 520,000 registration permits issued in 1985.

There are two reasons why informal enterprises may nevertheless not apply for commercial registration permits. First, the law exempts some activities, such as vending, from commercial registration. Second, if entrepreneurs want to go out of business or change the status of their companies, from, say, single-proprietorship firms to corporations, they will be subject to back-dated tax reevaluation. Sometimes, the past three to five years' financial records will be assessed by the Department of Internal Revenue. This imposes a high exit cost for an enterprise. Many owners of firms that have gone out of business have to pay unreasonably high extra taxes for the final few years of the firm's operation. Such exit costs deter people from starting or expanding their activities legally.

Import duties. Between 1974 and 1978, several government measures increased protection of import-substituting activities. Tariffs were raised for fifty-three industrial categories, which raised the average rates of nominal protection from 24.8–34.6 percent to 35.7–50.8 percent (World Bank 1980:ii). There were also reductions in the import duties and business taxes paid by a number of promoted firms, and the scope of the import control was broadened. Higher tariffs induced increased smuggling of products such as cigarettes, electrical appliances, and luxury canned foods.

After 1981, the government reformed its industrial policy, especially the tariff structure, with the aim of fostering efficient industrial growth, together with the expansion of small- and medium-size firms and improvements in the living standards of the poor. Changes included elimination of differences in business-tax rates on imports and on domestic products, and equalization of tariffs in a downward direction. Most tariffs on electrical equipment were brought down to a 20–50 percent range. Such changes effectively curtailed smuggling, especially of electrical appliances. However, tariffs on certain imported products remain high and there are still incentives for some smuggling. For example, many computers and computer parts are smuggled into Thailand. In 1988, the value of computer imports was 1.9 billion baht, while the total sales of all computer dealers were estimated at 4 billion baht. Although the tariff on computers and parts has been reduced from 40 percent to 20 percent since 1988, smuggled products are as much as 20–23 percent cheaper than legally imported ones ("Hia Kuang Computer Shop" 1990).

Labor costs. Most small-scale enterprises and informal enterprises do not comply with labor laws. More than 50–60 percent of all enterprises—most of which are small-scale enterprises with fewer than ten workers—do not pay the legal minimum wage rate (Nipon 1990). The difference between the minimum wage and the market wage ranges from 8 percent of the minimum wage in Bangkok to 38 percent in the upper northern region. Small-scale firms also generally fail to comply with other labor-protection laws, such as those requiring paid vacation, paid holidays, and paid sick leave. It is estimated that the saving in labor costs to small firms ranges from 2,600 to 4,400 baht per worker, or about 13–22 percent of an average year's wages for one worker (Nipon 1990).

It is difficult for small-scale enterprises to comply with labor regulations, because their average labor productivity rate is much lower than the large-scale enterprises (Chulacheep and Somsak 1988). Moreover, while large-scale firms enjoy low-cost credit and are entitled to government subsidies and privileges granted to firms promoted by the Board of Investment (BOI), small-scale firms are always subject to penalties imposed by government investment policy.

Costs of Informality

Informal enterprises incur special costs and experience some policy biases.

Bribery. Bribes are one of the most visible costs faced by many informal enterprises. As mentioned earlier, each motorcycle driver has to pay a monthly bribe, ranging between 100 baht and 200 baht, to the local police station, in return for an exemption from traffic fines.

Vendors on public streets also have to bribe officials of the Bangkok Metropolitan Authority and the police in order to avoid being arrested during periodic crackdowns. The average monthly bribe per vendor ranges from 200 to 300 baht. Since the amount of the bribe is small, relative to the fine of 500 baht per arrest, or to the vendors' sale revenues, which average several thousand baht per month, the vendors do not complain about the payment. In fact, as long as the police do not ask for too much, the vendors do not consider bribery unfair.[18]

Another cost that informal enterprises most often pay is rent. Rent is usually paid to the organizer of several vendors who together form a small group. The organizer has two main responsibilities: to protect each vendor's sales territory from competitors and to arrange with the police an exemption from arrest for each vendor. Usually the organizer will collect from ten to twenty baht per day from each vendor stall.

Cascading effect of business taxes on subcontracting. The most significant bias against small-scale enterprises in Thailand lies in the structure of the business tax. This tax is levied on all manufactured goods and on some categories of services. Its application to gross sales receipts of every transaction, wholesale or retail, results in a cascading effect that encourages vertical integration. Hence, the business tax has distorted the industrial structure by discouraging the use of subcontracting (World Bank 1989:86). A majority of self-employed workers complain that their main business problem is the heavy burden of the business tax (Pasuk and Pradith 1988:99).

Subcontracting is important for the Thai manufacturing sector in general, and for small-scale enterprises in particular, because most subcontracted work seems to occur among small firms. In their study of the self-employed workers, Pasuk and Pradith (1988) found that 30 percent of sample enterprises had subcontracting arrangements with larger firms.

Efficient subcontracting would enhance the competitiveness of Thai manufacturers. Subcontracting allows final assemblers greater flexibility in changing product lines and producing products with a variety of features.

It should be noted that the government is now planning to replace the current business tax with a value-added tax (VAT) in the near future. At first, VAT was to be used in 1989, but it was delayed as a consequence of political opposition and the public's lack of knowledge about its effects. When instituted, VAT, which will eliminate the cascading effect of business tax, will encourage subcontracting.

Policy bias toward large firms. The major incentives granted by the BOI to promoted firms are exemptions from and reductions of duties on imports of machinery and raw materials, and exemptions from income taxes for periods of from four to seven years. The BOI's investment-promotion system has been criticized for using high minimum-capital-requirement criteria and procedures that limit the availability of promotional privileges to small-scale enterprises. Although the minimum capital requirement for export-oriented projects has been reduced from 200 million baht in the 1960s to only 1 million baht today, the requirement still restricts the access of most small- and medium-size enterprises to the promotion system. Data collected since 1986 show that almost two-thirds of all projects smaller than 100 million baht that sought promotion were larger than 20 million baht. Only a few firms that sought promotion involved investments of less than 10 million baht, which is likely the maximum that firms with fewer than 200 employees would be able to invest (World Bank 1989:87). Since 1982, moreover, there has been a steady increase in the share of approved projects taken by firms with investments of over 500 million baht.

The BOI's administrative procedures are too costly for most smaller firms. For this reason, together with discretionary decision making in granting incentives, the promotion system tends to favor large-scale industry over small- and medium-size enterprises. To the extent the small-scale firms produce products similar to those made by promoted firms, the former will be in a much less competitive position.

Manufacturing-protection bias. As mentioned earlier, during the 1974–1981 period Thailand's level of import protection increased. Despite government willingness to reform the overall structure of tariffs in the early 1980s, revenue considerations generally muted such efforts. As a consequence, the average levels of effective protection in the mid-1980s were essentially as high as they had been earlier in the decade.

The heavy and highly variable protection provided to import-substituting activities is also harmful to small-scale industries. There is a bias in protection toward import-substituting industries that make heavy use of imported raw materials and machines, against the resource- and agriculture-based industries dominated by the informal sector. The bias in industrial protection, furthermore, favors capital-intensive, import-substituting industries over labor-intensive, small-scale manufacturing.[19]

Capital costs. The effects of investment policy, tariff protection, and other government policies[20] can be summarized in terms of the annual rental costs for a machine costing 100 baht, as faced by firms of different sizes and locations, with and without the benefit of incentive policies (see Table 5.7). Government policies tend to reduce the actual rental cost of a 100-baht-machine by from 30 to 46 baht for large firms in Bangkok. The implied capital subsidy is, thus, 16 baht, which can be broken down as follows: subsidy from overvaluation of the baht, 37 percent; interest subsidy, 13 percent; tariff and tax exemptions on machines, 25 percent; and income tax subsidy, 25 percent.[21] Firms in Thailand's special investment promotion zones have the lowest rental cost and receive the largest subsidy. The informal sector receives a small but positive subsidy if one assumes that these firms do not pay corporate income tax. But our interview with informal actors whose enterprises are not registered found that they do pay individual income tax. The actual rental cost of the informal sector, therefore, should be closer

TABLE 5.7   Annual Rental Cost of a Machine Costing 100 Baht for Different
Types of Firms (baht)

Firm size/location	Actual rental cost	Rental cost without incentive	Implied subsidy
Large–Bangkok	30	46	16
Large–Investment promotion zones	27	46	19
Informal sector[a]–Bangkok	45	54	9
Small-scale firms[b]–Bangkok	60	72	12

a. Employing fewer than ten workers.
b. Employing ten to fifty workers.
SOURCE: World Bank (1983:147).

to the no-incentive rental cost shown in Table 5.7. In any case, informal and small firms have the highest rental cost of capital, because they have access to neither investment incentives nor subsidized loans from public financial institutions.

Scarce access to formal sector credit. There are four possible formal sources of credit for informal enterprises: commercial banks, the Small Industrial Finance Organization (SIFO), the Bank of Thailand's refinancing scheme, and the Industrial Finance Corporation of Thailand (IFCT).

Although commercial banks provide more credit to small-scale firms than any other source, the access of the informal enterprises to commercial bank credit is very limited.[22] In 1983, only 6 percent of bank loans were for amounts less than 3 million baht, which is the maximum that could be borrowed by most small-size firms. In a survey of self-employed workers, it was found that less than 4 percent of them borrowed from financial institutions (Pasuk and Pradith 1988:98). There are at least two reasons. First, high administrative and screening costs limit the lending of commercial banks to small firms. Second, government policies that have limited competition within the banking sector, as well as the use of interest-rate ceilings, have further restricted the role of commercial banks. At the low rate of interest imposed by the government, banks tend to ration credit to large-scale firms with secured collateral. They have no incentive to lend to informal and small-scale enterprises. Although there has been no study of the difficulty and cost of obtaining loans faced by urban informal enterprises, a look at the rural credit market may shed some light on this problem.

Since 1975, commercial banks have been required to provide a certain percentage of their total loans to the agricultural sector. But the banks find that this business is a losing proposition, because the interest rate for agricultural loans is also regulated. Banks, therefore, try to shift the transaction costs to the borrowers.

Banks usually extend loans only to rich farmers who have title to their land. More than 90 percent of commercial bank loans to the agricultural sector are collateralized (Ammar 1987:12). The average annual household income of formal-sector borrowers is 47,673 baht, and they have landholdings averaging 34 rais;[23] those forced to borrow from the informal sector average 30,626 baht in annual household income and have landholdings averaging 16.4 rais (Nipon 1987). Extending loans only to wealthy farmers not only reduces the commercial banks' loan-default rate, but it also means the banks assume lower enforcement and information costs.

Even when it is possible for farmers to get bank loans, the application procedures are complicated. The farmers must first contact the loan officer at the bank office in town. It will then take a few weeks— or sometimes more than a month—for the loan officer to visit the farmers in order to assess the value of their land. The farmers must then wait a few more weeks before the loan is approved. Altogether, it takes from one to two months to get the money. When mortgaging their land, farmers not only bear all legal fees, which are typically set at about 1.5 percent of the land value, but also pay for the transportation and other expenses of the bank officers. A study by Nipon and Prayong (1989:151) found that the average time spent to obtain a loan from the formal sector was almost 711 working hours, compared with only 80 hours for a loan from the informal sector. In terms of expenses and the opportunity cost of time (but excluding delay costs), a formal-sector loan costs about 161 baht per contract, compared with 20 baht for an informal loan.

Most poor farmers and urban informal entrepreneurs, therefore, have to use their own savings or informal credit to finance their projects. The interest cost of borrowing from the informal sector ranges from 2 percent to 5 percent per month in urban areas, and from 3 percent to 10 percent per month in rural areas. But it is very convenient to obtain an informal loan, since it involves no complicated application procedures.

Other financial assistance available to small-scale industries is quite limited and occasionally may not even reach the informal borrowers at all. The volume of lending provided by the SIFO to small-scale industry was only 37.3 million baht in 1987.

The second formal credit scheme for small-scale firms is the refinancing facility that the Bank of Thailand (BOT) issues to such firms through commercial banks and the IFCT. However, such loans still represent a negligible fraction of total BOT refinancing. Moreover, the spread available to commercial banks on such lending is too low to cover their costs of lending to small firms.

The third lending institution is the IFCT itself, which provides credits mainly to large firms. In recent years, however, the IFCT has increased its involvement in lending to small- and medium-scale firms by managing a scheme called the Small Industry Credit Guarantee Fund, or SICGF. The fund was established in 1984 as a joint public-private venture to provide access to commercial bank credit for viable small firms without collateral. While the fund guarantees over 80 percent of a borrower's collateral shortfall, it attempts to ensure the borrower's commitment by requiring an equity contribution of at least 20 percent and a guarantee fee of 1.5 percent, of the total project cost. Loan approvals have risen rapidly, from 8.5 billion baht in 1986 to 95 billion baht in 1988. But the fund still does not reach the informal sector.

Differential burden of income tax. On average, registered small-scale firms pay a higher rate of corporate income tax (35 percent) than do large-scale firms that are listed on the security-exchange market (30 percent). Although informal enterprises—those that do not have a commercial registration permit—do not pay corporate income tax, their owners must pay individual income tax. This method of tax calculation has, in practice, resulted in higher tax rates for informal entrepreneurs, for their taxable income is always estimated at 20 percent of their total revenue. If their taxable income is in the lowest, 7 percent tax bracket, they have to pay income tax of 0.014 percent of their revenue. They must pay this minimum tax even if they lose money, whereas registered firms do not pay any tax if they lose money. Moreover, if the taxable income of informal entrepreneurs exceeds 400,000 baht, they must pay income tax at a higher rate than do registered firms.

The Political System and the Informal Sector

Before moving from analysis to prescription, it will be useful to describe some of the inherent weaknesses of the Thai legislative and political system. It should be cautioned that the solution is not simply to sweep away all bad legislation. In fact, even imperfect laws serve useful purposes. Thus, this analysis will focus on means of improving the existing law as it affects the informal sector.

Weaknesses of the existing laws. A large number of existing laws were written long ago, are badly outdated, and now present obstacles to economic development. For example, the Customs Act was passed in 1926, when the structure of trade was completely different from today. Although the law has been revised on a piecemeal basis, it still creates so many problems that its total reform is called for (Bawornsak 1989).

Reform is not likely soon, however, because the Thai Parliament is very slow at producing law. During the 1983–1986 period, 832 acts were considered by the members of Parliament, but only 116 acts (or less than 14 percent) were passed. There are two possible reasons for such slowness. First, Parliament has only a three-month session each year. Second, all elected Thai governments have been coalition governments. Each piece of legislation must go through a process of lengthy bargaining and compromise among the ruling parties.

Once they are passed, Thailand's major laws (that is, legislative acts) are often brief and incomplete. This tends to leave excessive discretionary power in the hands of bureaucrats. For example, the Export and Import Act contains only twenty-four articles, but there are more than one hundred subordinate laws. Table 5.8 shows that, in addition to 350 acts and revolutionary decrees (which are equivalent to acts) currently in effect, 18,744 subordinate laws have been passed by regulatory agencies and the executive branch. The executive branch enjoys an overabundance of power, which can be abused to generate economic rents for government officials and politicians.

Too many laws. Table 5.8 also reveals that there is a large number of laws—and the table does not include the countless bureaucratic memoranda, internal notes, advisory notes, and so on. Compliance is seriously affected, because most people, including the bureaucrats, do not know the law. The excessive number of laws means that some laws may be applied only at the whim of bureaucrats. Some people may be discriminated against, while others may be favorably treated by the bureaucrats.

In addition, the law is often so complicated that businessmen have to hire lawyers. Lack of clarity also results in business uncertainty. These costs have to be borne by those who choose to operate in the formal sector. Moreover, many laws are suddenly changed or enforced retroactively (Surakiat 1986). All of these uncertainties in the law allow bureaucrats to exert their own value judgments.

Overregulation and complicated bureaucratic procedures. Bureaucrats and legislators seek to control all economic activities. This is why it is necessary for even a tiny family factory to have a factory permit. Moreover, since every government office wants to exercise its power, a small factory may have to obtain several permits from various agencies, including a commercial registration permit, a factory permit,

TABLE 5.8   Major and Subordinate Legislation in Thailand, 1957–1986

Major legislation	
Legislative acts	327
Revolutionary decrees	23
Subordinate legislation	
Royal decrees	2,691
Ministerial regulations	4,027
Ministry notifications	6,272
Statutes	175
Municipal ordinances	80
Regulations (provisions)	46
Rules of procedure	287
Regulations	328
Committee notifications	1,289
Office notifications	1,543
Appointment announcements	1,351
Others	655
Total	18,744

SOURCE: Bawornsak (1989:72).

a health and sanitation standard permit, and so on. Finally, regulations by different government offices may overlap.

An important characteristic of the Thai legal system is that the power to make final decisions lies in the hands of high-level government officials in Bangkok. This explains why so many steps must be taken before a permit is granted. Unfortunately, there is usually no time limit on each procedure. For example, it can take several months to get a refund for the import duty on export goods. Such complicated procedures raise the cost of doing business.

Inadequate political participation. Before the student uprising of 1973, Thailand was governed by dictatorial regimes. Policy decision making and legislation were carried out by the bureaucrats. Such a political system is called a "bureaucratic polity," that is, a state of the bureaucrats, by the bureaucrats, and for the bureaucrats. The cabinet was dominated by the military and civil servants. Popular participation hardly existed, because most information on government policy was kept secret. Since 1973, elected representatives have begun to generate law in response to public demands. As a result of rapid economic growth and structural change in the economy, business organizations and practices have become more complicated. The bureaucrats now realize that they must have more contacts with the business community, in order to learn how business is carried out. At the same time, the business community is frustrated about red tape, bureaucracy, and complicated regulations. Besides providing funding support for the political parties, some businessmen enter the politics themselves. In the present Parliament, 68 percent of members are businessmen.

Another important factor that enhances the influence and role of business interest groups is the law. In 1966, the government enacted a law allowing businessmen and bankers to form trade and bankers' associations. Then in 1981, a joint private-public committee was set up to give advice to the government on economic policy and to notify the government of bureaucratic problems faced by the business community and suggest appropriate remedies.

The Thai people have begun to gain more political participation through direct demand, mass media, and interest groups. It should be noted, however, that there is asymmetrical participation among different interest groups. Until 1972, labor unions and farmers associations were banned, because the government feared such groups would be hotbeds of communism.

Although political participation has grown, there is still widespread corruption and rent-seeking behavior. In theory, elected representatives have to depend on the voters; in practice, there is such fierce competition for offices that if candidates do not have enough campaign funds, they may lose the elections. Politicians, therefore, have to establish a patronage relationship with businessmen who can provide them financial support.

Solution

The most serious barriers preventing informal actors from doing business legally or from expanding their businesses are the laws that prohibit certain activities and fail to recognize others.

Vendors must contend with laws prohibiting all obstacles from the streets and sidewalks, and laws that regulate polluting activities in public places. Although vendors are implicitly allowed in some areas, they are subject to certain regulations, including limits on the size of vending booths and bans on vending activities on certain days. The governor of Bangkok has issued an order prohibiting vending activities at bus stops and on narrow sidewalks. Discretionary enforcement allows some police officers to collect bribes from the vendors. Therefore, the Police Department has to closely monitor the behavior of its officers. Between January 1988 and October 1989, twenty officers were found guilty of receiving bribes or not acting according to the rules, and six of these were fired.

A new law was drafted in 1987 by Bangkok's Office of the Juridical Council that would permit vending activities in public places, subject to regulations concerning cleanliness and safety; the proposed law would not allow the Bangkok Metropolitan Authority to collect rent or tax from the vendors.[24] The law has not yet been scheduled for consideration by Parliament, however. In this case, the BMA must ask the Ministry of Interior to propose the new law to Parliament. Since the Parliament only reconvenes once every year for a period of three months, however, there is already a long queue of proposed legislation awaiting it. In addition, since the governor of Bangkok, who proposed the law, is the head of the opposition Palang Dham party, the coalition government is not eager to support the law.

At least two policy implications can be drawn from this case. First, Thailand needs more powerful, decentralized local government, which can better serve the interests of local population. So far, however, there has not been enough political will to move the country toward decentralization. Second, if the vendors would organize to demand changes in the law, their problems might be solved faster.

After the Metropolitan Police Bureau and the Land Transport Department ruled that motorcycle transport was not illegal, the police began unofficially registering drivers, and the motorcycle business has expanded rapidly ever since. Because there is still no law legalizing motorcycle transport, however, drivers must pay bribes to the police. This situation has several negative consequences. The drivers who pay the bribes can violate traffic laws without punishment. Since the business is not legally recognized, moreover, no tax is collected. Finally, since it is not possible to legally establish a motorcycle transport service, entrepreneurs cannot expand their businesses to take advantage of economies of scale.

It will be difficult to solve the problems, because most government officials will not interfere with the vested interests of other government agencies. The only possibility is for the motorcycle operators to organize and lobby for a new law that recognizes their business and allows free entry of new drivers. So far, there is no sign of such a movement, perhaps because the cost of organizing a lobby is thought to exceed the benefits.

If motorcycle transport is to be licensed, there should be no quota on the number of drivers and routes. A quota would only generate economic rent for the existing owners; society would be worse off than under the current practice, which allows nearly free entry.

Of the schemes that currently provide financial assistance to the small- and medium-scale firms, the Small Industry Credit Guarantee Fund, operated by the Industrial Finance Corporation of Thailand, is the most promising. The Small Industrial Finance Organization, which is designed to provide financial assistance to small firms, still faces both organizational and financial problems; but if it is reformed, the SIFO can also help provide funds for the informal sector. The possibility of designating the SIFO as an official financial institution should be considered, along with proposals to strengthen its personnel and funding sources.[25] The SIFO could also provide credit for viable small firms without collateral by imitating the loan-screening and loan-guarantee scheme of the SICGF.

Such a proposal has been suggested several times by Thai academicians, as well as by the World Bank (Somsak and Chesada 1983; World Bank 1983), and yet the proposal has never been seriously considered by the government. One reason is that the IFCT, which is the SIFO's main rival, always objects to the reform of the SIFO. The second, and more important, reason is a lack of political power on the part of the small firms.

Financial markets should also be liberalized, by allowing new entrants into the industry and by lifting the government controls on deposit and lending interest rates. If these two measures are carried out, more institutional credit will be available to informal enterprises.

Since the deregulation of 1982, it takes less time and fewer steps to obtain a commercial registration permit or factory permit. However, there is still room for improvement. First, the process of issuing commercial registration permits could be shortened if a computer system were established and if there were additional changes in the procedures for establishing corporations. Second, since the main reason for delay in obtaining factory permits is difficulty meeting pollution standards, Factory Department officials should be allowed to provide technical pollution-reduction advice to applicants for factory permits for a fee. This would speed issuance of factory permits, as well as provide officials with supplemental income and incentive to work harder. Moreover, favoritism and bribery would be minimized, because every applicant could legitimately hire officials as consultants.

It is also important for the government to reform policies that currently discriminate against small-scale firms and the informal sector. The need for such reform is underscored because the government has few other industrial and business policies with which to promote small firms or informal enterprises. Drawing from studies of Japanese promotion of small- and medium-scale enterprises, the World Bank has concluded that

> Support to some industries alone may not be effective and may not occur at all, if there is no political and social demand for them. In

this regard, it is encouraging that "the politics of small firms" is beginning to play an important role in Thailand, much as the politics of export promotion has done since the late 1970s. The government as well as political and business leaders are advocating support for small firms (and small entrepreneurs). Therefore, the political climate seems right for a strategy that encourages the removal of biases against these firms. However, reaching the smaller firms in particular poses a special challenge to the government (World Bank 1989:92).

Most Thai technical experts believe that the small firms' major problem is a lack of technical know-how (in both production and management) in responding to government assistance. What perhaps is more imperative, however, is the lack of an organization representing small firms' interests. The most useful way to aid small entrepreneurs may be to encourage and assist them in forming local trade or industry associations. These can then be used as means of determining needs and channeling technical assistance to small firms and informal enterprises.

Finally, there must be legal reform. Good laws must have the following properties: transperancy, certainty, flexibility, legality, and simplicity. More popular participation in the process of legislation is also required.

Conclusions

The informals are not only uneducated rural migrants. Some are highly educated; others acquire their skills from work experience. Their common characteristic is that they are hard-working persons who seek to improve their economic status. Extensive experience, patience, and diligence are the keys to their success.

The informal sector's share of total employment is now less than 50 percent and has shown a declining trend because of rapid economic transformation. The size of the informal credit market has also declined, largely because of government policy. However, the number of informal actors in some occupations, especially vending and transport, has increased, because of rapid urbanization and failure of government policy.

There are many reasons for informality. The number of vendors has increased rapidly because entry is easy, required investment is small, and the rate of return is attractive. But the law banning vending on public streets and sidewalks is the most important reason that small traders do business illegally. Although government officials have agreed that motorcycle transport is not illegal, there is not yet any legal status for motorcycle operators. Informal moneylenders exist because by avoiding government regulations, they are able to provide convenient credit service without complicated loan procedures.

Other causes of informality include import duties, labor protection laws, and costs of registration. But these reasons, especially the last, have become less important in recent years.

Informal entrepreneurs not only have to pay bribes to government officials, but are also subject to policy discrimination. Because of various policy biases, informal and small-scale enterprises incur higher costs of capital. Their capital cost is 80–100 percent higher than that paid by large-scale enterprises.

Popular participation, elected representatives, and increasing accountability of bureaucrats are factors that would contribute positively toward the well-being of informal actors. However, informal enterprises still face some problems and policy biases that can be solved only when they can organize themselves and press for changes in laws that limit or affect their activities. Finally, the informals could organize themselves more easily if the law were to recognize their associations just as it allows the formation of trade associations.

"Informality" in Development: The Poor as Entrepreneurs in Bangladesh

Bangladesh is one of the poorest countries in the world, with an annual per capita income of about US$165. Its population is about 110 million, of which about 85 percent live in rural areas. More than 50 percent of the population live below the poverty line. Ten million of the country's 18.5 million families are landless and without assets. The able-bodied labor force represented by these families is largely unemployed, underemployed, or without stable or regular sources of income. The women are mostly without paid employment, and the men are employed primarily as casual agricultural or nonagricultural laborers. They are usually illiterate and have no prospects of employment in the organized, or "formal," sector of Bangladesh's economy.

The efforts to overcome Bangladesh's poverty have focused on industrial development and, in recent years, have emphasized export-oriented growth and the development of the private sector (primarily medium and large-scale urban enterprises). Agriculture, from which the majority of the population draws its subsistence, and all types of micro and small-scale industry have been neglected. However, these

The views expressed in this chapter are those of the authors and do not necessarily reflect the views of Grameen Bank, where they both work.

sectors, and the 90 percent of people dependent on them, have survived, even if only marginally, thereby demonstrating remarkable resilence and powers of creativity and survival that have been overlooked by development specialists, planners, and administrators.

The donor-initiated and donor-driven development policies that were welcomed by the national elite (as in many parts of the third world) have brought about only marginal rates of economic growth. Both absolute and relative poverty have continued to increase, although there has been a slight improvement in real wages recently. It remains to be seen, however, whether this increase is sustainable.

Although increasing lip service is paid to poverty alleviation, as it is to environmental concerns and women in development issues, the poor are left out of development planning. There is, therefore, an urgent need to draw attention to the existence of poverty and the necessity of eliminating what is an insult to human dignity and a violation of basic human rights.

There is no one easy remedy for poverty. The answers, or at least some of them, can be found by examining how the poor have been surviving or coping by themselves. For them the search for an end to poverty is not a mere intellectual exercise, but a question of where their next meal will come from. It has more urgency for them than for those who hold seminars on development issues or write policy papers on poverty alleviation. It is an immediate problem necessitating an immediate answer.

Observers have finally started to look at what the poor do by and for themselves, and one of their "discoveries" has been the "informal sector." This is not to say that informality did not exist or function before being discovered and labeled by economists or social scientists. It is one of the socioeconomic phenomena that have existed from time immemorial: people undertaking various activities to survive and earn a living, without coming under the purview of any regulation or restriction imposed by the state (which does not mean that there are not various social and cultural norms regulating such activities and behavior). What has made this sector "informal" is the gradual buildup of regulations and formalization of various other sectors of the economy—for example, large-scale industry and foreign private investment.

While some regard the informal sector as an anomaly or an anachronism, something that should disappear with modernization, or as a problem (involving tax evasion, the unauthorized use of electricity, water, and gas, and other defiance of regulations), others have recognized the positive contribution it makes, not only in keeping people alive, but also to the national economy and to overall development. Furthermore, the informal sector has the potential for contributing even more if some of the constraints facing it can be removed.

This is the perspective from which Grameen Bank in Bangladesh operates. Much of its justification and success comes from its recognition of the needs and potentials of the poor in the informal sector. Many of Hernando de Soto's concepts regarding informality, developed in Peru, apply equally well to Bangladesh. There are, however, important differences, due to historical differences between the two countries. First, Peru is a highly urbanized country, while Bangladesh is a predominantly agricultural one. Poverty and industrialization in the two countries are at different levels. Second, Bangladesh is, on the whole, not as highly regulated a society and economy as Peru. Bangladesh does not have a mercantilist economy as does Peru, mercantilism being defined as "the belief that the economic welfare of the State can only be secured by government regulation of a nationalist character" (de Soto 1989:201). While Bangladesh is not fully a market economy, in which anyone is able to enter the market, produce, distribute, or obtain government authorization without the intervention of third parties, most regulation there is restricted to large industries. Small and micro-entrepreneurs do face a certain amount of harassment from government authorities in their attempts to obtain permits and basic facilities, such as electricity, gas, water, and telephones. Such entrepreneurs often ingeniously find ways around the problems. However, informal activities are more seriously constrained by other obstacles and conditions, such as difficulty of access to institutional credit and government policies that cater to the trade lobby and favor export-oriented growth, thus unfavorably affecting the poorest segments of the population.

Both de Soto's analysis and Grameen Bank's experience have shown that the poor should not be viewed as passive victims, but as fighters with basic survival skills and vast potential. De Soto documented the amazing creativity and tenacity of the urban poor in Peru under adverse conditions; Grameen Bank has demonstrated that the poor can improve their own lives and situations, especially if given access to certain resources, in particular financial means, on fair terms and conditions. This chapter will present Grameen Bank's experience working with the rural poor and the lessons that can be derived from this experience. This will be preceded by a brief discussion of key concepts and a description of urban and rural employment, including the informal sector. Finally, we will conclude with a discussion of the constraints faced by the informal sector and of government policies for this sector and the poor.

Some definitions. The informal sector and microenterprises have become much debated themes and are widely promoted as means of reaching the poor. The 1988 World Conference on Microenterprises referred to the informal sector as "the major development agent for employment creation, income generation and social stabilization in the next decade." The informal sector is composed of microenterprises of the urban or rural poor that do not fall under government rules and regulations. Social scientists and economists seem to have discovered the informal sector belatedly, and then only from the perspective of a formal economic theory that gives precedence to the "mainstream economy," that is, sectors that have formal requirements, are legally recognized by the government, are capital-intensive and often dependent on imported technology, require formally acquired skills, and comprise individual units with sufficient "stature" and "status" to have access to government bodies and resources. The informal economy has often been defined in opposition to all this, in negative terms: by illegality, lack of access to resources, lack of skills, marginality, and so on.

However, if one analyzes the economy within a larger time frame and does not restrict oneself to industrialized countries, the weight and status of normality given to the "formal" sector does not seem justified. Formalization was a historical process by which various rules and regulations were gradually imposed, first for fiscal purposes and gradually for other reasons. In Bangladesh, in recent years, urban large-scale industry has received the most attention and benefited from various incentives and government measures. However, large-scale industry accounts for only 5 percent of Bangladesh's GDP.

Broadly defined, the informal sector is the portion of economy characterized by family ownership (the family as a unit of production as well as of consumption), small scale of operation, labor intensity, use of adapted or indigenous technology, skills acquired outside the formal schooling system, ease of entry, and an unregulated and competitive market. This definition would seem to cover the largest part of the economy in its unrestricted, unformalized (or natural) state. A more neutral term for the informal sector might be the microenterprise sector, with microenterprise defined as any undertaking or activity by a poor person to generate an income to improve his or her social or economic condition. Such undertakings might include manufacturing, trading, processing, service delivery, or other activities.

This sector is not illegal but is, for the most part, outside of or untouched by the administrative framework that has formalized a (minor) part of the economy. The government knows that the microenterprises exist but usually lets them conduct their business without interruption. There may be a few rules, regulations, and measures that are supposed to concern such enterprises, but they are often totally ignored, partially acknowledged, followed intermittently, or even followed by default. The same enterprise may, at different times, shift among these different positions. What, for analytical purposes, is conceptualized as a dichotomy between informal and formal is, in reality, a continuity, not only in static but also in dynamic terms.

What must be stressed is the natural durability, pervasiveness, and flexibility of the informal sector and the resourcefulness of the people who survive in it. The dynamism of the sector is remarkable, in view of the lack of support it receives from government and the frequent implementation of policies that often go against its interests. The micro-enterprise sector is valid as an organizational form, in its own right.

Another definition that must be clarified at the outset is that of development. For the purposes of this chapter the perspective adopted will be as follows: poverty is a basic violation of fundamental human rights, and the central objective of development should be the elimination of poverty in all its dimensions. Development should mean positive change in the social and economic status of the bottom 50 percent of the population in any given society. Any measure or program for this section of the population should address it exclusively.

The right to work and earn an income is an important human right. Those who lack gainful employment use their time to whatever benefit possible—doing housework, scavenging in garbage dumps, or endlessy searching for work. As the World Commmission on Environment and Development wrote, "Most of the so-called unemployed are in fact working 10–15 hours a day, six to seven days a week. Their problem is not so much unemployment as underpayment." The poor in the low-income countries comprise self-employed subsistence farmers, landless laborers, sharecroppers, artisans, and traders. Young people and women are disproportionately represented. The root problem is poverty or low-productivity employment, not unemployment. Some people without jobs have an income from other sources and do not rank among the poorest. Many very poor people work long and hard in unremunerative activities throughout their lives (Streeten 1989:9).

"Employment per se does not remove poverty," Muhammad Yunus has argued. "Unless designed appropriately, employment can turn into a mechanism that perpetuates poverty" (Yunus 1987a:144). One of the basic reasons why people become poor, remain poor, and continue to get poorer is that they have very little economic maneuverability. Their economic base consists only of physical labor. Part of the process of impoverishment is the transformation from self-employment to wage employment. For example, a skilled, self-employed weaver who cannot keep himself afloat as an independent under adverse financial circumstances sooner or later turns into a wage laborer for a moneyed man who owns a dozen or so looms. As a wage laborer he earns a daily wage of between 20 and 30 takas, whereas if he had done the work for himself with his own inputs he would have earned a wage of between 60 and 90 takas (US$1 = 36 takas in December 1990). Futhermore, his family income would have been higher because his wife and children could have added to family income by participating in the production process. A great transformation could take place in poor people's lives if they could add financial resources to support their physical resources. "The removal or reduction of poverty must be a continuous process of creation of assets. Self-employment, supported by credit, has more potential for improving the asset base than wage employment has" (Yunus 1987a). Any program that can provide adequate support to microenterprises can help create or strengthen self-employment, increase assets, and increase incomes, thereby empowering the poor.

To recapitulate, there are three main reasons for paying attention to the informal sector: first, the majority of the population are poor and most of them are in this sector; second, the formal sector is structurally incapable of absorbing the existing large number of unemployed and underemployed, not to speak of the increase in the labor force projected for the next twenty years; and third, the informal sector is a reserve of productivity, creativity, initiative, and earning power, and it provides opportunities for self-employment, and thereby empowerment, for the poor. The sector's potential is still far from being fully exploited.

Poverty and unemployment. Bangladesh faces problems of widespread poverty, unemployment, underemployment, and landlessness. Rapid growth in population has led to a deteriorating amount of land per person. The ability of the landless poor to improve their standard of living is limited by inadequate resources, especially financial; the bias of various institutions against them; exploitation by existing social and economic structures; poor infrastructure and inappropriate technology; inadequate nutrition and health care; and the inadequacies of the projects, programs, and institutions that are supposed to assist them. Various government policies working at cross purposes may also adversely affect the poor and landless.

According to Bangladesh's Household Expenditure Survey for 1985–1986, 44.2 million rural and 7 million urban people, representing 51 percent and 56 percent of the rural and urban populations, respectively, live below the poverty line, as measured in terms of the internationally accepted minimum calorie intake. The disastrous floods of 1987 and 1988 caused a slowing down of agricultural production and investment, resulting in a further decline in real wages and an increase in unemployment.

The country's potential labor force is 50.85 million (the portion of population between fifteen and sixty-four years of age), which is 50 percent of the population as estimated in 1986. However, the official

Labour Force Survey of 1985–1986 (LFS 1985–1986) estimates a total civilian labor force of 30.9 million (of which 27.7 million are men and 3.2 million are women). Out of the 30.9 million, 30.5 million are considered active, of which 0.4 million are unemployed. Labor force participation rates are therefore low: 45.6 percent of the total population (81.4 percent for men and 9.9 percent for women), which implies a high degree of economic depencency of the nonworking on the working population. However, the official statistics are biased against women's economic participation and grossly underestimate their contribution, a common fault of statistics around the world. The statistics we will use to discuss occupations and economic sectors must therefore be regarded with caution.

Some 57.2 percent of Bangladesh's working population is employed in agriculture, and 42.8 percent works in the nonagricultural sector (LFS 1985–86). The share of agriculture in the 1987–1988 GDP was 38.7 percent, and of manufacturing 8.5 percent (which was divided into 4.8 percent of GDP contributed by large-scale industry and 3.7 percent contributed by small-scale industry). Trade, professions, and miscellaneous services together account for 18.9 percent of GDP. Table 6.1 shows the percentages of employed persons aged ten years and over arranged by employment status in 1984–1985.

It is not possible to identify the poor by occupation groups, as information on cross-classification of income and occupation categories is not available. Furthermore, the poor are most often compelled to pursue more than one occupation at the same time, for basic survival.

Urban Bangladesh

Urban employment. During the past decade the growth of employment in modern industry in Bangladesh has been limited. The modern industrial sector currently employs only about 500,000 persons, which

---

TABLE 6.1   Employment Status of Employed Persons 10 Years and Over, 1984–1985 (percentage)

Employment status	Bangladesh	Urban	Rural
Self-employed	38.8	33.3	39.7
Employee	11.6	28.6	8.9
Day laborer	28.4	23.6	29.2
Unpaid family helper	17.9	8.6	19.4
Not reported	3.2	5.9	2.8

SOURCE: Bangladesh, Bureau of Statistics, *Labour Force Survey, 1984–85.*

is less than 2 percent of the officially recognized labor force. Huge investments would need to be made in order to absorb a significant proportion of entrants into the labor force into the sector. Since 50 percent of the total population of the country is under age fifteen, new entrants pose a significant problem. As pointed out by Paul Streeten:

> In an economy in which 80 percent of the labour force is in agriculture and services and 20 percent in urban industry, and in which population and labour force grow by 3 percent per year, urban industrial employment would have to grow by 15 percent per year in order to absorb only the new entrants into the labour force, leaving the pool of unemployed untouched. In no country has industrial employment grown by anything like this rate (1989:64).

Increasing landlessness is leading to a migration of the rural population to urban centers at an approximate average annual rate of 2.2 percent. The urban population rose at an annual rate of 10.6 percent between 1974 and 1981, compared with 2.3 percent for the nation as a whole.

The Labour Force Survey of 1985–1986, which classifies employed persons (aged ten and over) by broad occupation categories, shows that in urban areas 22.7 percent of the population is employed in sales, 13.2 percent in services, 10.8 percent in production and transport, 10.5 percent in clerical occupations, and that as much as 24.2 percent could not be classified. Classification by industry showed that 24.5 percent were employed in trade, hotels, and restaurants, 21.6 percent in community and personal service, and 17.4 percent in manufacturing. As can be seen from these various statistics, a significant percentage of the urban population cannot find wage employment or even self-employment in the formal sector. A large number of people in the urban areas have to earn their livelihood wherever they can, from a wide variety of trades and services. As stated by the government in its *Memorandum for the Bangladesh Aid Group* (1989–1990):

> Regardless of policies followed, micro-industries continue to multiply. In 1985 there were about 28,000 small-scale enterprises, employing about 380,000 persons, and about 370,000 cottage industries, employing about one million. In addition there were 320,000 hand-looms, producing nearly 60 percent of the cloth requirements of the country and giving direct employment to over 1.2 million people. Nearly one-half of the total industrial production comes from these units and they account for two-thirds of the total urban employment (p. 106).

The urban informal sector. Of the two-thirds of total employment in Dhaka city in 1980 estimated to be in the informal sector, some

70 percent was estimated to be in manufacturing, trade, and nongovernment services. While it was found that the structure of employment in the urban informal sector was similar to that in rural areas, a major difference was that more than 16 percent of urban informal employment is in transport, mainly operating rickshaws (International Labor Organization 1988:36). The average income of self-employed persons in the informal sector in Dhaka in 1979 was estimated at 960 takas per month, which was considerably higher than the income of an agricultural laborer.

According to a 1979 sample survey of informal sector units (defined as units with fewer than ten workers, either not registered, or in unauthorized locations, temporary structures, or the owner's home) in Dhaka, one-fifth of all workers in such units were family members of the owner and 55 percent were owners (or proprietors). Only a quarter of the informal workforce was hired labor. Nearly one-third of the workforce in the informal sector had never been to school and half had had only primary education. Two percent had acquired their skills through technical schools and 7 percent through apprenticeship in large enterprises. Most of the workers had acquired their skills through apprenticeship within the informal sector or through the help of friends. Over three-fourths of the workers were born outside Dhaka city, suggesting that a majority came from rural areas, particularly in the past fifteen years. More than half the migrants did not possess any land at all, and 22 percent owned less than one acre prior to migration (Amin 1987).

The average income in the urban informal sector of 960 takas per month in 1979 was, as we have mentioned, much higher than the average agricultural wage of 585 takas per month in the same year. It also exceeded the average income of factory workers in urban areas, which was 590 takas per month. However, there were, and there remain, variations in incomes in the informal sector: the self-employed (or owner) earned a monthly net income of 1,083 takas per household, while hired labor earned 498 takas. More wage laborers than owners in Dhaka's informal sector were recent migrants (64 percent of workers had been in the city for less than five years, while only 31 percent of owners had been there for so short a time). Furthermore, a larger majority of recent migrants belonged to the unskilled category, as compared to those who had been longer in Dhaka. Seventy percent of the self-employed studied had previously been employees. This seems to indicate that the informal sector served as a training ground and people were able to progress from being employees to owners.

Significant variations in income between informal subsectors were also found: an owner's net monthly income in manufacturing was 1,038 takas, compared with 767 takas in trade or 796 takas in transport.

While manufacturing seems more profitable, entry is more difficult, as the capital requirements are higher and access to credit more problematic.

In spite of the various constraints, informal manufacturing units in Dhaka were found to be more efficient generators of income and employment than those in the formal sector. For a given investment of 1 million takas, the informal sector is estimated to generate 418 jobs and 5.26 million takas in value added, compared with 55 jobs and 741 thousand takas in value added in the formal sector (International Labor Organization 1988:38).

The informal transport sector is also important and is comprised essentially of cycle rickshaws. A study undertaken in 1981 showed that the number of registered transport vehicles in 1981 in Dhaka was only 26,925, but the actual number was estimated to be three times higher, or about 80,000. Informal transport was estimated to carry between 2.6 million and 3.5 million passengers every day, compared with 150,000 by government-owned public buses (Kalambu 1987). With 2.5 pullers per rickshaw (working on a shift basis), the activity accounts for 220,000 jobs in the city, which also includes 20,000 engaged in support services (such as license brokers, rickshaw builders, and mechanics). By 1988 it was estimated that there were 100,000 rickshaws providing employment to 250,000 people, and that as many as one million people were involved in one way or another with the activity (Centre for Urban Studies 1989).

In spite of the size and importance of the informal transport sector, public policy has not been supportive. On the contrary, there have been attempts to ban cycle rickshaws, certain important roads have been closed to rickshaw traffic, and the pullers are subject to continuous harassment by the police. Although Dhaka's municipal license fee is only 9 takas per puller, the license could be obtained only through a broker who charged (in 1981) 40 takas to obtain a new license and 30 takas for renewal— amounts that covered the broker's fee and payments to others involved in the process. Besides licenses for pullers there is also a registration fee ranging between 25 and 30 takas per vehicle.

Rural Bangladesh

Rural employment. In spite of the adverse ratio of land per person, the majority of Bangladesh's population is engaged in agriculture. Classification by broad occupational category shows that 65.9 percent of rural workers are engaged in agriculture, forestry, and fishery, 9.6 percent in sales, 6.5 percent in production and transport, and 5.3 percent in services. Eight percent could not be defined. Classification by industrial sector confirms the dominance of agriculture, forestry, and fishery, with trade, hotels and restaurants (10.4 percent), and manufacturing (8.5 percent) being the only other sizable sectors.

The Labour Force Survey statistics, however, categorize people by their primary occupation. Persons who are principally agricultural labors are not likely to be fully employed as such throughout the year. On an average they are generally employed 185 days per year, including 115 days in crop production and 70 days in other allied activities, which leaves 180 days free. The laborers therefore require either high wages for agricultural work to carry them through the lean period, or additional nonfarm jobs.

In addition, it is estimated that 85 percent of farm workers belonging to farms operating on less than 2.5 acres are surplus in the sense that they have to depend on other farms or other activities for their livelihood. Even on farms operating on 2.5 to 5.0 acres and 5.0 to 7.5 acres, 12.11 percent and 2.35 percent of farm workers, respectively, are surplus (Masum 1989:22).

While the landless and nearly landless poor supply over 80 percent of the required labor in the agricultural sector, they probably use barely one-fifth of their labor in agricultural activities. If we refer to the landless and nearly landless as farmers, we commit the mistake of categorizing them by a single and often minor characteristic. Also, categorizing the landless and functionally landless as farmers steers the discussion into male issues, since the universally accepted image of the farmer is male. Therefore half of the population—the female half—which is disproportionately affected by poverty, is ignored. Women of poor families in Bangladesh are far more economically active than the women from higher income families. There are proportionately more female heads of household among the poor women than among the nonpoor. It is estimated that about 40 percent of destitute women are heads of households.

The Bangladesh Census of Agriculture and Livestock (1983–84) showed that 39.8 percent of total rural households are involved in agricultural labor and only 6.7 percent are households with cottage industry. The same census showed that 28.3 percent of the national population had no land or only homestead land, and that an additional 28.2 percent could be considered functionally landless, having less than 0.5 acres of cultivable land.

If we restrict ourselves to the rural poor, to the bottom 50 percent of the rural population, we find that a majority of them are landless or marginal farmers and are self-employed. Most rural poor are not farmers. They may be employed only for part of the year as agricultural labor or subsist by carrying out agriculture-related activities. Therefore, the predominance of agriculture in rural Bangladesh, as shown in the national statistics, needs to be kept in perspective.

The rural nonfarm sector. Comprehensive information on rural small enterprises was collected in 1978–80 through the Rural Industries Study Project (RISP). It was found that a large proportion of workers in such enterprises, 44 percent, were "unpaid family" laborers, of which two-thirds were women. Over 80 percent of the rural small industrial units had fewer than five workers, with an average of 3.8 workers per unit. Of the thirty-odd percent of workers who are hired, the majority are on a casual or piecework basis. The average wage of workers in rural enterprises would seem to be 20 percent lower than in urban areas, with salaries for women being substantially less than those for men. However, rural prices also seem to be 20 percent lower than in urban areas.

It is generally believed that most of the cottage and small industrial units in rural Bangladesh are established by their owners as a matter of family tradition. However, the RISP study found that only 45 percent of those interviewed stated that they were pursuing the family tradition. Fifty-five percent of the owners had parents who were engaged in agriculture or trade.

Handlooms are a major component of rural small industry. According to RISP data, half the value added in rural small industry can be attributed to handloom products. Other dominant sectors are food, wood, and cane and bamboo.

Available macroeconomic data suggest that service is among the three most important nonfarm activities in terms of employment. However, there are no studies that provide information on the structure and composition, earning levels and returns, linkages, constraints, and growth potentials of the subsector.

A valuable insight into the enterprises in which the rural poor are engaged can be gained by analyzing the data of Grameen Bank on activities for which loans are taken out by its members, who are among the poorest of the rural poor. The choice of the activity is left up to the borrower and his or her group. The activity is generally one the borrower is familiar with. The only restriction imposed by the Bank is that the loan must be used for income-generating activities, that is, not for consumption.

As of December 1990, members had taken out 3,631,388 loans totaling 7,590.66 million takas (US$210.85 million) for 442 different activities, of which 149 were classified as processing and manufacturing; 40 as agriculture and forestry; 16 as livestock and fishery; 39 as services; 156 as trading; 23 as peddling; and 19 as shopkeeping. Table 6.2 shows the disbursement of loans since inception through December 1990 by broad categories. One observes different patterns for men and women, and we will analyze them separately.

From Grameen Bank's inception through 1990 the largest number of loans and a major portion of the credit disbursed have been taken

TABLE 6.2 Disbursement of Grameen Bank Loans, 1976–1990

	Male borrowers		Female borrowers		Total	
Purpose of loan	Number of loans	Amount (in takas)	Number of loans	Amount (in takas)	Number of loans	Amount (in takas)
Processing and manufacturing	83,871	221,039,080	1,066,613	1,862,189,610	1,150,484	2,083,228,690
Agriculture and forestry	28,544	53,234,150	96,140	234,937,763	124,684	288,171,913
Livestock and fisheries	90,828	248,109,796	1,369,082	2,964,075,657	1,459,910	3,212,185,453
Services	30,905	102,804,300	23,002	65,064,681	53,907	167,868,981
Trading	185,123	573,251,384	350,689	739,204,911	535,812	1,312,456,295
Peddling	8,502	24,919,703	25,918	52,502,915	34,420	77,422,618
Shopkeeping	30,001	101,794,587	96,855	227,394,663	126,856	329,189,250
Collective enterprises	51,900	49,595,000	93,415	70,545,000	145,315	120,140,000
Total	509,674	1,374,748,000	3,121,714	6,215,915,200	3,631,388	7,590,663,200

SOURCE: Grameen Bank, Annual Report, 1990.

TABLE 6.3   Sectoral Distribution of Grameen Bank Loans to Women, 1976–1990
(percentage of total loans)

Sector	1976–1981	1982	1983	1984	1985	1986	1987	1988	1989	1990
Processing and manufacturing	49.0	48.3	38.8	36.4	37.2	37.4	35.1	34.0	33.7	32.6
Agriculture and forestry	0.4	0.8	0.9	1.2	1.4	1.3	2.4	4.5	3.5	3.2
Livestock and fisheries	39.5	37.4	43.4	37.1	38.8	46.9	45.6	43.5	43.3	45.0
Services	0.0	0.5	0.1	0.3	0.5	0.5	0.7	0.6	0.8	0.9
Trading	5.7	6.9	10.9	9.7	8.8	7.3	8.8	10.8	13.2	12.7
Peddling	2.6	1.2	0.5	1.0	1.1	0.8	0.8	1.0	0.8	0.7
Shopkeeping	2.8	4.1	4.5	3.1	2.8	2.6	2.7	3.0	3.4	3.3
Collective enterprises	—	0.8	0.9	11.2	9.4	3.2	3.9	2.6	1.3	1.6

— = not applicable.
SOURCE: Grameen Bank, *Annual Report*, 1990.

out by women for investment in livestock and fisheries, followed by investment in processing and manufacturing (see Table 6.3). These two sectors account for 72 percent of all loans (77 percent of loan disbursements), with another 11 percent of loans (12 percent of disbursements) taken out for trading. Comparing data from the period preceding 1981 with data from 1990, the percentage of loans taken out for processing and manufacturing has declined, whereas the livestock and fisheries sector has increased. Trading rose, and agriculture and forestry increased until 1988 but fell in 1989 and 1990. Services have remained relatively unimportant over the years, as has peddling.

In spite of the multiplicity of activities for which loans are taken out, there is a concentration on a limited number of activities. Table 6.4 shows the twenty-five most common activities for which women took out loans in 1990. These accounted for 84 percent of total disbursements to women during the year. Such a concentration has been observed since the bank's inception, when the percentage share of twenty-five activities was 94 percent of loan amount disbursed. The activities in the "top twenty-five" list have changed only slightly, with raising milk cows, husking paddy, and fattening cows remaining favorites. These three items accounted for 70.1 percent of disbursements in 1981, but their share was reduced to 51.4 percent in 1990. Other livestock activities such as goat, bullock, and poultry rearing have increased slightly in importance, as have some trading activities, such as rice and flour trading and grocery and stationery shops. Bamboo work is also slightly more important than before.

From inception to 1990, 44 percent of the loans disbursed to men were for trading, peddling, and shopkeeping, and accounted for 51 percent of the amount disbursed (see Table 6.5). Livestock and fisheries accounted for 18 percent and processing and manufacturing for 16 percent of the total disbursement from inception. The percentage of loan disbursements for services, although relatively small (8 percent), is higher than for women (1 percent).

Between 1981 and 1991, the percentage share of the number of loans disbursed for trading has decreased. The share of processing and manufacturing fell until 1984, but was back at its 1981 level of 22 percent in 1990. Agriculture and forestry increased in importance, as did livestock and fisheries. The share of services was reduced slightly.

The activities pursued by male borrowers are more diverse than those pursued by female borrowers. Table 6.6 shows the twenty-five most common activities for which men took out loans in 1990, which accounted for 69 percent of total disbursement to men during the year. This concentration has been variable and fell to 64 percent in 1983. The male "top twenty-five" list contains a number of activities that are also

TABLE 6.4   Leading Activities for Which Women Borrowed from the
              Grameen Bank, 1990

Rank	Activity	Number of loans	Amount (in takas)
1	Milk cow raising	124,539	437,975,253
2	Paddy husking	179,920	347,114,138
3	Cow fattening	127,672	270,831,300
4	Rice/paddy trading	42,817	99,757,245
5	Bamboo works	29,814	74,371,285
6	Goat raising	64,663	62,410,673
7	Poultry raising	59,741	59,822,565
8	Bullock raising	19,352	51,066,270
9	Grocery shop	16,777	37,284,728
10	Stationery shop	11,082	28,369,830
11	Mat (*pati*) making	10,423	24,263,900
12	Land cultivation	6,887	23,997,400
13	Land lease	5,859	22,831,300
14	Cane works	11,467	19,978,650
15	Wheat powder (*ata*) trading	10,729	18,866,990
16	Sewing machine purchase	5,014	17,947,310
17	Sheep raising	5,425	16,897,250
18	Pisciculture	4,070	15,857,600
19	Betel leaf cultivation	4,787	15,693,400
20	Fishing net making	8,264	14,896,563
21	Vegetable trading	7,266	14,768,481
22	Puffed rice making	7,942	13,470,885
23	Cloth trading	4,560	13,220,139
24	Trading of seasonal agricultural products	4,169	9,925,040
25	Garment making	2,970	9,219,800
	Total	776,209	1,720,867,995

SOURCE: Grameen Bank, *Annual Report*, 1990.

on the female list: rice and paddy trading, milk cow raising, and paddy husking. Other male borrowing is characterized by the preponderance of trading activities (of cloth, cattle, vegetables, fish, timber, tobacco, wheat, firewood, betelnuts, mustard, flour, sarees, garments, and jute) and the purchase of rickshaws and bullocks.

In 1982 Grameen Bank started providing loans to collective enterprises. Such loans quickly became popular but for several reasons their relative importance decreased after 1985. In 1984, 32 percent of Grameen Bank members participated in collective enterprises, but

TABLE 6.5   Sectoral Distribution of Grameen Bank Loans to Men, 1976–1990
(percentage of total loans)

Sector	1976–1981	1982	1983	1984	1985	1986	1987	1988	1989	1990
Processing and manufacturing	22.4	20.8	18.2	12.1	13.3	14.8	15.9	16.2	18.2	22.0
Agriculture and forestry	5.2	3.6	1.6	2.3	2.9	3.6	5.8	10.1	8.1	8.0
Livestock and fisheries	15.0	14.5	14.7	15.0	18.9	22.4	19.4	19.0	18.0	16.5
Services	8.4	5.3	8.4	5.9	5.6	6.3	6.4	5.7	5.8	5.5
Trading	41.3	41.1	38.5	33.8	35.6	38.0	36.1	34.7	38.2	35.4
Peddling	12.4	2.0	2.2	1.3	1.5	1.8	1.7	1.7	1.4	1.9
Shopkeeping	5.3	5.4	5.8	4.3	4.9	6.2	6.3	6.4	6.5	7.4
Collective enterprises	0.0	7.3	10.6	25.3	17.3	6.9	8.4	5.2	3.8	3.5

SOURCE: Grameen Bank, *Annual Report*, 1990.

TABLE 6.6   Leading Activities for Which Men Borrowed from
             the Grameen Bank, 1990

Rank	Activity	Number of loans	Amount (in takas)
1	Paddy husking	6,739	19,265,900
2	Rice/paddy trading	5,168	18,619,008
3	Milk cow raising	3,852	14,211,392
4	Trading of seasonal agricultural products	2,332	8,908,800
5	Rickshaw purchase	2,176	8,734,000
6	Cow fattening	2,669	7,658,710
7	Stationery shop	1,860	7,648,735
8	Bamboo works	1,882	6,731,200
9	Grocery shop	1,713	6,608,100
10	Bullock purchase	1,908	6,329,000
11	Cloth trading	945	4,300,500
12	Vegetable trading	1,187	3,892,300
13	Fish trading	897	3,455,900
14	Saree weaving	587	3,157,658
15	Timber trading	737	3,137,700
16	Wheat powder (ata) trading	881	2,814,500
17	Fertilizer (for cultivation)	2,255	2,707,650
18	Cattle	512	2,488,500
19	Land cultivation	855	2,458,500
20	Betel leaf cultivation	646	2,157,300
21	Tobacco trading	761	2,094,800
22	Molasses (gur) trading	374	1,551,000
23	Stationery goods	427	1,501,740
24	Van purchase	408	1,464,500
25	Firewood trading	315	1,446,200
	Total	42,086	143,343,593

SOURCE: Grameen Bank, Annual Report, 1990.

by 1985 this group declined to 17 percent. The share of collective enterprises in total loans jumped from 1.9 percent in 1983 to 8.2 percent
in 1984, but fell to 5.1 percent in 1985 and further to 1.4 percent in
1986. Between 1982 and 1984, nearly one-half of the total loan amount
was taken for joint crop cultivation or pisciculture. In 1985 crop
cultivation accounted for about three-fourths of the loans disbursed
for collective enterprises. In 1990, 1.6 percent of all loans disbursed
were for collective enterprises; the percentage was higher for men than
for women.

The literature on rural nonfarm activities in Bangladesh has put emphasis on "supply side determinants" of productivity and returns. Raw material supply, credit, and technology have been identified as the dominant constraints. Rural industries have been found to have strong backward and forward linkages with the local agricultural economy.

Constraints Faced by the Informal Sector

The vast multitude of poor people are endowed with useful skills which are considered to be of little use, because it is conventionally believed that people who are illiterate are devoid of skill. Illiterate they may be, but certainly not without useful skills. The very fact that they are still alive despite the severely adverse and outright hostile circumstances they face throughout their lives demonstrates beyond any doubt that they are endowed with a very useful skill—the skill of survival. This skill has passed the test of the centuries and can provide an excellent time-tested foundation for establishing a microenterprise development program.

To take this position as a starting point means that one should not impose unfamiliar ideas on poor people, but rather carefully observe

Anser Ali, a rickshaw puller, purchased his rickshaw with a loan from the Grameen Bank branch in Shekerchar Narsindi. Many of the bank's loans to men are used to buy rickshaws.

their circumstances, how they keep themselves afloat, and their upward mobility. A planner's job is to design a program that will make constraints give way, in order to assist the poor to use their full potential and to further develop their capabilities.

One of the most formidable constraints poor people face is the lack of financial resources. Under adverse and hostile socioeconomic circumstances, individuals have often been forced out of their traditional trades. It is inappropriate to argue that all able and willing people are prevented from pursuing their respective chosen pursuits only because they lack financial capital; there are indeed many other constraints. What we argue here is that the unavailability of financial resources at a reasonable cost (monetary, nonmonetary, expressed, and hidden) constitutes the single most overwhelming constraint preventing people from pursuing known and feasible activities. If financial resources can be made available to them under reasonable terms and conditions (that is, at the commercial rate), "these millions of poor people with their millions of small pursuits can collectively create the biggest development wonder" (Yunus 1982:6).

Various studies and practical experience (such as that of Grameen Bank) show that the informal sector is starved of credit and could easily absorb substantial amounts. "The marginal rate of return on investment is estimated at 67 percent as compared to 12 percent interest charged by commercial banks on loans" (International Labor Organization 1988:32). The RISP data showed that only 6 percent of informal units relied on institutional and noninstitutional sources for loans to finance *initial* investment. Over 70 percent of the requirements for additional investment (expansion) came from profits. The few enterprises that were successful in obtaining loans from institutions could do so only by offering collateral worth two to three times the loan amount. Others who depended on noninstitutional sources, such as moneylenders, wealthy individuals, and friends and relatives, paid between 48 percent and 100 percent interest, if one excludes rare interest-free loans. Besides interest, the poor also pay hidden charges, such as unofficial payments or bribes and the loss of up to twelve working days in getting a loan sanctioned. What is still worse is the long delay in obtaining loan amounts. This delay varies between different institutional sources: commercial banks, 72 days; cooperatives, 32 days; Bangladesh Small and Cottage Industries Corporation (BSCIC), 20 days; and other government agencies, 157 days. However, to the poor, timely receipt of the money is more important than the interest charged, as is evidenced by their willingness to avail themselves of loans from noninstitutional sources. Yet another disadvantage of credit from institutional sources is the range of stringent terms and conditions attached to loans, including the precondition of literacy. In a country with a national literacy rate of 28 percent, filling in countless forms is not possible for everyone.

Noninstitutional sources of credit meet about 80 percent of the need for credit in rural Bangladesh. This credit is supplied in both cash and in-kind debts, and is often carried over to succeeding generations. The most significant feature of the informal credit market is its close integration into the village power structure.

Another estimate says that the informal credit market (urban and rural) lends 37 percent as much capital as the institutional market does (Rahman 1989:4). According to a recent survey, 35 percent of households participated in the informal credit market, compared with 8.5 percent that borrowed from the formal credit market (Rahman 1989:5). (Formal-sector loans tend to be larger than informal sector ones.)

With appropriate credit and resource support, millions can create self-employment by working in their familiar processing and manufacturing trades; providing transport services; storing agricultural produce; marketing agricultural and nonagricultural inputs, outputs, and supplies; providing maintenance services; and so on. The availability of financial resources to the lower half of the population will solve one layer of economic problems, but it will bring into sharper focus a new generation of problems, such as poor input-delivery systems and inadequate linkages across the board. The precise nature of these problems will emerge as economic activities are undertaken by the self-employed poor. Some of these problems will be resolved by the people themselves through experience coupled with indigenous knowledge. Solving the remaining problems will require national policy support.

Government Policies, the Informal Sector, and the Poor

One of the major thrusts of the Third Five-Year Plan, covering the period from July 1985 to June 1990, was poverty alleviation. The strategy identified to achieve this objective was to provide "productive employment" to the population so that people could increase their income and their command over resources and so satisfy their basic needs. The plan aimed to develop rural industries, rather than large-scale firms or "technologically moribund" cottage industries, as the sector that would provide dynamism to the entire economy. Employment was to be generated by increased investment in agriculture and rural development, assistance to small-scale industries, and various social programs. However, the plan identified no detailed strategy to promote rural industry, and intersectoral and interindustry links received inadequate attention. Among the linkages neglected were those between large- and small-scale industries, between the formal and informal sectors, and between the informal sector and construction and industry. Public-sector resource allocations to rural industries were also minimal.

The New Industrial Policy, formulated in 1986, provided policy guidelines for the entire manufacturing sector, from large modern industry to small cottage units. It placed increased emphasis on private-sector participation; promoted small, cottage, and handloom industries and agro-based and agro-supportive industries; encouraged geographic dispersal of industries; and sought to create employment opportunities in rural areas. Its objectives also included promoting import substitution, supporting export-oriented and export linkage industries, and encouraging foreign investment.

A number of measures were formulated specifically for small and cottage industries. The BSCIC was to create infrastructural facilities, such as industrial estates, to provide developed industrial areas with power, water, sewerage, telephone service, and various other common facilities. BSCIC was to provide marketing information, and the government's purchase policy was to be formulated with a view to ensuring marketing of the products of small and cottage industries. Banks were instructed to open separate windows for financing small and cottage industries and were asked to set apart a definite percentage of their resources to provide such loans. An advantageous debt-equity ratio of 80:20 was declared. Small and cottage industries located in less-developed areas were declared entitled to income tax rebates scaled to production. Banks were also instructed to make funds available for ailing small industries and to finance subcontracting. "The policy of linkage between large/medium and small industrial units will be consciously pursued so that in course of time small units could act as 'sub-contractors' to the bigger ones," the 1986 policy document declared. "In giving sanctions to new units, particular care should be taken to see that entrepreneurs are encouraged to manufacture/fabricate only core items in their premises, leaving the peripheral items to be manufactured by other smaller units" (p. 20).

The main objectives of the Fourth Five-Year Plan, which extends through mid-1995, are poverty alleviation, increased self-reliance, and employment generation. Employment generation is considered both an objective in itself and a strategy for achieving the other two objectives. A sector-based approach is to be complemented with a group-based approach so that the poorest groups can be identified and concerted efforts can be made to improve their socioeconomic situation. Included in the ten groups identified for support are rural formal (the upper 40 percent of the rural nonfarming group); rural informal (the lower 60 percent of the rural nonfarming group); urban formal (the upper 40 percent of the urban employment group); and urban informal (the lower 60 percent of the urban employment group). The definitions of these groups seem somewhat inadequate, and the utility of these categories is therefore doubtful.

A growth rate of 3.5 percent per year is expected in agriculture. This growth will stimulate effective demand and push the industrial growth rate to an expected 10 percent. In order to develop agriculture and industry, the plan will stress infrastructure, both physical and social. The plan proposes special efforts to make more investment funds available to the poor and disadvantaged, drawing on the experience of programs such as Shawnirvar (an indigenous nongovernmental organization) and Grameen Bank.

Although the plan recognizes the importance of the informal sector and allocates some resources to it, the sector has not received adequate attention in the planning process. It has not been structurally integrated as a productive sector, along with other sectors. Policies that affect the structure and growth of other sectors, or that determine the composition and levels of imports and exports or fiscal policies, have not been influenced by consideration of their probable effect, positive or negative, on the growth of the informal sector. Policies currently in force are not always consistent with regard to employment and poverty alleviation. In fact, there has not been, until now, a national policy or program for the informal sector; it survives at the microeconomic level in virtual segregation.

Construction and housing, which have strong linkages with the informal sector, receive low priority in the development plan. Import

Weaving sarees is a common activity for both women and men in Bangladesh. Weaving microenterprises, however, face stiff competition from protected large-scale textile firms.

policies for industrial goods, yarn, and milk powder, to take a few striking examples, all adversely affect local industrial workshops, handloom enterprises, and dairy producers. Although manufacturers in general enjoy a high degree of protection in Bangladesh, rural industries are discriminated against in favor of large-scale manufacturing. For example, weavers in the handloom sector, the largest rural industry in Bangladesh, use yarn as their basic raw material. Yarn, being an intermediate product, is subject to a high tariff rate of 50 percent, and with a 20 percent sales tax on duty-paid value, a 6 percent development surcharge, and a 2.5 percent import permit fee, the effective tariff rate becomes as high as 88.5 percent. Cotton textile mills, however, have to pay only a 10 percent tariff on imported raw cotton, along with a 6 percent development surcharge and a 2.5 percent import permit fee. Locally produced yarn is insufficient in quantity and costlier than imported yarn. For production of fabric, textile mills have to pay an excise duty of 0.75 takas per yard and 3 takas per loom per month. The handloom sector is not subject to any excise duty, but the potentially favorable impact of the differential excise duty is nullified by contradictory trade policies. In other sectors as well, the potential use of fiscal policies to promote local, small-scale, or informal-sector production has not been exploited.

The government's credit policies have also been ineffective in meeting the needs of the microentrepreneurs. In rural areas, the "large farmer" bias of institutional credit is evident, as is the bias toward large-scale industrialists and entrepreneurs in urban areas. In addition, there is a bias against rural areas, with relatively more credit available to urban areas. Commercial banks and specialized farm-credit organizations possess limited information about rural customers. Their credit-allocation policies tend to be based on observable wealth or ability to provide collateral. They do not ration credit to large farm holders, but credit to medium-sized landholders is rationed and small farmers are screened out.

In order to promote small-scale and cottage industries, Bangladesh Bank (the central bank) instructed the commercial banks to advance at least 5 percent of their total loans to this sector at a subsidized rate of 10 percent. Because of the commercial banks' preference for lending only against collateral, they have not fully complied with the instruction. Also, more credit has gone to urban small industry than to rural small industry (Masum 1989:74). Under the Rural Transport Credit Program, rickshaws became eligible for bank loans, but despite repeated instructions from the central bank to increase the volume of loans to this sector, the role of commercial banks in financing rickshaw activities remains marginal (Masum 1988).

What is perhaps most crucial to the informal sector is not whether such policies exist but how they are implemented. It is important to note in this context that the vast majority of the informal sector consists of poor and illiterate persons who remain often uninformed of the institutions that have been created to help them, let alone the policies formulated. This implies that the institutions responsible for implementing policies should take into consideration the differences between the formal and the informal sectors and modify and simplify their procedures accordingly, rather than harassing the poor and illiterate with paperwork and procedural delays. This is only possible within the framework of democratic institutions that are accountable to the people they are meant to serve.

Microenterprises as Bankable Clients: The Case of the Grameen Bank

The 869,538 borrowers of the Grameen Bank, mostly women, who meet weekly to pay loan installments and deposit savings in 34,206 meetings held in more than 19,536 villages throughout Bangladesh are challenging the conventional wisdom on poverty and the informal sector. These borrowers, who are increasing at a rate of over 15,000 a month, are the poorest of the poor in one of the poorest countries in the world, yet they are proving themselves to be commercially viable clients for a banking institution. They are also, to the surprise of many, proving their ability to accumulate savings totaling more than US$21.62 million, an average of about one month's wages per borrower. The Grameen Bank demonstrates the powerful impact on the lives of the poor that guaranteed, equitable, and dependable access to capital can have.

There is a question that inevitably arises concerning the Grameen Bank: is it the exception that proves the rule, or does it represent a new rule that demands adherence? That the Grameen Bank should be increasingly considered the rule rather than the exception is evidenced by the results of a number of similar experiments in the developing world.

The popular beliefs, that the poor people are not bankable, that they cannot find a way to earn a living outside agriculture, that they cannot save, that they quickly run out of ideas, that the rural power structure will not allow the poor, particularly women, to borrow from financial institutions, have all proved to be myths.

The beginning. The origin of the Grameen Bank dates back to 1976, when Dr. Muhammad Yunus, a professor of economics at Chittagong

University, launched an action-research program to design a comprehensive banking framework to bring the rural poor within the framework of viable financial institutions. He was convinced that the traditional banks were structured in such a way that they would never do business with the poor, who constitute the largest segment of society in Bangladesh and who are desperately in need of credit. He identified the following problems:

- The basic design of conventional banks was wrong. In order to borrow money from a bank, one has to have collateral.

- The poorest of the poor in Bangladesh do not possess land or other assets that they can use as collateral for borrowing.

- Most of the Bangladesh's banks discriminate against women. Any woman wanting to borrow has to have her husband or father provide security for loans.

- Conventional banking requires literacy. "When you apply for a loan, they make you fill out an application," Dr. Yunus said. "Could you imagine a grocer or a butcher requiring his customers to take a literacy test before he did business with them? Well, this is the situation we have with the banks. They have created this myth that you need education to borrow money."

Thus, Dr. Yunus reasoned that if financial resources could be made available to poor, landless people at existing commercial terms, then "millions of poor people with their millions of small pursuits can add up to create the biggest development wonder."

The project first demonstrated its strength in the village Jobra (a village adjacent to Chittagong University—the initial site of the action-research project) and some of the neighboring villages during 1976–1979. It was then extended to Tangail (a district near Dhaka) in 1979, and from there spread to the districts of Chittagong, Dhaka, Rangpur, and Patuakhali. Table 6.7 shows the year-by-year expansion of the Grameen Bank from 1976 to 1990.

In October 1983, the Grameen Bank Project was transformed into an independent bank by a government ordinance. Presently the government provides 25 percent of the paid-up share capital of the bank, while the remaining 75 percent is held by the borrowers of the bank.

Borrowers are landless men and women who must form themselves into groups of five in order to receive loans, for which no collateral is required. The group members should belong to a similar

TABLE 6.7   Grameen Bank Performance, 1976–1990

Performance indicator	1976	1977	1978	1979	1980	1981	1982	1983	1984	1985	1986	1987	1988	1989	1990
Number of members[a]															
Female	2	10	70	903	4,655	9,356	11,785	26,538	68,045	112,362	173,885	275,600	420,965	588,802	791,606
Male	8	60	220	1,297	10,175	14,772	18,631	31,782	53,006	59,260	60,458	63,556	69,398	73,461	77,932
Number of groups[a]	—	—	—	377	2,935	4,818	6,243	11,664	24,210	34,324	46,869	67,831	98,073	132,453	173,908
Number of centers[a]	—	—	—	36	326	482	780	2,443	4,763	7,210	10,279	14,390	19,663	26,976	34,206
Number of villages covered[a]	1	2	4	17	363	433	745	1,249	2,268	3,666	5,170	7,502	10,552	15,073	19,536
Number of branches[a]	1	1	2	7	25	25	54	86	152	226	295	396	501	641	781
Number of borrowers[a]															
Female	n.a.	n.a.	n.a.	800	3,171	8,253	9,400	20,991	59,714	99,332	155,142	265,415	403,625	575,117	775,547
Male	n.a.	n.a.	n.a.	1,134	8,473	13,451	14,777	25,964	47,229	53,131	54,325	63,142	68,805	73,150	77,075
Total loan amount disbursed during the year (millions of takas)	0.008	0.007	0.268	3.03	17.11	33.53	41.91	99.34	304.36	428.45	541.73	810.03	1,280.43	1,768.28	2,262.47
Number of activities	n.a.	n.a.	n.a.	87	110	196	201	331	481	534	451	464	462	463	459
Amount of balance in Group Fund (millions of takas)	—	—	—	0.22	1.46	3.89	5.92	11.22	26.65	49.16	75.01	113.35	165.47	226.73	294.85
Amount of balance in Emergency Fund (millions of takas)	—	—	—	0.01	0.04	0.34	1.44	3.38	6.25	12.67	22.01	33.81	52.70	81.79	122.01
Number of employees	1	1	5	41	140	208	401	824	1,288	2,777	3,315	4,637	7,035	9,737	13,626

n.a. = not available. — = not applicable.
a. Cumulative figures.
SOURCE: Grameen Bank.

economic and social background. Any person whose family owns less than 0.5 acres of cultivable land and the value of whose family assets does not exceed the market value of one acre of medium-quality land in the local area is eligible to take loans from the bank for any income-generating activity.

Before loans are given to the eligible borrowers, they have to undergo an intensive training for a period of one to two weeks in the philosophy of the Grameen Bank, its rules, and its procedures. The group members have to pass a test before they are granted recognition and become eligible for loans. During the test the members must satisfy the bank staff of their seriousness, their understanding of the principles and procedures of the bank, and their ability to write their own names.

Each group elects its own chairman and secretary, who must hold weekly meetings, at which attendance of all the members is compulsory. Several groups in a single village are federated into a center. From among the chairmen of the groups a center chief and a deputy center chief are elected to conduct the weekly meetings of the center, recommend loan proposals, supervise loan activities, and assist bank workers in their efforts.

Savings. The bank encourages its members to participate in savings schemes such as the Group Fund and Emergency Fund. The importance of savings can hardly be overemphasized, in the lives of individuals or nations. One of the most intractable problems of development is the failure of the rural sector to generate surplus capital for investment. In theoretical discussions, savers (lenders) and borrowers are usually imagined as two separate groups of people. Savers deposit their savings in the bank, borrowers borrow the savings of others at a price. Not much attention is given to the fact that a saver can also be an investor. For the poor this is the most usual case. Their investments can be calibrated in very small amounts. Any small savings can be plowed back into investment at any time.

The multiplier effect of investment can clearly be demonstrated in a credit program for the poor through continuous expansion of the economic base of poor, as incomes rise with additional investment through borrowing. The vicious cycle of "low income–low savings–low investment–low income" can be broken by injecting credit into the cycle, which becomes "credit–more income–more savings–more investment–more income."

Group-based savings in Grameen Bank serve a wide range of purposes other than immediate investment:

- Discipline is imposed on group members, who develop the habit of saving regularly.

- Saving enhances self-confidence. Having been nonsavers all their lives, individuals in a group find it encouraging to become habitual savers.

- Savings provide protection against normal business risks; seasonal variations in income; natural calamities such as floods, famines, cyclones, droughts, and diseases; and political disturbances. Group members can afford to take greater risks because they have a "cushion" in their savings.

- Group-based savings of the poor can demonstrate the strength found in numbers. Even if each poor person regularly saves a very small amount each week, altogether their savings add up to large amounts in a short time.

That their collected number is a great source of strength to themselves and to the nation is strikingly demonstrated to the poor by a simple savings program. Such savings empower microentrepreneurs to obtain control over various productive assets and make them less vulnerable to various risks to their enterprises.

Current operations. The Grameen Bank now operates through ten zonal offices. Beneath the zonal offices are area offices, each supervising ten to fifteen branch offices.

A branch office usually has nine persons to carry out its business: a branch manager, a senior assistant, six bank workers (three male and three female), and a guard. According to the principles of the Grameen Bank, the bank should go to the people rather than the people coming to the bank. All banking transactions are done at center meetings attended by borrowers and bank workers. The branch borrows from the head office whenever it needs funds, at the rate of 10 percent, and on-lends these funds at the rate of 16 percent. A branch is expected to earn a profit by the end of its sixth year of operation.

At the end of December 1990, the bank, through its 781 branches, was serving 869,538 members. It had disbursed, by December 1990, 7,590.66 million takas (US$210.85 million). Its recovery rate is close to 98 percent. Group members had saved more than 765.36 million (US$21.62 million) by December 1990. The bank's operations have reached 19,536 villages, out of about 64,000 in the country. It hopes to be operating 1,000 branches by the end of 1992.

The Grameen Bank presently has a staff of about 14,000, who together put in 40,000 miles of legwork per day. Staff who are committed and personally involved in what they do are essential for the success of a program such as the bank's. Staff training is therefore crucial.

The bank has also introduced housing loans for the poor. A durable shelter is one of the basic requirements for people to be able to organize their thoughts, discipline their actions, and undertake plans and programs for creative pursuits. People without a home tend to be uncertain, worried, and unstable, which affects their every action. The ownership of a house infuses people with a sense of confidence and honor that enables them to start dreaming of a better life. Furthermore, homestead is also often the workplace for the rural poor. A bank member can borrow up to 18,000 takas (US$500) for constructing a simple tin-roof house. Housing loans are paid back over ten to fifteen years, in weekly installments. More than 91,157 such houses had been constructed by December 1990, for which a total amount of 798.53 million takas (US$22 million) has been disbursed. The average size of housing loans was only 8,761 takas (US$243). This experience proves that, given the opportunity, the poor can provide decent houses for themselves.

The role of women in the Grameen Bank. The Grameen Bank has gradually come to pay increasing attention to women, who constitute the vast majority of its members. This is the result of deliberate efforts, which were guided by a consideration of the status of women of Bangladeshi society and their developmental role.

Rural women, either married to poor, landless, and assetless men or widowed, divorced, or abandoned, face the constraints of the society particularly harshly, for they lack the social and economic power to improve their situation. Although they work for long hours, their contribution is all but invisible (it does not appear in any national statistics) and unrecognized. One of the most important reasons why this is so is that traditionally their work was unremunerated. Although it contributed to family income, their work did not directly bring in an income that they could claim as theirs and over which they would retain control.

Although the participation of women in activities outside the household was traditionally minimal, growing poverty and changing customs have resulted in the greater participation of women, especially in the more disadvantaged categories, in various types of employment outside the home, including agricultural activities, earthwork, vending, and factory work. However, the opportunities open to women are much more limited then those available to men, and they are also paid much lower wages for the same kinds of work.

The inferior social status of women in traditional Bangladeshi society, together with their limited access to any kind of resources (including financial resources), makes women particularly vulnerable to the effects of poverty. The situation is worsened by the fact that increasing poverty leads to higher rates of divorce, remarriage, and desertion of families by the male head of the household.

In spite of efforts undertaken by both the government and other, private organizations, the situation of women in contemporary Bangladesh is a cause for serious concern. By promoting the participation of women in its credit operation for income-generating activities, the Grameen Bank seeks to improve both the economic and the social status of rural women, by enabling them to earn incomes by which they can support their families and therefore to be recognized as contributing and productive members of the family, which will provide them with a say in family matters.

By December 1990, 91 percent of the bank's borrowers were women. Grameen Bank loans have now been extended to more than 791,606 women, who together have received total loans of more than 6,215.9 million takas. Bank statistics further show that the disbursement level of loans to women has increased at a higher rate than for men and that discipline and repayment records of female borrowers are better than those of males. Women borrowers have saved more than 624.7 million takas in their savings accounts.

Although economic activities financed through loans constitute the core of the Grameen Bank, the bank has sought over the years to broaden its concerns and add new dimensions to its activities. Apart from the promotion of cooperation and solidarity through its institutional

Anita used credit from the Grameen Bank to help her set up a small grocery shop in Keraniganj Upazila.

framework, the bank has gradually introduced a range of subsidiary activities, including improvements in housing, personal hygiene and sanitation, health care, nutrition, family planning, and literacy, through workshops and exchange visits, mostly with women borrowers.

The role of women in the Grameen Bank is reflected in an ordinance entitled the "Grameen Bank Ordinance" (revised in 1986 and 1990), which provides for 50 percent of shareholders to be women. At present all nine of the board members representing the borrower shareholders are women. Women, many of whom were destitute before joining the bank, are now members of the board of directors, along with senior officials nominated by the government.

In economic terms, women (like their male counterparts) have an opportunity to undertake a productive activity, with the possibility of developing an independent economic base. The actitivies undertaken by women borrowers are largely similar to what they previously did for others in return for wages or food or for themselves on a smaller scale. Previously, however, they were paid less than one-third of what would be due to them if they had had the resources to work for themselves. It is clear from the diversity of their activities that women's traditional household role has not prevented them from developing marketable skills.

Furthermore, the economic benefits realized as a result of these activities are not limited to the women themselves but are spread to their families, especially their children. Many husbands of women borrowers have now taken up activities to complement their wives' new businesses. In a society where women still find it difficult to venture into public places alone, these complementary activities are particularly important. Experience also shows that women exhibit greater bias toward the family unit in distributing their new income, preferring to improve household living standards in terms of improved nutrition, sanitation, and education of children.

Impact on women borrowers. The relatively high rate of participation of women in the Grameen Bank's credit scheme has brought about certain lasting changes in the lives of these women. This impact is both social and economic. The various aspects of the economic impact are as follows:

- Women are carrying out transactions independently with the bank, and in almost all cases for the first time dealing directly with a formal institution independently of their fathers, brothers, or husbands. In many cases, women are handling large amounts of cash for the first time.

- The loan investment brings in an income that is visibly the woman's, as distinct from the household's. This means that, for her personal expenditures at least, she does not have to ask her husband or father.

- Compulsory weekly saving means that the woman has a growing savings account at the bank that only she can operate or withdraw from. Her rights of use or possession of that amount are ensured formally.

- Membership in a group and a center imply active and regular association with others in the group and the center through which the woman learns with other women about banking and investment.

- The existence of a group fund provides access to a kind of mini-bank fund that the woman can utilize individually or together with other members of her group.

The social impacts are as follows:

- The association with the bank, groups, and centers has increased the physical mobility of women beyond their villages, unions, and even districts.

- Association with other women through groups, centers, and workshops has paved the way for a wider social exchange and greater flow of information, knowledge, and, most important, organizational skills.

- Greater mobility and a wider scope for association have resulted in a general elevation of self-confidence. Women's self-awareness itself has led to increased female participation in decision making within the household.

- Meeting regularly with women who share the same kind of life and the same problems makes the women realize that they are not isolated and that they are part of a larger community. The women often develop a sense of solidarity with other center members.

An illustration of the potential impact of the Grameen Bank on social change for women can be seen from the resolutions adopted by

women borrowers (mostly center chiefs) at the national workshop held
in March 1984. The resolutions covered subjects such as sanitation,
education of children, family planning, and the dowry system. The
very awareness of such issues is an indication of the potential social
benefits that can be derived.

Conclusions

Self-employment and credit. In seeking solutions to poverty, economists often recommend wage employment for all, that is, full employment. They hardly realize that most of the jobs offered to the poor
ensure that they remain poor for the rest of their lives. For example,
a factory worker has wage employment, but in the normal course of
events will not be able to progress from there. Economists do not talk
about forms of employment other than wage employment because their
world is made up of "firms" and "farms" that hire different quantities
of labor at different wage levels, according to their requirements. There
is hardly any room in economic literature for people, especially the
poor, doing things they are familar with to make a living. This is, and
has been, the natural way for most people (outside the organized sector), in most regions of the world, to earn their livelihoods. The base
for this natural way of doing things is the household. Economics as
a discipline, by not recognizing the household as a production unit
and self-employment as a natural way for people to make a living, has
missed essential aspects of economic reality.

Self-employment is a way people can organize their social and
economic lives in conformity with the resources they can command.
Self-employment enables people to make their own decisions to their
own advantage, thereby restoring human dignity and self-respect.

It is generally believed that, because of resource constraints, under
the existing global economic framework, it is not possible to make
resources available to the majority of the population who happen to
be poor. This perception persists because the role of credit in economic
development, through the creation of self-employment, has not been
fully perceived or recognized. Perhaps the reason for this is that
economists have played a dominant role in shaping concepts and
developing models since the 1940s. They perceive themselves to be
social scientists, without in fact being so. If economics were a genuine
social science, it would have realized the role that credit can play toward
economic and social development through self-employment. In
economic literature, credit has been assigned a neutral or docile
role as a facilitator of trade, commerce, and industry. A genuine
social science would have discovered that credit is economic, political,

and social power, all combined in one. Unlike any other asset, credit—that is, cash—can be converted into any kind of asset or power almost instantaneously.

Credit is perhaps the only affordable resource that can be made available at commercial rates to satisfy any quantum of demand—by creating self-employment for the poor to pursue microenterprises of their own choosing, with which they are already familiar and for which they possess the required skills. In order for the 10 million poor families of Bangladesh to take up various microenterprise projects, the total amount of funds needed would be approximately US$1 billion, which is less than the cost of a single Trident nuclear submarine!

The unfortunate part of this proposition is that conventional financial institutions do not regard poor people as bankable. In fact, it is the financial institutions and their rules that have created the myth that the poor are not bankable. The myth has primarily been created by financial institutions through the legal requirement of collateral. In their logic, since the poor cannot offer collateral, they are not creditworthy. This myth has now been exploded by institutions such as the Grameen Bank of Bangladesh, Badan Kredit Kecamatan (BKK) of Indonesia, and ACCION in many Latin American countries, which have drawn worldwide attention.

At the "World Conference on Microenterprises" organized by the World Bank in 1988 in Washington, the following remarks were made

Rekha has a business making rubber sockets, assisted by loans from the Basta Keraniganj branch of the Grameen Bank.

by U.S. Representative Benjamin Gilman, a member of the House Select Committee on Hunger: "One of development's best-kept secrets will soon be public knowledge, namely investing in poor people is good business. Not only are the poor bankable, they may be one of the most productive and safest investments today."

The poor are not unproductive. In fact, they are the most productive segment of the population. Unfortunately the fruits of their labor are usurped by wealthier segments of the society through economic, social, and political manipulations. All these manipulations find their strength in their absolute control over financial and other resources. If the control of the powerful segments of society over resources can be loosened, the poor can at the very least begin to enjoy some of the fruits of their labor, expand their economic base, lead a life of dignity, and look forward to building a better future for themselves and their children.

The experience of the Grameen Bank has shown that placing a strategic input—credit—within the reach of the poor enables the poor to unleash their creative energies and productive powers by engaging in, or expanding, self-employment opportunities, thereby improving simultaneously their own economic and social conditions and the wealth of the country.

Conceptualization of poverty-focused programs. While the Grameen Bank and other similar programs have demonstrated how the provision of credit can promote microenterprises and enable the poor to be come entrepreneurs, there are a number of safeguards that must be observed if such programs, and the policies that might inspire them, are to meet the ultimate development objective: elimination of poverty and positive change in the status of the bottom 50 percent of the population in any country.

The most important precondition is avoiding conceptual confusion, which is an important reason why even well-intentioned legislation, policies, or programs often go astray and fail to meet their goals.

Conceptual vagueness has done great damage in the formulation of projects for the poor. When a basic concept lacks sharpness in its definition, it can lead to strange situations. Quite frequently one will find development literature in which rural and poor are being used interchangeably. Another common practice, which has been mentioned earlier, is the use of the term "small" or "marginal" farmer as a synonym for the poor. "The poor" may or may not include marginal and small farmers, depending on the definition decided upon before the analysis begins. But in any case, "the poor" are a much larger collection of people than small or marginal farmers alone. At the very least, women and children are left out when one defines small or marginal farmers as the poor.

Instead of using occupation or location to define the poor, a conceptually safer policy would be to use income/asset criteria. Each country should have its own definition of the poor. International organizations could accept these definitions as given, instead of imposing new ones.

Theoreticians sometimes stretch debates over definitions until they become exercises in hairsplitting. We are not arguing for a sharp definition in order to achieve some theoretical perfection, but for the sake of achieving operational strength. No society provides a sharp demarcation line between poverty and nonpoverty. Unless a firm demarcation line is laid out to guide policy makers and program implementors, it is easy for them to mistarget programs without even realizing it.

Definitions are like navigational markings in unknown waters. They need to be clear, distinct, and unambiguous. Any definition that is not clear and precise is as bad as none. If it is felt that a separate program for the poor is needed, then it is imperative that one have a clearly defined boundary line so that it becomes easy to recognize nonpoor people seeking to take advantage of the program. Any hesitation or confusion in recognizing such "trespassers" will erode the strength of the program.

When we know clearly the poor population we are trying to reach, the definition of microenterprise is also sharpened. We have defined it as any undertaking or activity wherein a poor person generates an income to improve his or her social and economic situation. We do not limit it to any particular sector or type of activity (such as manufacturing, trading, processing, or service delivery), nor do we define it in terms of capital invested or number of workers employed. In the context of Bangladesh, the microenterprises of the bottom 50 percent of the population are, for the most part, family-based activities with minimal capital investments.

Units employing five to ten workers, with capital of up to 15 million taka (the government's definition of small industry), are the target of some programs. While these programs may be justified in themselves, we do not feel that they should be put in the same category as poverty-focused programs. Such small units, which are closer to establishments in the formal sector, are in many ways easier to deal with; they are units to which planners and program administrators can apply familiar concepts such as productivity and cost-efficiency, and they can, with relatively little effort, be assisted to "take off" as profitable ventures. There is, therefore, a danger that planners and program adminstrators may slide over from poverty-focused microenterprise programs into small-enterprise assistance programs or, worse still, confuse the two, in which case the absolute poor will lose out to the relatively less poor or, as some call them, the "viable poor."

Most development programs are, in fact, omnibus programs, offering aid to poor and nonpoor. Whenever a project allows the nonpoor to be copassengers one can safely guess the outcome. The poor will soon be elbowed out. As in Gresham's Law, it is useful to remember that, in a world of development, if one mixes the poor and the nonpoor within the format of a single program, the nonpoor will always drive out the poor.

Exclusiveness should not be limited only to the client level. It should extend down to the level of implementation machinery. A delivery mechanism that is entrusted with the responsibility of delivering all kinds of goods to all kinds of people will only end up delivering all kinds of goods to one kind of people: the richer clientele. This is another inexorable law of nature. If one has to deliver anything to the poor, the delivery mechanism must be designed and operated exclusively for them.

Creating poverty-focused programs. Specialized delivery mechanisms will require specialized people, from the planning and design level, down to the person-to-person contact at the field level. If one accepts the proposition that programs for the poor are a new breed of policy, then one also has to agree that they need a new breed of people to design and manage them.

Myths and half-truths about the poor have been promoted by institutions that have never had any participation from the poor. Any "expert" will say with absolute certainty that the poor need to be trained before they can undertake any income-generating activity, that the poor cannot save, that poor women have no skills, that the poor cannot make rational judgments, that they have a narrow view of life, that they are uninterested in change, that it would be impossible for the poor women to keep their incomes to themselves, that husbands will torture them to appropriate any income the women make—all of which the Grameen Bank's experience has proven to be largely false.

To make microenterprise programs for the poor realistic and effective, it is imperative that the gap between the designers and implementors on the one hand and the clientele on the other hand be bridged, and the myths exploded. This requires bold steps. Project personnel should shift their attention from the particular product or service they are offering to the people they are serving. They must learn to look at the poor as total human beings. They must remember that it is their job to help change the lives of the people they are serving. Toward that end, experiments may be undertaken to initiate institution building exclusively by the poor, to ensure fear-free interaction between them and formal institutions.

Microenterprise programs for the poor can be meaningful and effective only within a supportive national policy framework. In the absence of a supportive policy framework, development programs can easily work at cross-purposes. One agency of the government may be trying to build something for the poor, while another agency may be destroying it, all without even realizing what is happening.

Government policies may, in certain cases, act against microenterprises and the "informal sector"—either intentionally or unintentionally. There is a need to revise such policies. A more positive measure required is the formulation of policies that are supportive of the informal sector and recognize that the formal and informal sectors are often complementary to each other.

Microenterprises and the informal sector as solutions. Informality in development and microenterprises of the poor are not problems to be addressed by policy makers and program implementors. They are part of the solution that the poor have found for themselves and by themselves, and can be seen as part of their survival strategy. On the whole, they are untouched by direct government interventions or measures, although they are obviously influenced by larger government policy decisions, often adversely.

An African proverb states: "Things done without me are done against me." This seems to be true of the poor. They have virtually no say in the formulation and functioning of the political and legal institutions that affect their lives. Since there are no institutional arrangements allowing the poor to participate meaningfully in decision making, and since most governments feel no compulsion to be accountable to the poor, the natural beneficiaries of most policies and institutions are the various elites. This is true of most countries. Serious political commitment to creating truly democratic and representative institutions that will be accountable to the majority, who happen to be poor, seems to be a precondition for meaningful national development.

Given appropriate resources and support, the poor are able to help themselves, at very little cost to the government or society as a whole. Not only do they thereby improve their own socioeconomic status, but they contribute to national development, not merely growth. In the process the poor gain dignity and self-respect, which, combined with a more secure economic base, empowers them to gain control over their own lives. This empowerment is also likely to enable them to participate meaningfully in the political process and will lead toward more just and humane development.

A. LAWRENCE CHICKERING
AND MOHAMED SALAHDINE

The Informal Sector's Search for Self-Governance

The informal sector raises issues of great importance to developed and developing countries alike. Informal markets facilitate a cooperative entrepreneurship that allows the poorest people around the world to assert themselves economically and politically. This silent revolution is changing societies everywhere. It is confronting them with extraordinary challenges to expand opportunities by establishing institutions and policies that will permit full participation of their citizens in all aspects of economic, social, and political life.

The informal sector revolution can provide important lessons to governments, aid agencies, and voluntary organizations trying to work for economic growth, human development, and political democracy. These lessons are especially important now, when traditional regimes in many countries are searching for new sources of political legitimacy. They are especially valuable in developing countries and in the former Marxist countries, which are trying to manage transitions to democratic pluralist and market economic systems.

The challenge presented by the informal sector arises out of the postwar history of development, which focused on institutions and policies that would build a modern, industrial sector. This sector was capital-intensive in countries that were labor-intensive in their resources, and its concentration in urban centers encouraged a large migration of people from the countryside to the cities in search of work.

In this context, at least four different sectors have emerged in developing countries: a modern manufacturing sector, which is both government-owned and private; an infrastructure sector, which includes public utilities and financial services, and is also both government-owned and private; an agricultural sector, which is mostly private; and a sector made up of small- and medium-scale enterprises, which are also private. Finally, there is a disorganized sector of individual proprietorships and individual workers who do many different things.

Most developing countries have focused nearly all of their attention on encouraging and subsidizing the first two sectors in a variety of ways, while ignoring the agricultural and small-enterprise sectors. These countries vested their hope for development in the modern, industrial sector, but the capital-intensive industries in that sector could not absorb enough labor to reach the great majority of people.

The result of this concentration of effort was the emergence in these countries of a *dual economic and social structure*—the modern, "formal" sector of industrial, urban enterprise and the traditional, "informal" sector of agricultural and largely rural enterprise. One sector is legal and privileged. The other is "off-the-books" and poor.

The challenge the informal sector presents to developing country governments is to end this pattern of discrimination favoring the modern, privileged sectors and reform institutions and policies to expand opportunities for the informals. The challenge is to end the dual structure of development that is so common in developing countries.

One can examine the informal sector from different perspectives. Economists look through an individualist lens and see informal entrepreneurs pursuing self-interest while searching for economic and social progress. Sociologists and anthropologists look through a "communitarian" lens and see them in relation to traditional communities and culture. Each of these perspectives—one emphasizing individuals, the other emphasizing groups—has important things to say about the informal sector, about development, and about what nearly all societies are struggling to achieve.

Most of the contributors to this volume are economists, and their conclusions reflect the rationalist individualism that animates their discipline. Yet their policy conclusions could as easily have come from the group-oriented disciplines of sociology and anthropology. This multidisciplinary feature of their analysis highlights the power of the conclusions suggested by their chapters.

Both of these perspectives are important because nearly all societies are engaged in a search for a way to integrate the modern commitment to freedom, individualism, and rights with the older, traditional commitment to obligation, community, and order. They seek, that is, to integrate the individualistic perspective of economists with the group or community perspective of sociologists and anthropologists. The key to this integration is self-governance.

The informal sector in fact achieves a substantial, effective integration of these two perspectives. It does this by combining tradition and culture with the entrepreneurial energy necessary for economic growth. The informal sector thus embodies the social and economic search for both economic growth and human development, the twin purposes of all serious development initiatives.

The contributors to this book agree about the nature of the informal sector and its role in development. They agree about the informal sector's important contributions to development, and they agree about its healthy and dynamic nature. All of them also see opportunities for policy reform, but there is some difference in the reforms they emphasize. Muzammel Huq and Maheen Sultan, in their chapter on Bangladesh, focus on the importance of providing credit to empower informal entrepreneurs; the others emphasize policy and institutional reforms to create opportunities (as does the study on Egypt; see Toubar 1991). They also encourage implementing policies that would expand the formal sector, thus increasing job opportunities in it.

Despite the contributors' basic agreement about the value of the informal sector, many of the major parties to the debate on development feel great ambivalence toward it. It is important to reflect on the sources of this ambivalence to understand the problems faced both by the informal sector and by many countries seeking development. It is important to ask why so many countries have perpetuated the dual economic and social structure.

In pulling together our conclusions about this project, we will summarize the participants' observations about the informal sector in these five countries, with occasional references to the study on Egypt. Considering the substantial differences between these countries in history, culture, language, and religion, as well as in economic circumstances, the similarity of the authors' general perspectives and conclusions is in fact quite remarkable (see the Appendix for comparative social and economic statistics).

Recalling that one major purpose of this volume is to explore the issue in relation to Hernando de Soto's research in Peru, the reader will be able to compare the results here with Peru by referring to our summary of de Soto's studies in the Introduction. Where the circumstances and conditions in these countries seem to us similar to those in Peru, we draw on the Peruvian experience to muse on future implications.

Let us begin by summarizing our principal conclusions from the chapters, both for the informal sector and for general development policy.

Principal Conclusions

The size and role of the informal sector. Our first (and most obvious) conclusion is that in all of the countries studied here the informal sector is enormously important, both economically and socially. This suggests that it is probably just as important in most, if not all, developing countries. These chapters present estimates of informality exceeding 50 percent of the labor force, producing 40–60 percent of GDP. In Bangladesh, with a per capita income of only US$165 per year, the numbers are much higher. There, more than 70 percent of the urban work force is informal, as are an even larger percentage of rural workers. Only 5 percent of GDP is produced by large-scale industry, which employs less than 2 percent of the work force.

The number of informals working in particular industries is extraordinary. One approach to measurement of the sector in the Philippines, for example, produced estimates that in 1983, 73 percent of non-agricultural employment was informal, including 93 percent of people working in the trade sector, 86 percent of people in transportation, and 78 percent of those in construction. These numbers have actually increased substantially compared with measurements made in the early 1960s and early 1970s.

In addition to these sectors, informal employment is greatest in catering, garment manufacturing, repair services, financial services, small manufacturing, and a wide range of middleman services.

In the Introduction, we discussed various approaches to the problem of definition. We noted that most traditional studies of the informal sector have focused on functional attributes such as size, complexity of operation, source of capital, family relationships, and so on. Beginning with the International Labor Organization's 1972 study, defining the informal sector in terms of such functional attributes has taken on a strongly sociological tone. Since most of these attributes tend also to describe traditional (that is, predeveloped) society, it is not surprising that studies emphasizing them tend also to see dysfunction and pathology in informal behavior.

Most of the participants in this study emphasize *legal status* as the touchstone of informality. Although this view does not reject the sociological perspective, it does reject the critical judgment that often goes with it. Huq and Sultan's chapter on Bangladesh focuses more on poverty and household work as the bases of informality, but their overall view of the informal sector's role in development is the same as that of the other authors.

The vitality of the informal sector. Our second conclusion, shared by our contributors and already mentioned, is that, although overwhelmingly poor, the informal individuals and firms described in this volume have almost none of the dysfunctional and pathological qualities that traditional development theories take to be the cause of their poverty. On the contrary, the informals described here show themselves to be among the most extraordinarily entrepreneurial groups in their societies. This suggests that if encouraged and given real opportunities, they could make an even greater contribution to economic and social progress.

These analyses reject the belief that poverty is caused by the pathologies of the informal sector or by "what the poor lack." The perspective presented here is that poverty is not primarily a "technical" problem (as the Newtonian model would have it), based on lack of skills. Many informal entrepreneurs who are extremely successful are in fact illiterate. The most dramatic testament to the skills, talents, and energies of poor people in developing countries is given in the chapter on Bangladesh, which relates how the Grameen Bank has used small amounts of credit to help hundreds of thousands of the poorest rural people to gain control over their own lives and develop productive means of self-support.

The emphasis on pathology comes from across the political spectrum, and it is very much related to the ambivalence that many people feel toward the informal sector. If the informal sector participants embody an integration of modern individualism and entrepreneurship with traditional values and culture, their more "modern" critics across the political spectrum tend to see either pathology or unreality in *both* elements in the integration. On the one hand, the oligarchic right fears both the competition posed by informal entrepreneurs and—in many places—the destabilizing effects of traditional society, especially religion. On the other hand, leftist and liberal critics see in the informal sector only pathological artifacts of larger social processes, especially of the class struggle.

That both the right and the left should fear the informal workers makes a great deal of sense, because those workers represent a live refutation of almost all of the principal ideas about development held by both sides. The informal workers also refute the commitment to centralized economic and political power.

The roots of informality. If the poor's incapacities are *not* the ultimate cause of their poverty, we must rethink both the causes of poverty and strategies for escaping from it. If poverty is not caused by technical deficiencies such as lack of skills, what is the problem?

The problem (for most of the contributors) is that *the poor lack opportunities.* The most fundamental problem is the lack of jobs in the modern, formal, capital-intensive sector. Alonzo summarizes the reasons economists give for the failure of this sector to absorb more employment. He mentions an overvalued exchange rate, which hurts exports; import-substituting protection of inefficient domestic enterprises; a biased fiscal structure that promotes excessive capital intensity; a repressed financial system that allocates credit to large enterprises and thus discriminates against small firms; and large and inefficient government enterprises that waste scarce resources.

Overall, that is, bad economic policies, which inhibit the growth of export sectors, retard employment opportunities, forcing people to scramble for work in the informal sector. Only Nipon's chapter on Thailand tells a different story. That country has implemented generally good policies and has had strong growth, which has resulted in a steady decline in the informal sector there.

The contributors describe the absence of opportunity in other, different ways, although the spirit of their recommendations is the same. Most of the studies (on Morocco, the Philippines, Sri Lanka, and Thailand, as well as the one on Egypt) conclude that although the disadvantages and costs associated with informality are great, the laws and institutions make it *even more costly* for poor individuals and firms to be formal. They focus, that is, on the problem of policy and institutional failures that prevent the poor from using their entrepreneurial talents to improve their own lives. The informal workers lack access to formal institutions that facilitate commerce, including formal legal systems and credit institutions.

Although informal sector participants do not pay income taxes in most countries, income taxes (as we noted in the Introduction) tend not to be a very important source of revenue in developing countries. Informal entrepreneurs do pay regressive sales and value-added taxes, which are much more important. They must also pay high tariffs on inputs they need for their businesses, in contrast to large enterprises, which the tariffs frequently protect. Nipon reports that in Thailand informal entrepreneurs must pay individual income taxes, and they face higher overall taxes than large, registered firms as well.

In addition, many informal workers have to pay significant bribes to the police and other officials to stay in business. Nipon describes in some detail the bribery system that allows Bangkok's informal motorcycle operators to continue operating, and most of the other contributors mention bribes that informal entrepreneurs must pay as well.

In summary, informal entrepreneurs are informal either because the government makes it difficult and expensive for them to register their businesses, or difficult and expensive to abide by rules and regulations imposed on them after they are registered. In his study of Sri Lanka, Sanderatne thus concludes that although the costs of registration are very low, the costs of being formal are such that unless they want to grow a great deal, most informal businesses never even consider going formal. If they grow to a certain size and need, for instance, a bank account, then they will register and go formal. He illustrates his point with his narrative on Pala, an informal entrepreneur who supported himself with a number of different activities until he finally started a successful business making jewelry boxes. At that point, he finally registered his business in order to be able to open a bank account and cash checks from customers.

In their chapter Huq and Sultan argue that although informal workers are unnecessarily harassed by government regulations, in Bangladesh they are *more* harmed by lack of access to institutional credit and by general government policies favoring large enterprises.

Another thing informal workers lack, in a larger context, is the sense that what they are doing represents a valuable contribution to economic and social progress in their countries. This point may seem abstract, but we return to the experience of the Grameen Bank to illustrate its importance. In the bank's experience, the moment of empowerment occurs for their borrowers not when they get their initial loan; it happens *when they make their first payment to repay the loan* (Huq 1988; Yunus 1984). It is the moment when they know that all they have heard about their own incapacities—from policy makers, scholars, and even their own neighbors—is untrue. When they start to repay, they are in control. They are free.

The other chapters cite a number of institutional and policy problems that cause informality. They include cumbersome and expensive registration procedures; costly regulations, including paperwork, to remain formal; legal barriers to doing business (which may also be regarded as barriers to registration); and other high costs imposed on formal businesses through regulations on labor, health, and other areas.

These problems were evident in the case of Nipon's motorcycle transport workers, who were prohibited by Bangkok's regulation of transportation. They were a factor for Salahdine's informal truckers, who were avoiding the high costs of getting and maintaining permits. They were present in Alonzo's description of the transportation sector in the Philippines, encumbered by burdensome registration requirements and onerous paperwork and other regulatory requirements after that. And they were the very heart of the elaborate facilitation process in Egypt, where much of that country's entrepreneurial talent is consumed in circumventing that country's nightmare bureaucratic regulatory system.

On the issue of avoiding labor regulations, 50–60 percent of all enterprises in Thailand—most of them small enterprises employing fewer than ten workers—do not pay the country's legal minimum wage. Low productivity makes such payments impossible. The saving of labor costs ranges from 13 to 22 percent depending on sector and region.

One other regulatory problem is also implicit in the reasons why informal entrepreneurs elect to remain outside the formal sector. It involves their access to credit. A major inducement to formality *should* be the opportunity to raise capital from formal institutional sources, such as banks. Unfortunately, almost every chapter herein reports complaints that banks will not consider lending to small businesses without long credit histories. Informal entrepreneurs complain that banks do not see them as active, progressive parts of their economies, worthy to be considered for bank loans.

Part of the problem here is broad development strategies that allocate credit to large, established enterprises, thus reducing the pool of capital available to smaller firms. In several of the countries, the government tries to compensate for this with special loan programs for small businesses. Unfortunately, the bureaucratic and paperwork requirements to qualify for these are so onerous that most informal businesses are effectively excluded from access to the programs.

Beyond this is the problem caused by most countries' bank regulatory systems, which set ceilings on the interest rates that banks can charge. Small businesses without credit histories, like start-up companies, are inherently riskier than large, established companies. The cost of administering their small loans is also very high. If banks are not allowed to charge an interest rate high enough to accommodate the increased risk and higher costs, they will lend only to the most creditworthy borrowers. The regulations therefore effectively eliminate access to formal credit as an inducement to formality.

And of course the same interest rate ceilings also lie behind the creation of informal credit markets, which service informal businesses. Although interest rates are higher in informal markets, Nipon points out that informal moneylenders provide an essential service because their loans are easily available without complicated procedures. In fact, his studies in Thailand show that the average time necessary to get a loan from formal lending sources averages more than 700 working hours, compared with only 80 hours to get an informal loan.

It is important to mention one additional reason for informality: the natural consumer efforts to circumvent government rules and regulations that unnecessarily raise the costs of things they want. In a sense this point simply restates the points made earlier about restrictions on the opportunities available to informal businesses.

But those businesses would not continue if there were no buyers for their products and services. Consumer demand explains informal smuggling of imports facing high tariffs. When tariffs can increase the price of imports 50 percent and more, it becomes easy to see why consumers—including many consumers who work in the informal sector—look to informal markets to provide such imported goods. This was true in Thailand during the 1970s for things such as cigarettes, electrical appliances, and luxury canned goods; smuggling declined after 1981, when tariffs were reduced. Nevertheless, tariffs remain high on certain items, such as computers and computer spare parts, and they continue to be the basis of major smuggling trade.

The role of the informal sector in economic and political change. Our final major conclusion is that the informal sector holds the key to the search for economic and political transformation by many traditional regimes—both traditional developing countries and developed Marxist countries. The informal sector holds this key because it represents the sociological "bridge" between traditional values and culture and modern individualism and entrepreneurship.

Informal markets provide an organic instrument for social evolution from traditional to modern society. They provide both the freedom and the order that all people need, and governments—of developing countries, of Marxist regimes, and even of developed countries—have only gotten into trouble when they denied the self-governing capacities of people and imposed large bureaucratic structures on them.

Governments that support and encourage this process of development, with the full participation of the informal workers, will have an opportunity to gain a new form of political legitimacy, supported by a broad, new political base. Not incidentally, such governments will also have a chance to build political coalitions that will support sound economic policies.

Feedback and Institutional Problems

We perceive several problems related to the absence of feedback and corrective mechanisms for bureaucratic rule making. First is the absence of good information on how various policies affect different groups. Second is the absence of institutions of feedback and accountability.

We saw an example of the first problem when our study group was in Peru in April 1989. The Instituto Libertad y Democracia (ILD) had just completed a study of the costs of automobile tires under the country's high tariff barriers, which effectively prevented the importation of tires. The study concluded that Peruvians were paying two and a half times as much for tires—or about US$101 million per year—as they would have to for imported tires. The policy had been sustained through lobbying by Peru's inefficient, import-substituting tire industry, which employed 1,258 people. When the figures became known, 300,000 informal transport workers pushed successfully for reform.

Information was the missing piece in altering the political forces on which the policy depended. The problem of misinformation is obviously honeycombed throughout the policy processes of developed and developing countries alike. This is especially true for the informal sector, which lacks resources to research and understand its own true interests.

Even where information is available, the ability of informal workers to use it depends on organization. In his discussion of Thailand's policy bias toward large firms, Nipon summarizes the effects of investment policy incentives, tariff protection, and other government policies in terms of the very different costs faced by different sized firms in renting a machine worth 100 baht. To rent the same machine, in Bangkok, a large firm will pay 30 baht per year, a firm with ten to fifty employees will pay 60 baht, and a firm with fewer than ten employees will pay 45 baht. These seem like shocking discriminations against those least able to pay. Unfortunately, they are probably typical of discriminatory policies in many developing countries. Information about such effects is just the beginning, however. Organization of public protest and debate then becomes necessary to generate suffi-cient pressures to achieve reform.

Hernando de Soto has emphasized a second feedback problem: the absence of mechanisms that allow real public comment and response to bureaucratic rules. Such feedback is needed both for rules currently promulgated and for rules instituted in the past, even under previous legal systems. For example, Nipon argues that in Thailand incomplete drafting of laws tends to vest excessive power and authority in administrative agencies, which must promulgate rules. These rules or subordinate laws provide the real content for the primary laws. For example, although the Export and Import Act currently in force has only twenty-four articles, more than one hundred subordinate laws have been implemented by administrative decree, without public feedback or accountability. He provides a chart showing that for the 350 acts now on the books, 18,744 subordinate laws have been passed by executive or regulatory order.

The problem of feedback and accountability also operates for past laws on which there is no current debate. This may be a special problem in many developing countries, which developed their bureaucratic and regulatory systems under colonial regimes and never reformed them after independence. In Morocco, for example, the legislation granting a merchandise transport monopoly to a small (and currently insuffi-cient) number of truckers has its origin in French colonial law. The French legislated a transportation monopoly during World War II to keep tight control of the transport of goods, and the law has not been changed since.

At least one of these countries has experienced significant reform in this area. For example, as Ruperto Alonzo writes in his chapter, "In the Philippines, for almost fifteen years before 1986, almost every law was issued by presidential decree or executive order. The Parliament served merely as a rubber stamp for the president. Initially this system was lauded by many as providing 'dynamic flexibility' and a quick response mechanism for any situation. Only much later did people realize that this also meant bad laws could be passed as easily as good ones." A new constitution, established in 1987, has restored an independent bicameral legislature in the Philippines. In addition, informal transport workers, retailers, and squatters have begun to form associations, not only to meet members' need for services but also to lobby for their political rights. Since 1987, some policy reforms reducing regulations for small enterprises and simplifying procedures have taken place, but much more remains to be done. In general, we wish there could have been more discussion of this issue in the chapters.

A final set of institutional problems concerns how formal institutions and laws are administered. Feedback and other kinds of checks on arbitrary government power depend in the first instance on formal rules and laws. However, the ultimate efficacy of formal institutions must lie in how they are implemented—how fairly justice is administered by administrative bodies and by courts. In many countries corruption enormously retards the effectiveness of institutional protections of citizens. This is far too complex a problem for us to do more than mention here. We do mention it, however, because it is a crucial issue in thinking about institutional reform.

The History

To understand the full implications of the analysis presented here, it is important to recall how we got where we are. This means recalling the philosophical/ideological, economic, and political histories of development and informality. For traditional development theories evolved in ways that encouraged informality by making it economically difficult for informal workers to become formal. Both the underlying ideas and the power relationships are important.

In the Introduction, we summarized the philosophical history, animated by the mechanistic assumptions of Newtonian physics.

Looking at development in the model of a machine means analyzing the machine to see what needs fixing. The whole tradition of import substitution, and of central planning itself, sprang directly from this underlying belief. In the past two decades, economic theory has moved away from this model.

The informal sector, in fact, *mocks* the idea of societies and economies as machines. In the process, the informal entrepreneurs also refute one of the most important artifacts promoted by this "scientific," Newtonian view, which is heavy reliance on economic statistics and official data as guides to policy and to reality. The reliance on such symbols of certainty is part of what Arnold Harberger has called the "false technicism" associated with much traditional policy making.

The economic and political histories of institutions and policies are also important, and they synchronize with the Newtonian worldview. In many developing countries, policies were formulated by colonial governments to protect the nationals of the mother countries, who were a minority—often a very small minority—compared with the indigenous peoples. An example was the French in Morocco, whose colonial laws and regimes protected French prerogatives in all aspects of economic and financial life—entrepreneurship, investment, rights to export, rights to import from the mother country, and so on. The laws had limited vision, developed as they were to help specific groups of people, in a context of conflict between indigenous peoples and foreigners.

It is easy, in this light, to see how top-down development policies evolved, with little belief or confidence that ordinary people could play an important part in the economic and social development of a country. After independence, these countries continued to be governed by people who received elite educations in the former colonial countries— that is, by elites on both the left and right who were often notably alienated from their own people, especially from ordinary people who make up the great majority of the population.

It is hard to avoid the conclusion that paternalistic, bureaucratic development policies allowed these elites to perpetuate some of the more unattractive qualities associated with colonialism. This problem continues in many developing countries even today, long after independence; and it explains a large part of the struggle they are having in moving to a new base of legitimacy, supported by a broad coalition of political constituencies.

Rethinking the Vocabulary of Development

The informal sector may exert its most powerful influence on the debate about development by forcing a rethinking of the entire vocabulary used to talk about the subject. We mean a rethinking of the most basic words in the debate, including even words like "capitalism," "socialism," "left," and "right." It would be hard to overstate the importance of such a rethinking. For even today, the debate on development is greatly influenced, if not dominated, by words that do not describe anything real. The reason is that there is no agreement about what they mean.

The collapse of socialism in the Soviet Union and Eastern Europe has made it far easier to rethink capitalism and socialism than was possible five years ago. Until very recently, most intellectuals believed that socialism represented and embodied the most idealistic vision of development and of society. That belief alone—however crudely held or understood—was a crucial factor in sustaining all bureaucratic theories of development (even, arguably, development based on import-substituting industrialization). The crisis of Marxism in the Eastern bloc countries has now greatly weakened if not destroyed that belief for many people. Nevertheless, it continues to have surprising strength in many places.

In the Introduction, we noted how Hernando de Soto has used language to change the terms of political debate in Peru. The same situation is evident throughout the chapters here. In the traditional view, "capitalism" was associated with the old, oligarchic sectors of society, and "socialism" represented the forces of justice, pushing for opportunities for the poor. It is clear from the chapters in this book that the ruling classes of these countries are mercantilist, not capitalist, and that the socialists are doing almost nothing for the poor. In all of these countries the poor—the informal workers—must be included among the true entrepreneurs and capitalists of the country. They are fighting an unholy alliance between the socialists and oligarchic mercantilists, who continue, in the name of "the people," to exclude the disadvantaged from real opportunities.

In any case, in all developing countries, the poor are outside of the ideological and political sphere of traditional socialist concern. For socialists, society is reduced to two social classes: the bourgeoisie and the proletariat. The proletariat is made up of salaried workers working for large industrial enterprises and organized into unions. The activities of nonsalaried and informal workers have no place in the traditional socialist's ideological concern. At best, socialists believe that the informals occupy temporary, provisional jobs that will disappear with the worsening contradictions of capitalism. According to the Marxist vision, the small entrepreneur is condemned to become a member of the proletariat, working for the owners of capital.

In our conception, the poor are not a *proletariat*; they are *entrepreneurs*. And if their energies are released from the weight of the bureaucratic, feudal system that weighs on them, they will transfuse a new entrepreneurial energy and vitality into systems held back by the coalitions of the traditional left and the traditional right.

We do not mean that there are no people who can be described as a proletariat. Nor do we mean that there are no poor who should get traditional kinds of assistance. Our point is that these people are far fewer than is commonly thought, and there is no way to know who they are and what they may need until institutions and policies are reformed to open opportunities for the large number of poor who are entrepreneurs.

The informal sector has also influenced our perceptions of the political vocabulary in the Marxist countries. For there is no doubt that informal workers played a major role in the collapse of socialism and of the centralized systems in those countries. The real economy in those countries was and is not the visible, formal sector of centrally planned socialism, but the informal sector of unplanned economic activity and cooperation.

The informal entrepreneurship described throughout these pages stands in stark contrast to the "capitalism" of large-scale enterprises, which in most developing countries are sustained largely by subsidies and favors from governments. The purpose of policy reforms should be to end such subsidies and create a level playing field for all enterprises, large and small alike. Serious policy reform will release the entrepreneurial energies in both the large enterprises of the formal sector and the small enterprises of the informal sector.

Political Implications

Talking about implications means speculating about the future. The conventional wisdom on development begins with the observation that politics will drive economics, in several senses: narrowly, by influencing economic policy; more broadly, by determining whether a government enjoys enough political stability and legitimacy to have a *chance* to implement sensible policies.

The dilemma of legitimacy presents a great challenge to many developing countries and to the Marxist or formerly Marxist countries. In many of them, newly elected democratic governments are struggling to achieve economic transformation and a new foundation of political legitimacy. Throughout the 1950s and 1960s it appeared possible that these two objectives were readily compatible. The import-substituting development policies then in favor seemed a perfect instrument for constructing a foundation for nationhood: centralized economic policies would reinforce and sustain a stable political order. It seemed especially true for countries torn by tribal conflict, which were looking for a basis of unity and nationhood.

In the early 1970s, import-substituting industrialization began to lose favor; as more market-oriented policies returned to vogue, conventional wisdom shifted and began to hold that the objectives of economic and political transformation were in fundamental conflict. The reasoning was that the special, concentrated interests of the few in maintaining special favors and subsidies from government would always overwhelm the diffuse, general interest in a free, open economy. Thus, the belief grew that economic reform depends on "buying off" the political interests that obstruct it.

Countries that still pursue centralized, import-substituting development strategies try to buy support in a much bigger way, but the cost is enormous. If this strategy has produced poor economic policy, it is now clear that it has not worked very well politically either. Ethnic and tribal conflicts continue unabated in many places with centralized economic and political systems, and the search for modernization in many countries is today threatened by fundamentalist religious movements that seem to mock the very idea of modernization. The political stability and legitimacy of the Arab countries, especially, have been threatened by Islamic fundamentalism symbolized by the late Ayatollah Khomeini in Iran.

The chapters in this book suggest another means by which the informal sector can become the basis for implementing sound development policies and can build a stronger foundation of legitimacy for democratic governments, even for countries torn by ethnic and tribal conflict. The solution to both economic and social problems is basic institutional reform, encouraging full informal participation in society and self-governance for all cultural, ethnic, and economic groups.

The emergence of the informal sector will almost certainly change the political environment for policy reform in many countries. Peru is the model, showing how the informals can become a rallying point around which to organize people who in the past were disorganized and unrepresented. They can become a powerful constituency that will support sound policies.

Studies of the informal sector, such as those in this book, that examine its role in society and the policies that discriminate against it, can play an important role in this process. Such studies, like the ILD's study of the Peruvian tire industry, highlight the sector's common interests and thus provide a rallying point for organizing them.

A serious policy agenda for the informal sector must include basic institutional reform, broad policy reform, and specific programs. First, basic institutional reform, guaranteeing full participation in the economic and legal institutions of the formal economy, is essential. It must include real opportunities to comment on and critique rules that in many developing countries are made by executive order without real accountability to voters. Second, policy reforms are needed that reduce unnecessary and burdensome government regulations and taxes on economic activity. Third, policy reforms must reduce active encouragement of large-scale enterprises, which acts as an implicit (and sometimes explicit) form of discrimination against the informal sector. Fourth, programs that encourage informal entrepreneurship, such as agricultural extension services and special credit programs (the Grameen Bank is a model), should be initiated. Fifth, programs that will help build institutions of civil society, to assist the informals become full, participating members of society, should be started. These include especially programs of private voluntary organizations, which work for both economic growth and human development.

The dilemma facing many Arab governments is noteworthy in this context (we write this at the end of the Gulf War). There is no reason to believe the outcome of the war will alter the Islamic fundamentalist threat to destabilize more than a few Arab governments. We believe that the informal sector holds the key for most Arab governments to achieve a new kind of legitimacy. By reaching out to the informal workers and encouraging their full participation in the social and economic life of society, these governments could strengthen their popular support. Such a policy, we believe, would reduce the appeal of Islamic fundamentalism, which at present offers much more to participants in the informal sector than do remote central governments, seeking to impose bureaucratic modernization from above.

Finally, by opening up their economies, producing according to comparative advantage, and expanding exports, developing countries can create opportunities in the formal sector and reduce the appeal of the informal sector. It is no accident that Thailand provides the only clear case in this book of a declining informal sector, for it has pursued the best overall economic policies and has enjoyed, as a result, the best overall economic performance.

Policy Recommendations

The following specific policy recommendations, based on the chapters here and on other sources, are directed to three important institutional actors. These are the principal institutions that can influence the future of the informal sector in developing countries: the governments of developing countries, private voluntary organizations, and the aid agencies of both the developed countries and international organizations.

Recommendations for governments of developing countries. It is time for governments of developing countries to end the dual economic and social structures that are the result of their development policies and to extend full rights and opportunities to all economic sectors and classes. They can achieve these goals in several ways.

Our *first* recommendation on the informal sector is to implement sound, outward-oriented development policies, which will stimulate overall economic growth and increase employment opportunities in the formal sector. More than anything else, this will expand opportunities for the informal workers and will encourage them to become formal.

Our *second* recommendation is to recognize and accept the informal sector, which holds important keys to solving the economic and political problems of developing countries. Although poor and apparently marginal, the informal workers represent 50 percent or more of full-time work forces and much larger fractions counting people working part-time and in certain sectors. They produce between 40 and 60 percent of national income. Most remarkably, they do this in an environment that gives them little assistance, since they are largely excluded from access to the principal legal and financial institutions that facilitate commerce. In fact, they represent one of the most dynamic entrepreneurial parts of the economies of perhaps most developing countries, often in the face of policies that actively discriminate against them.

Contrary to traditional beliefs, informal workers are not dysfunctional. Their poverty is not caused by pathology. In most countries it is caused by great institutional failure that limits their ability to improve themselves economically and politically.

Our *third* recommendation is to eliminate institutions and policies that discriminate against the informal sector, such as the following:

- Excessively difficult or onerous procedures to register or operate a business.

- Excessively difficult or onerous procedures to establish title to land or to get a permit to build.

- Burdensome regulations on economic activity.

- Policies that indirectly discriminate against informal workers and the poor.

Business regulations, which are often developed from models created in developed countries, may range from labor conditions to health and safety requirements to rules on pricing, and so on. While some of these regulations may be worthwhile in more developed countries, in a developing country they often price the poor out of the formal sector.

In addition, developing countries have a wide range of policies that do not discriminate directly against informal workers, but which raise the cost of joining the formal sector and thus impose the costs and disadvantages associated with informality on them. Many developing countries, for example, have policies that promote large enterprises, including tariffs, direct allocation of credit, and trade restrictions protecting their production from competition. Although not aimed at the informal sector, these policies nevertheless affect it in important ways—especially by diverting scarce resources away from it in favor of largely unproductive activities. This problem was emphasized in the chapters on Bangladesh, the Philippines, and Thailand.

We have also mentioned another policy that frequently hurts informal entrepreneurs: strict regulations on the interest that banks may charge its borrowers. Such regulations again price the informals out of the market, ensuring that bank loans will all go to large enterprises with long credit histories.

Other kinds of policies also hurt informal workers and the poor. We have mentioned trade restrictions that raise the cost of inputs for informal businesses. Huq and Sultan note that weavers in Bangladesh's handloom industry, the largest rural industry in the country, face effective tariff rates of nearly 90 percent for yarn, their basic raw material. Such restrictions are a frequent cause of smuggling as an informal business. We have also seen that tariffs as an instrument of import-substitution policy retard growth in export industries, which are the major potential source of expanding formal employment opportunities. While higher input costs hurt all businesses, they hit the poor the hardest, and most poor in these countries work in the informal sector. At the same time, the informal sector is often the only group potentially strong enough to exert the political pressure necessary to reform the policy.

Our *fourth* recommendation is to prepare for greatly increased demand for government provision of basic services once the informal sector has been integrated into the society. It will be extremely difficult for most developing country governments to meet this demand, and a major issue will therefore be how to respond to it. One possibility, which should be given serious consideration, is having the government oversee competition in the private sector to provide public services. Chile provides an excellent example of ways in which this can be done (Castañeda n.d.).

A *fifth* recommendation is to create institutions guaranteeing citizens' rights, including the right to comment on and criticize government rule making, and effective mechanisms to review violations of rights. Opening up the process of rule making will enable people to fight effectively for their interests and will protect citizens, including those in the informal sector, from the rules imposed by executive fiat, without benefit of a full public hearing and comment—which is common practice in many developing countries. Without making government accountable and providing for feedback from people to government, economic reforms stand in jeopardy of being removed by special interest rule making.

In addition, it may be even more important to create active opportunities for comment and criticism on rules instituted in the past, especially in colonial periods prior to independence.

Creation of strong, independent judiciaries is also essential. This is a goal that goes beyond constitutional empowerment of the judiciary; it entails creation of an institution that is free from the special interest corruption that affects other parts of governments. Although this enormous subject is beyond the parameters of this study, its importance impels us at least to mention it.

Our *sixth* recommendation is to encourage establishment of institutions that will facilitate economic, social, and political self-governance.[1] The aim here is to promote mechanisms that decentralize power and authority, giving local communities the power to govern their own lives. It means allowing local governments and local communities to control all aspects of public administration other than those that clearly involve transjurisdictional issues and that therefore require the involvement of higher authority. Nipon endorsed this idea in relation to Thailand, and it is implicit in all of the other chapters.

This point is especially important for construction of infrastructure that is crucial to economic growth. In the United States, particularly in rural areas, much of this infrastructure was built by single-purpose public sector enterprises in the form of special districts providing services such as water, power, fire protection, airports, hospitals, road construction, and other infrastructure that facilitates commerce.

The attractions of special districts are several. First, they are oriented toward benefits. A community can invest in itself and then pay for those investments. Second, special districts can provide valuable training in the art of self-governance. Third, since they have a single purpose, they do not threaten other governmental entities. And finally, they are oriented toward enterprise, teaching people how individual and local effort can make a difference and showing that such services need not be dictated from above.

The great value to governments of developing countries here is that they can begin building a civic culture of self-governance while investing in infrastructure that is benefit oriented. Therefore, individuals and local communities will have a reason to want these enterprises.[2]

The great antagonist to this process will always be the tradition of the strong central state as the backbone of development. Everywhere this symbol is crumbling because it denies self-governance to people who demand it. The need for self-governance is especially great where ethnic and tribal tensions threaten the stability of the nation state.

Our *seventh* and final recommendation for governments of developing countries is to encourage institutions that will support economic empowerment. Huq and Sultan's discussion of the Grameen Bank in Bangladesh presents one celebrated model of how small amounts of credit can empower even the poorest people to work for economic independence. Similar models are the Bank Rakyat Indonesia and Badan Kredit Kecamatan in Indonesia, which have also been extremely successful. Other institutions that provide technical information and know-how to informal enterprises and firms, similar to agricultural extension services, would also be valuable.

A major challenge in creating such services—and indeed in creating most other kinds of assistance programs for informal workers and the poor—is communicating their existence and value to their intended beneficiaries. The chapter on Bangladesh points out that most people in the informal sector, who are poor and illiterate, are completely uninformed about the policies and programs that have been created to help them.

All of these recommendations imply a fundamental change in the image of what government should be—from the benevolent protector of one's interests to guarantor of the rule of law and of equality before it. As the experience of the informal sector demonstrates so well, governments almost never fulfill the promised role of benevolent protector. But this failing is only the initial reason why governments should stop trying to play this role; the other reason is that all people, including the poor, need opportunities to realize the cooperative entrepreneurship and self-governance that will give them control of their own lives and will allow them to maximize their contributions to economic and social progress. The government-as-protector merely gets in their way.

The problem of formal codification is only the beginning of a process of creating institutions that realize the purposes outlined here. After codification, the challenge is to create living institutions that serve the purposes for which they were created—to protect the rights of both individuals and groups—free from interference by special interest groups and other forms of corruption.

Recommendations for private voluntary organizations. Alexis de Tocqueville remarked on the extraordinary degree of voluntary association he found in the United States following his travels there in the

1830s. We believe that private voluntary organizations (PVOs) can be powerful vehicles for organizing shared interests and objectives and for encouraging cooperation and participation by the informal sector in the economic and social life of developing countries. PVOs can play an important role in encouraging the informal sector to organize itself, to promote its own interests, and to gain recognition as an important force in the development process.

To help informal workers organize, PVOs must first change their view of the informal sector. Many foreign development workers have been taught by certain development theories to recognize only the contributions of official commercial and government sectors to the economic growth of a country. Informal activities, such as handicrafts, street food vending, and equipment repair, while perhaps important economic activities for an individual poor person, are not seen as important in an overall economy. PVOs must recognize the creative entrepreneurship and economic vitality that exist in the informal sector and seek ways to help remove obstacles to the full participation of informal workers in the national economy.

The Catholic Relief Services in Morocco is trying to do this by focusing its efforts on encouraging economic independence. On a broad scale, it is studying the entire system of social services in the country for the purpose of recommending wholesale reforms that will promote independence and self-governance. It is also promoting professional training that is targeted to the labor market and providing a professional qualification that will facilitate access to remunerative jobs.

The following are some recommendations on how PVOs could help facilitate a more complete integration of informal workers into the economic and social life of developing countries:

- *Develop models of social service institutions that respond to low-income people's articulated needs.* In particular, PVOs should rely on informal workers' knowledge of local communities when developing social assistance programs.

- *Target assistance programs for microentrepreneurs.* Despite financial and administrative constraints, these entrepreneurs have developed successful businesses without government subsidies, but they could still benefit from information services on basic skills that are necessary in operating a business, similar to agricultural extension services.

- *Develop nonacademic training programs for informal workers.* Such programs would enable them to improve both their skills and the quality of their services.

- *Identify activities and organizational models that allow informal workers to organize themselves around shared interests.* The purpose would be to expand the PVOs' traditional approach (doing things for the poor) and create institutions that would facilitate and encourage participation by the poor themselves in various community service programs, including health, education, and so on.

- *Develop models of institutional feedback that permit informal workers to respond to government rule making.* This might include work both with governments, to create opportunities and occasions for feedback, and with the informal workers, to create mechanisms that could process community reactions and feelings in response to governmental actions and then communicate those reactions to policy-making bodies.

PVO activities designed to assist the informal sector should be targeted to informal workers' needs. PVOs should not try to control the informal sector and artificially organize programs and services. Rather, they should encourage the informal workers' initiatives, help them organize and cooperate to defend their interests, formulate their demands more clearly, and promote leaders that can represent their interests before policy-making bodies. Sanderatne cites some interesting examples of reform initiatives that failed in Sri Lanka because they tried to impose economic structures on informal markets without understanding their real needs.

Recommendations for aid agencies. A major purpose of the aid agencies of both developed countries and international organizations is to support and reinforce institutional and policy reforms by developing countries. Rather than repeat the recommendations presented above (that is, by encouraging aid agencies to support the reforms we have suggested for the governments of developing countries and for PVOs), we would like to put our conclusion for aid agencies in the form of a question. In their commitment to encouraging development, what higher calling could aid agencies have than to encourage institutions and governments to promote the self-governance of poor and disadvantaged groups? Since economic and political independence may be considered the ultimate object of development, there can be no higher calling than this.

As we have already argued, we think that PVOs have a special and important role to play in regard to encouraging self-governance for the informal sector, and aid agencies can play an important role in assisting the PVOs. In addition to recommendations already mentioned, aid agencies could promote self-governance by aiding PVOs that help the poor by measuring their success not only in terms of the number of poor people served, but also especially by the numbers who achieve independence and no longer need aid.

In many developing countries there are very few PVOs. The state is all-present and (often) all-powerful, and even prevents the development of PVOs. Aid agencies should encourage the creation of PVOs throughout the developing world, because if they are organized in the right way, PVOs can augment the state's resources in working for economic and social development. One way they can do this is by intervening at the local level to that end. PVOs can do things that aid agencies cannot do because they can operate closer to the people and especially the poor than the state can, thus better responding to their needs.

We must also mention the value of reducing the bureaucratic maze that characterizes many aid programs. Informal firms have difficulty complying not only with government lending programs for small business but also with the requirements of aid agencies and PVOs. We hope especially that the review and finance procedures for project proposals might be streamlined, since local PVOs often lack qualified permanent staff who can comply with the complex administrative procedures that aid agencies frequently require.

A final series of issues concerns unanswered questions about the informal sector. The aid agencies have assumed important leadership roles in encouraging and supporting studies of the sector, and we hope they will continue and maintain their leadership in this area. We especially hope they will continue to sponsor studies that try to answer important questions that remain about the informal sector and to sponsor studies in new regions. The most obvious regions of interest are Central and Eastern Europe and Africa, where the need for economic and political reform is great, where the informal sector is large, and where the role of aid agencies in the reform process is potentially extensive.

Future Subjects of Study

Among the most important questions for future study are those related to the costs of formality and the opportunities to reduce them, thus encouraging people to become formal. One question, for instance, concerns the costs of staying in business for formal enterprises once they are registered. The ILD has estimated that in Peru about 40 percent of administrative time in small formal businesses is devoted to dealing with paperwork required by the government. We would like to know what this level is in other countries and to what extent it is a cause of informality.

The question of how *general* costs of formality influence the decision to remain informal is rather straightforward, and much of the recent discussion of the informal sector has focused on it: how much does it cost to register a business, how much does it cost to get title to undeveloped land, and how long does it take, and so on. Our sense from the chapters in this book, however, is that the greatest causes of informality are not related to these problems of general cost. The cases cited in this volume involve regulations for *specific* sectors: regulations on the number of truck licenses, regulations on the kinds of public transportation that are allowed, and so on. These chapters give illustrations of this problem. It is difficult to imagine how many areas of economic and social life are dominated by regulations of this kind throughout the developing world.

It is likely that in most places where public regulations can be found, informal entrepreneurs are operating outside the law, avoiding them. The problem of regulation avoidance as a motive for informality raises a dilemma for governments trying to balance two conflicting policy values. On the one hand, governments have important and legitimate responsibilities for public health and welfare, which means imposing costs on workers and firms. On the other hand, they should not want to impose regulations so strict that they push both businesses and the public to ignore them and to do business underground. If regulation drives a lot of businesses underground, effective regulation is not only lost; many businesses have also left the formal sector, with all other consequences attaching to that, both for the businesses and for the society at large. One of the most serious consequences for the society is the general decline of respect for law and public authority.

Where should a government draw the line and how? Putting the question more generally: how much regulation genuinely serves the public interest in its broadest sense? How much, to put the question more provocatively, is just an excuse to protect monopolists and avoid competition?

Our bias on this issue is that governments should keep their interventions to a minimum and therefore keep the costs of formality as low as possible. It is certainly true, however, that the task of drawing a precise line is a complicated technical and political one that almost certainly should (and will) depend on the level of a country's development. If poor countries try to impose on their people environmental and health standards like those in rich countries, they will encourage avoidance and informality and will in the process retard economic and social progress. They will also postpone the time when they could establish and maintain higher standards. We think that a great deal more work should be done on this issue.

We are also interested in other issues that go beyond the informal sector (at least defined in terms of legality), but that do affect most informal businesses. For instance, what costs have the strategies of encouraging large firms and import substitution imposed on informal sector participants and the poor? These costs include everything from the increased costs of buying high-priced domestic inputs (such as tires) to blatant discrimination against small firms in favor of large ones (through, for example, credit subsidies), to more indirect costs associated with the myriad other distortions commonly found in developing country policies.

What have been the results for small and informal businesses of the general developing country practice of subsidizing large enterprises at the expense of small ones? Although a great deal of work has been done on these issues from a macroeconomic viewpoint, we think it would be valuable to know about its effect on the informal sector. The few references to this problem in the chapters of this book suggest that the effect is substantial, but it would be useful to know more as informal workers and firms gain a more self-conscious understanding of their own interests.

Other issues with important implications for the informal sector include the broad subject of transaction costs and their impact on informal firms and workers. Lee and Alexandra Benham have undertaken some studies of the costs in time and money of specific transactions, such as getting a telephone, buying spare parts, obtaining credit, and other such activities (Benham and Benham 1991). Their studies measure, that is, the "friction" in exchange in different countries. For example, they have studied the costs of getting a distributor cap for a Caterpillar tractor, which is crucial to operate the tractor. In St. Louis, where they live, this cap can be obtained in one hour for US$2,000. In Lima, Peru, the same distributor cap costs US$10,000 and takes forty-seven weeks to get. The reason for the enormous cost difference lies almost entirely in Peru's policies, which raise the cost of imports. To get a telephone (to give another example) costs about US$85 in St. Louis and takes about two and a half days. Sanderatne notes that in Sri Lanka new phones cost about US$25, but installation can take two to three years. Even paying US$500 for a "priority" installation does not guarantee quick service. The same is true in most developing countries. In Bangladesh there are more than 100,000 names on a waiting list for phones; the government has announced they will issue no new phones for ten years until they have converted the phone system to fiber optics. To get a phone immediately requires enormous pull and costs tens of thousands of dollars. People there get phones by buying houses that happen to have them.

The pattern of policies that influences these transaction costs is determined by political forces in each country. We would like to know how these policies and costs affect the informal sector and small firms compared with large enterprises. We suspect that policy-influenced transaction costs are heavily weighted to benefit large firms at the expense of small ones. Again, it would be valuable to understand the specific effects, as informal workers gain a more self-conscious understanding of their own interests.

Beyond all of these questions about cost, we must also repeat our interest in Sanderatne's comment that formality does not make sense for many in the informal sector. While he acknowledges that reducing the costs of formality would encourage informals to become formal, he raises an interesting and important question about the value of the *benefit* side of formality. He believes that almost no matter how low the costs of formality fall, the benefits of formality would still not be sufficient to encourage many in the informal sector to go formal. The reason, he argues, is that formality is a benefit only to a certain size of operation, and until a firm decides it wants to grow to that size it will remain informal.

This point seems persuasive to us, at least in the abstract. The point is ultimately a philosophical one, having to do with what motivates people to make the transition from traditional to modern styles of work and life. We believe, however, that it would be impossible to be confident about it until a society had removed all unreasonable costs that now discourage people from formality. Moreover, our intuition is that really open economic and political systems would encourage many more to choose the expansion and growth that formality would make possible than would choose to remain in a static, traditional condition. His point is interesting, and it would be valuable to know more about it in order to understand the limits of the overall approach argued in these pages.

It is important for us to say in closing that we have no illusion that the reforms we have recommended, encouraging informal workers and firms to join the formal sector, will provide a miracle cure for the economic and social challenge of development. Although we do think these reforms will encourage economic progress, especially for lower income groups, in the best of circumstances development will continue to be a long, hard process, which will ultimately depend on working, saving, and investing—as it has always.

In many ways the political implications of this analysis may be the most important. Bringing informal workers into the formal economy would not only encourage political conditions that are conducive to good economic policy, but also strengthen the legitimacy and authority of many governments. As this book is going to press, these issues are looming larger than at any time in memory. This is true for the countries trying to rebuild after the Gulf War and also for the countries in Central and Eastern Europe, including the Soviet Union, trying to accomplish economic and political transformations to market economies and democratic pluralist systems. We believe that the informal sector holds an important key to solving the problem of legitimacy facing many countries.

The challenge for developing countries is ultimately to stop their policies of discrimination, which are perpetuating the dual economic and social structure that defines their development dilemma. The challenge is to open their societies and expand opportunities for those in the informal sector, who are some of the most dynamic entrepreneurs in those countries.

In reality, the question is not whether they will expand opportunities, but when. Economic and political participation and self-governance represent the highest aspirations of development. Real development cannot happen without them.

Appendix

Morocco: Selected Social and Economic Statistics, 1988

Area	711,000 square kilometers
Irrigated or arable land	12%
Population	
Total	24 million
Growth rate	2.6%
Under 20 years old	52%
Active (employed and unemployed)	30%
Urban	46%
Major cities (population)	
Casablanca	2.2 million
Rabat/Sale	1.1 million
Fes	0.5 million
Marrakech	0.4 million
Meknes	0.3 million
Tangier	0.2 million
Rural population	54%
% of rural employment in agriculture	47%
Farm animal population	16 to 17 million (60% sheep)
Literacy	28%
Religion	97% Moslem
Natural resources	Phosphates, lead, manganese
Exchange rate (dirham per US$1)	8
GDP	DH 176 billion (US$22 billion)
GNP per capita	DH 7,693 (US$950)
GDP growth rate	3.6%
Structure of GDP	
Agriculture	18%
Industry	17%
Commerce	20%
Services	12%
Government	10%
Exports	22%
Balance of payments (before debt repayment)	
Exports	DH 29.75 billion (US$3.7 billion)
Imports	DH 39.13 billion (US$4.9 billion)
Trade balance	–DH 9.38 billion (–US$1.2 billion)

(table continues)

(continued)

Net transfer	DH 7.7 billion (US$1.0 billion)
Remittances	DH 11.68 billion (US$1.5 billion)
Debt service/exports	46%
Tourism as export	DH 9.1 billion (US$1.1 billion)

Major exports

Phosphoric acid, phosphate, fertilizers, garments, crustaceans and mollusks, citrus fruit, hosiery, fish, preserved and canned vegetables, carpets and rugs, paper pulp, shoes and leather goods, fresh tomatoes

Share of export value of
Phosphates and minerals	40%
Agriculture	28%

Major imports

Petroleum products, sulfur, other chemicals, machinery and appliances, wheat, wood, plastic materials, iron and steel, commercial vehicles, ships and boats, paper and paper board, consumable vegetable oils, textile machinery, cotton fabric

Share of import value of
Crude oil	12%
Sulfur and chemicals	12%

Major trading partners
Exports
France	26%
India	9%
Spain	7%
Germany	6%
Italy	6%
Japan	5%
Belgium	4%

Imports
France	22%
Spain	8%
Germany	7%
United States	7%
Italy	6%
Canada	5%
Iraq	5%

SOURCE: Direction de la Statistique, Ministère du Plan, Rabat; World Bank, *World Development Report 1990.*

Philippines: Selected Social and Economic Statistics, 1988

Area	300,000 square kilometers
Arable land	34%
Population	
Total	60.5 million
Growth rate[a]	2.3%
Under 14 years old	40.3%
Active (employed and unemployed)	40.3%
Unemployment rate	8.6%
Labor force participation rate	
(15 years old or over)	64.5%
Urban	41%
Major cities (population estimates)[b]	
Metro Manila (4 cities, 13 towns)	7.8 million
Manila	2.2 million
Quezon City	1.5 million
Kalookan	0.6 million
Davao City	0.8 million
Cebu	0.6 million
Rural population	59%
% of rural employment in	
agriculture	63.4%
Farm animal population (1986)	1.7 million cattle, 7.2 million pigs
Literacy[c]	86%
Religion	83% Roman Catholic, 9% Protestant, 5% Moslem
Natural resources	Gold, copper, nickel, forests, fisheries
Exchange rate (pesos per US$1)	20.5
GDP	US$39.2 billion
GNP per capita	US$630
GDP growth rate	
1980–1985	–0.6% per year
1985–1988	4.1% per year
1980–1988	1.1% per year
Structure of GDP	
Agriculture	27%
Industry	33%
Manufacturing	25%
Services, etc.	40%
Balance of payments	
Exports	US$7.1 billion

(table continues)

(continued)

Imports	US$8.2 billion
Current account balance	–US$694 million
Net workers' remittances	US$388 million
Total long-term debt service/	
exports	27.7%
Tourism as export[d]	US$647 million receipts

Major exports — Electric and electronic equipment, garments, coconut products, mineral products (copper, gold, chromite), forest products (lumber, plywood, logs)

Share of export value of	
Electric and electronic equipment	20.9%
Garments	18.6%
Coconut products	8.2%

Major imports — Raw materials (mineral fuels, textiles, chemicals, etc.), machinery and equipment, nondurable consumer goods

Share of import value of	
Raw materials	82.8%
Semiprocessed	65.8%
Unprocessed	17.0%
Machinery and equipment	10.3%

Major trading partners	
Exports[d]	
United States	35%
Japan	17%
Imports[e]	
United States	25%
Japan	16%

a. Average annual rate for 1980–1988.
b. 1990.
c. 1985.
d. 1986.
e. 1987.
SOURCE: World Bank, *World Development Report 1990;* National Statistics Office (NSO), *Population and Housing Census,* preliminary results, August 1990; NSO, *Integrated Survey of Households, January 1990,* preliminary; National Economic and Development Authority, *Philippine Statistical Yearbook 1987;* Asian Development Bank, *Key Indicators of Developing Asian and Pacific Countries, 1990;* National Economic and Development Authority, *Philippine Statistical Yearbook 1989.*

Sri Lanka: Selected Social and Economic Statistics, 1988

Area	65,608 square kilometers
Arable land	33%
Population	
Total	16.6 million
Growth rate	1.4%
Under 14 years old	35%
Urban	21%
Major city (population)[a]	
Colombo	0.7 million
Rural population	79%
% of rural employment in	
agriculture[b]	57%
Farm animal population[a]	1.8 million cattle, 0.97 million buffaloes, 8.83 million poultry
Literacy[c]	87%
Religion[b]	69% Buddhist, 15% Hindu, 8% Christian, 8% Moslem
Natural resources	Graphite, limestone, precious and semi-precious stones, phosphate, forests, rubber, illmenite, rutile
Exchange rate (rupees per US$1)	31.80
GDP	US$6.4 billion
GNP per capita	US$375
GDP growth rate	2.7%
Structure of GDP	
Agriculture	26%
Industry	26%
Manufacturing	12%
Services, etc.	48%
Balance of payments (1990)	
Exports	US$1.98 billion
Imports	US$2.68 billion
Current account balance	–US$240 million
Net workers' remittances	US$540 million
Total long-term debt service/	
exports	16.5%
Tourism as export	US$120 million
Major exports	Tea, textiles and garments, industrial exports, rubber, coconut, minor crops, minerals, petroleum re-exports

(table continues)

(continued)

Share of export value of	
Textiles and garments	32%
Tea	25%
Major imports	Petroleum, textiles, machinery, food and drink, transport equipment, fertilizer
Share of import value of	
Petroleum	13.3%
Textiles	10.2%
Major trading partners	
Exports	
United States	25%
Germany	6%
United Kingdom	5%
Japan	5%
Imports	
Japan	12%
United States	8%
Iran	8%
Taiwan	6%
South Korea	5%
United Kingdom	5%

a. 1989.
b. 1981.
c. 1985.
SOURCE: Central Bank of Sri Lanka, *Annual Report 1988, Economic and Social Statistics of Sri Lanka 1988-89*, and *Sri Lanka Socio-Economic Data 1990*; Department of Census and Statistics, *Statistical Pocket Book of the Democratic Socialist Republic of Sri Lanka*, 1988.

Thailand: Selected Social and Economic Statistics, 1988

Area	513,000 square kilometers
Arable land	46.9%
Population	
Total	54.9 million
Growth rate[a]	1.95%
Under 14 years old	34.6%
Active (11 years and older)	74.78%
Urban	18.10%
Major city	
Bangkok	5.72 million
Rural population	81.9%
% of rural employment in agriculture	78.0%
Farm animal population	89.8 million chickens, 9.1 million cattle, 5.7 million pigs
Literacy[b]	91.93%
Religion	93.3% Buddhist, 5.5% Moslem, 0.8% Christian
Natural resources	Limestone, tin, lignite, gypsum, iron, lead, manganese
Exchange rate (baht per US$1)	25.35
GDP	US$59.4 billion
GNP per capita	US$1,072.5
Real GDP growth rate (at 1972 prices)	10.7%
Structure of GDP	
Agriculture	16.61%
Industry	33.56%
Manufacturing	24.77%
Services, etc.	49.78%
Balance of payments	
Exports (FOB)	US$15.7 billion
Imports (CIF)	US$19.8 billion
Current account balance	−US$1.6 billion
Public long-term debt service/ exports	10.6%

(table continues)

(continued)

Tourism as export	US$3.1 billion receipts
Major exports	Textile products, rice, rubber, tapioca products, integrated circuits

Share of export value of
Textile products	14.5%
Rice	8.6%
Rubber	6.7%

Major imports	Machinery and parts, crude oil, steel and iron, chemicals

Share of import value of
Nonelectrical machinery and parts	17.7%
Electrical machinery and parts	10.6%
Chemicals	9.5%

Major trading partners
Exports
United States	20.03%
Japan	15.96%
Singapore	7.68%

Imports
Japan	29.08%
United States	13.56%

a. Average annual rate for 1980–1989.
b. 1985.
SOURCE: National Statistical Office, *Statistical Yearbook of Thailand,* 1980 and 1989, *Report of the Labor Force Survey,* August 1988, *Report of the Literacy Survey,* 1985; Department of Livestock, *Data on Economics of Livestock,* 1990; Institute of Population and Social Research, *Population and Development Newsletter* 9 and 11, 1988 and 1989; Office of the Secretariat, Ministry of Education, *Summary of Education Statistics 1985,* National Economic and Social Development Board, *National Income 1989,* Bank of Thailand, *Monthly Income Report,* June 1990.

Bangladesh: Selected Social and Economic Statistics, 1988

Area	144,000 square kilometers
Arable land	63%
Population	
Total	108.9 million
Growth rate[a]	2.8%
Under 14 years old	44.7%
Urban	13%
Major cities (population estimates)[b]	
Dhaka	3.4 million
Chittagong	1.4 million
Khulna	0.6 million
Rural population	87%
% of rural population in agriculture	18%
Farm animal population[c]	23 million cattle, 10.7 million goats
Literacy	23%
Religion	83% Moslem, 16% Hindu
Natural resources	Natural gas, offshore oil, coal
Exchange rate (takas per US$1)	35.9
GDP	US$19.3 billion
GNP per capita	US$170
GDP growth rate[a]	3.7%
Structure of GDP	
Agriculture	38.7%
Industry	14.4%
Manufacturing	8.5%
Services, etc.	38.4%
Balance of payments	
Exports	US$1.2 billion
Imports	US$3.0 billion
Current account balance	–US$1.1 billion
Net workers' remittances	US$737 million
Total long-term debt service/ exports	20.5%
Tourism as export[c]	US$14.6 million receipts
Major exports	Jute, tea, hides and skins, newsprint, garments

(table continues)

(continued)

Major imports	Machinery, fuel, wheat
Major trading partners	
Exports	
United States	30%
Italy	9%
United Kingdom	6%
Imports	
Japan	11%
United States	9%

a. Annual average rate for 1980–1988.
b. 1987.
c. 1986.
SOURCE: Bangladesh Bureau of Statistics; World Bank, *World Development Report 1990; World Almanac 1990.*

Notes and References

Chapter 1   A. Lawrence Chickering and Mohamed Salahdine, "Introduction"

References

Charmes, Jacques. 1982. "The Contradictions of Non-Structured Sector Development." *Third World Review* 21: 321–35.

———. 1986. "The Non-Structured Sector." *AMIRA* (Amélioration des méthodes d'investigation et de recherche appliquées au développement), no. 37.

de Soto, Hernando. 1989. *The Other Path.* New York: Harper and Row.

Hugon, Philippe, and Isabelle Deblé. 1985. *To Live and Survive in the African Cities.* Paris: Presses Universitaires de France (PUF).

Morice, A. 1983. "The Bicycles of Koalack." *African Studies Books* (Paris) 1–3: 197–210.

Sethuraman, S. V. 1976. "The Non-Structured Urban Sector: Concept, Measure and Action." *International Review of Labor* 1140, no. 1 (July–August).

Vekemans, Roger, and Silva F. Ismael. 1969. "El Concepto de Marginalidad." In *Marginalidad en América Latina*, Desal. Barcelona: Editorial Herder.

Vekemans, Roger, Jorge Giusti, and Silva Ismael. 1970. *Marginalidad, Promoción Popular e Integración Latinoamericana.* Santiago: DESAL.

Webb, R. 1975. "Ingreso y Empleo en el Sector Tradicional Urbano del Perú." In *América Latin: Distribución Espacial de la Población*, ed. Ramiro Cardona, 257–87. Bogotá: Corp. Centro Regional de la Población.

Chapter 2   Mohamed Salahdine, "The Informal Sector in
Morocco: The Failure of Legal Systems?"

Notes

1. These were the principal concerns of officials from the Ministries of
Planning and Economic Affairs during the last meetings of the Ministry of Planning in March 1990.

2. To measure the contribution of the informal sector to employment,
the ministry conducted a comparative analysis of population censuses and
the statistics on economic establishments drawn from the Office of Taxation
tax records. It includes in the informal sector (1) the employers and employees
in establishments of fewer than ten persons and (2) all people who are
classified, in terms of professional status, as independent workers, as family
employees, or as apprentices, as well as those who belong to other poorly
defined categories.

References

Ministry of Planning. Department of Statistics. 1980–1989. *Employment Surveys
in Urban Areas*. Rabat.
Salahdine, Mohamed. 1985. "La Signification du concept et les approches
méthodologiques." *Lamalif* (February).
———. 1988a. *Les Petits métiers clandestins au Maroc ou le business populaire*.
Casablanca: Eddif Maroc.
———. 1988b. "Combien y a-t-il de chômeurs au Maroc?" *La Vie économique*
(December).

Chapter 3   Ruperto P. Alonzo, "The Informal Sector in the
Philippines"

Notes

1. The *barangay* or village is the smallest unit of local government, with
a population of about 150 to 200 households. The village residents elect the
barangay council, and the councilman receiving the highest number of votes
serves as chairman.

2. A garment factory owner we interviewed donated 500 pesos (US$25)
to the *barangay* when she established her business in 1988. She had eight sewing
machines at that time.

References

Alonzo, Ruperto P. 1980. "The Informal Transport Sector in the Greater Manila
Area." *Philippine Review of Economics and Business* 17, nos. 1 and 2.
———. 1981. "Towards a Fair and Just Maximum 'Boundary' Rate for the
Jeepney Industry." Paper submitted to the Institute for Labor and Manpower Studies, Ministry of Labor and Employment, Philippines.

Alonzo, Ruperto P., and Maria Alcestis Abrera-Mangahas. 1990. *The Informal Sector in Metro Manila: Findings from a Recent Survey.* Geneva: International Labor Organization.

Arboleda, Heidi. 1989. "Measurement of the Informal Sector." Paper presented at the Fifth National Convention on Statistics, held in Quezon City, Philippines.

Asian Development Bank (ADB). 1988. "Road and Road Transport Sector Issues in the Philippines." Background paper submitted to the government of the Philippines for discussions on a proposed road and road transport program loan.

Bautista, Romeo M. 1973. "Employment and Labor Productivity in Small-Scale Manufacturing in the Philippines." *NEDA Journal of Development* 1, no. 1.

Biggs, Tyler, et al. 1987. "Small Business Policy Direction Study: The Philippines." Monograph submitted to the Ministry of Trade and Industry, Philippines, and USAID. Cambridge: Harvard Institute for International Development.

de Soto, Hernando. 1989. *The Other Path: The Invisible Revolution in the Third World.* New York: McGraw-Hill.

Guevara, Milwida. 1990. "Fiscal Policy for the Development of Small Enterprises: An Assessment and Proposals for Policy Directions." Paper submitted to the Congressional Economic Planning Staff, Congress of the Philippines.

International Labor Organization (ILO). 1974. *Sharing in Development: A Programme of Employment, Equity and Growth for the Philippines.* Geneva: ILO.

Licayan, Liza R., and Jennifer M. Sagun. 1984. "Tenure Security and the Value of Housing." Undergraduate paper, University of the Philippines, Quezon City.

Manasan, Rosario G. 1990. "An Assessment of Fiscal Policy in the Philippines, 1986–1988." PIDS Working Paper Series No. 90-06. Makati: Philippine Institute for Development Studies (PIDS).

National Statistics Office (NSO). 1983. *Integrated Survey of Households.* Manila: NSO.

———. 1983. *Census of Establishments.* Manila: NSO.

Santos, Maria Imelda, and Jonathan Serrano. 1990. "The Informal Sector: Focus on Four Vending Areas." Undergraduate paper, University of the Philippines, Quezon City.

Suarez, Ruby Lynn N., and Elsa Agustin. 1989. "Factors Affecting the Underground Economy in the Philippines." Paper submitted to the University of the Philippines School of Economics, Program in Development Economics.

Tanzi, Vito. 1982. *The Underground Economy in the United States and Abroad.* Lexington, Mass.: D.C. Heath and Co.

Tecson, Gwendolyn, Lina Valcarcel, and Carol Nuñez. 1989. *The Role of Small- and Medium-Scale Enterprises in the Industrial Development of DMCs: The Philippine Country Study.* Manila: Asian Development Bank.

Zamora, Elvira A. 1990. "Direct Regulatory Control Policies and Their Role in Small Enterprise Development: Analysis and Recommendations." Paper submitted to the Congressional Economic Planning Staff, Congress of the Philippines.

Chapter 4   Nimal Sanderatne, "The Informal Sector in Sri Lanka:
Dynamism and Resilience"

Notes

1. The problem discussed here could be formulated more precisely
as follows:

$$\text{GDP} = Y_f + Y_i + Y_0$$

where

Y_f = output in formal sector already included in GDP estimates

Y_i = output in informal sector already included in GDP estimates

Y_0 = output of informal sector not included in GDP

Since only Y_f and Y_i are included in GDP, the actual contribution of the
informal sector is

$$\frac{Y_i + Y_0}{Y_f + Y_i + Y_0}$$

2. For a discussion of this scheme, see Sanderatne (1989a).

References

Centre for Women's Research Sri Lanka. 1989. *Sub-Contracting in Industry:
Impact on Women.* Colombo: Centre for Women's Research Sri Lanka.

International Labor Organization/ARTEP. 1986. *The Impact of Economic Laborali-
zation on the Small-Scale and Rural Industries of Sri Lanka.* New Delhi:
ILO/ARTEP, May.

Kahagalle, S., and Nimal Sanderatne. 1977. "The Role and Performance of
Cooperative Rural Banks in Sri Lanka, 1964–1967." Central Bank of
Sri Lanka *Staff Studies* 7, no. 2 (September): 1–44.

Marga Institute. 1979. *The Informal Sector of Colombo City.* Marga Research
Studies no. 7. Colombo: Marga Institute.

Sanderatne, Nimal. 1988. "Cooperative Rural Banks: A Success Story?"
Economic Review 14, nos. 8, 9 (November, December).

———. 1989a. "Informal Lenders in Sri Lanka: Linking Formal and Informal
Markets." Paper presented to the Seminar on Informal Financial Markets
in Development, October 18–20, Washington, D.C.

———. 1989b. "The Nature of the Rural Informal Credit Market in
Sri Lanka." *Marga* 10, no. 4: 26–47.

Sri Lanka. Department of Census and Statistics. 1983. *Survey of Manufacturing
Industries.* Colombo: Department of Census and Statistics.

World Bank. 1978. *Sri Lanka: Plans and Policies for Industrial Development.*
Washington, D.C.: World Bank.

Chapter 5   Nipon Poapongsakorn, "The Informal Sector in Thailand"

Notes

1. Although there was a military coup on February 23, 1991, the military-backed civilian government has adopted the deregulation policy of the previous elected government.

2. Examples of ethnographic studies of the informal economy include work by Teilhet-Waldorf and Waldorf (1983) and a study of the informal moneylenders by Chirmsak and Prayong (1988).

3. The study by Larsson found that more than half of workers were female (see Table 5.1).

4. The owners of motorcycle routes do not have to own the motorcycles. But they own the uniforms (or jackets) that are required in order to operate a motorcycle on the route.

5. The underground economy includes all illegal activities such as narcotics, prostitution, and smuggling, and also nonmarket activities, such as housework.

6. Hawkers and vendors often must pay bribes to the police, since they illegally occupy public places.

7. This assumes that 7.0 million passengers used formal public transport, and that there were 10,000 *silorleks*, which took 130–180 passengers each per day, and 20,000 motorcycles, which provided service for 60–80 passengers each per day.

8. Between 1970 and 1986, Bangkok's population growth rate was 4.4 percent per year, compared with 3.9 percent for all urban areas (NESDB 1986).

9. The fare of *silorleks* and *samlors* is usually fixed at two baht for the whole route, a distance of about one to four kilometers. The motorcycle fare will increase from three baht for the first kilometer to five baht for the next kilometer, seven baht for the third, and ten baht for a longer distance within the route.

10. When motorcycle drivers are cited, they give the citation to their leader (or the owner of the route) who, in turn, gives it to the traffic police chief. In general, the drivers have to pay about one-fifth to one-third of the fine (for example, 100 baht for a fine of 500 baht).

11. Every motorcycle operator in Bangkok must wear a vest or jacket with a number on the back. The number allows policemen to identify the operator in case of a traffic violation or accident. It also allows the police chief to keep track of the size of the motorcycle fleet on each route, which, in turn, will determine the price of the approval.

12. The average group size is eighteen motorcycles in the group-owner firms and sixty-one in the single-owner firms. Entrance fees, as measured by the price of a jacket, are 24,000 baht and 12,700 baht, respectively.

13. In a thesis carried out in support of this study, Nuchjarin (1990) found that economic variables are the most significant factors explaining fare-setting behavior. A regression analysis showed that distance is the most important factor positively affecting fares. Fares were also found to be higher if an operator could not pick up passengers from the far end of a route, other things being equal. Presence of competitors and high population density can significantly reduce fares.

14. Gross daily income per driver is about 294 baht. The total annual figure assumes 20,000 drivers who work 300 days per year.

15. About 20.7 percent of route owners' income is paid to the police.

16. This assumes that each driver pays nine baht per day for the *win* fee and that there are twenty-five working days per month.

17. The courts will not enforce a loan contract with an interest rate higher than 1.25 percent per month. But informal lenders are smart enough to write contracts in such a way that the principal to be repaid includes the annual interest payment.

18. The system of paying bribes to government officials is not considered immoral in the Thai context. Historically, government officials were not paid by the king. Instead, the king would allow his officials to collect money from the people.

19. The price effect of tariff protection is the overvaluation of the currency.

20. Other policies include: (1) subsidized credit provided by the Industrial Finance Corporation of Thailand (IFCT) to manufacturers and (2) subsidized credit provided by the Small Industry Finance Organization (SIFO) to small-scale industries.

21. Currency overvaluation is the result of a mixture of three measures: (1) pegging of the baht to the U.S. dollar, which appreciated against other major currencies during 1981–1984, (2) tariff protection, and (3) export taxes on agricultural products.

22. It is estimated that in 1986 about 31 percent of all loans to small-scale firms were provided by commercial banks.

23. One rai is equivalent to 0.16 hectare or 0.395 acre.

24. According to the constitution, all of the laws that deal with tax and budget must be endorsed by the prime minister.

25. The SIFO has not been designated a financial institution, and it therefore lacks a branch network, which limits its ability to reach small borrowers.

References

Ammar Siamwalla. 1987. "Thai Rural Credit System: Some Empirical Findings and a Theoretical Framework." Paper presented at the Expert Meeting on Resource Mobilization in the Informal Sector, East-West Center, Honolulu, Hi., June.

Bhalla, A. S. 1973. "Self-Employment in Less Developed Countries: Some Aspects of Theory and Policy." In *Employment Creation in Developing Societies: The Situation of Labor in Dependent Economies*, ed. Karl Wohlmuth. New York: Praeger.

Bawornsak Uwanno. 1989. "Crisis of the Outdated Thai Law" (in Thai). *The Journal of Chulalongkorn* 68 (April–June): 68–78.

Bromley, Ray. 1978. "Introduction—The Urban Informal Sector: Why Is It Worth Discussing?" *World Development* 6, no. 9/10: 1033–39.

Center for International Private Enterprise. 1989. *Informal Sector Newsletter* (August). Washington, D.C.

Chalongphob Sussangkarn. 1987. "The Thai Labour Market." Paper presented at conference on Thai Studies, Australian National University, Canberra, July 3–6.

Chirmsak Pintong and Prayong Netayarak. 1988. *Portrait of the Lender* (in Thai). A research project on the rural credit market in Thailand. Bangkok: Thailand Development Research Institute and Thammasat University.

Chulacheep Chinwanno and Somsak Tambunlertchai. 1988. "Japanese Investment in Thailand and Its Prospects in the 1980s." In *ASEAN-Japan Relations: Investment*, ed. Sueo Sekigushi. Singapore: Institute of Southern Asian Studies.

Department of Commercial Registration. 1982. *Handbook of Registered Partnerships and Limited Companies* (in Thai). Bangkok.

Department of Labor. 1988. *Labor Statistics* (in Thai). Bangkok.

Department of Land Transport. 1982–1989. *Statistics Worksheet* (in Thai). Bangkok.

de Soto, Hernando. 1989. *The Other Path: The Invisible Revolution in the Third World*. New York: Harper and Row.

Duangmanee Wongprateep and Suchada Traikoon. 1985. *The Informal Financial Market at the Macro Level* (in Thai). A research report prepared for the Informal Financial Market Project, Bank of Thailand, Bangkok.

El-Shaks, Saral. 1984. "On City Size and the Contribution of the Informal Sector: Some Hypotheses and Research Questions." *Regional Development Dialogue* 5 (Autumn): 77–81.

International Labor Organization (ILO). 1972. *Employment, Incomes and Equality: A Strategy for Increasing Productive Employment in Kenya*. Geneva.

International Labor Organization (ILO) Asian Employment Program. 1988. *Urban Self-Employment in Thailand*. A report prepared for the National Economic and Social Development Board, Thailand. Geneva.

Krittaya Achavanijkun, Napaporn Havanon, and Sivaporn Pokpong. 1981. *46 Slums* (in Thai). Bangkok: Institute for Population and Social Research, Mahidol University.

Kunda, Amitabh, and P. N. Mathur. 1984. "Informal Sector in Cities of Different Sizes: An Explanation within the Core Theoretic Framework." *Regional Development Dialogue* 5 (Autumn): 82–85.

Kuroda, Akira, and Shuji Kasajima. 1987. *Development Strategies for Small and Medium Scale Industries in Thailand*. Bangkok: Ministry of Industry, Small/Medium Industry Promotion and Finance Project.

Larsson, Jan E. 1980. *Skill Acquisition by the Self-Employed: A Case Study of Small-Scale Entrepreneurs in Bangkok*. Islamabad: Asian Skill Development Program.

Main, Jeremy. 1989. "How to Make Poor Countries Rich." *Fortune* (January): 101–2, 106.

Malee Suwana-adth. 1989. *Women and Small-Scale Enterprise Development in Asia: The Thailand Experience*. A paper presented at a seminar on the Asian informal sector. Bangkok: SVITA Foundation.

"Hia Kuang Computer Shop." *The Manager* 7 (March 1990): 62.

Manop Pratoomtong. 1988. *Breath of Bangkok* (in Thai). Bangkok: Institute of Social Development, Chulalongkorn University.

Mathur, Om Prakash, and Caroline O. N. Moser. 1984. "The Urban Informal Sector: An Agenda for Future Research." *Regional Development Dialogue* 5 (Autumn): 9–21.

Methvin, Eugene H. 1989. "Crusader for Peru's Have-Nots." *Reader's Digest* (January): 37–40.

Metropolitan Police Bureau. 1988. *The Role of Hired Motorcycles in Urban Areas and the Control and Supervision of the Royal Thai Police Department.* A seminar organized by Economic and Social Cooperation in Asia and the Pacific (ESCAP) in cooperation with the Bangkok Metropolitan Administration. Unpublished.

Mingione, Enzo. 1984. "The Informal Sector and the Development of Third World Cities." *Regional Development Dialogue* 5 (Autumn): 63–76.

Morell, Susan. 1972. *Six Plans in Bangkok.* A report prepared for the United Nations Children's Fund. Bangkok: UNICEF.

Moser, Caroline O. N. 1984. "The Informal Sector Reworked: Viability and Vulnerability in Urban Development." *Regional Development Dialogue* 5 (Autumn): 135–83.

Nat Tapasanan. 1985. *An Individual Share (Mutual Finance)* (in Thai). A research report prepared for the Informal Financial Market Project, Bank of Thailand, Bangkok.

National Economic and Social Development Board (NESDB). 1986. *Proposals on Development of Bangkok and Surroundings: The Guidelines of Major Development and Investment Plans* (in Thai). In the Sixth National Economic and Social Development Plan (1987–1991), Planning and Development of Bangkok Project. Bangkok.

––––––. 1988. "Report of the National Seminar on the Urban Informal Sector in Thailand." Report to a seminar organized by the Human Resource Planning Division, NESDB, and the ILO.

National Statistical Office (NSO). 1971–1987. *Report of the Labour Force Survey.* Round 2: 1971–1985, Round 3: 1986–1987. Bangkok.

Nattrass, Nicoli Jean. 1987. "Street Trading in Transkei: A Struggle against Poverty, Persecution, and Prosecution." *World Development* 15, no. 7: 861–75.

Nipon Poapongsakorn. 1987. *Informal Credit Market in Thailand: A Case Study of Contracts, Market Structures, Behavior, and Interest Rates* (in Thai). Bangkok: Thailand Development Research Institute and Thammasat University.

––––––. 1990. "Labour Law: Role and Economic Impacts (in Thai)." A paper presented at the Annual Symposium on Law and Economics. Faculty of Economics, Thammasat University, Bangkok, February 14–15.

Nipon Poapongsakorn and Prayong Nettayarak. 1989. "Regional Variations in Rural Interest Rates." A research report submitted to the Asian Development Bank and the Thailand Development Research Institute.

Nuchjarin Kasemsukworarat. 1990. "The Economic Analysis of Hired Motorcycle Service in Bangkok." M.A. thesis, Thammasat University.

Pasuk Phongpaijit and Pradith Charsombat. 1988. "Report of the National Seminar on Urban Self-Employment in Thailand." Bangkok: National Economic and Social Development Board and the International Labor Organization.

Pawadee Tongudai. 1982. "Wage Migration and Employment: A Study of Migrant Workers in Bangkok." Ph.D. dissertation, New York University.

Prachoom Suwattee. 1980. "Hawkers in Metropolitan Bangkok" (in Thai). Bangkok: School of Applied Statistics, National Institute of Development Administration.

––––––. 1984. "Informal Sector: Concept and Appropriate Policy." A paper presented at a conference on World Structural Change and Its Impact on

ASEAN's Employment and Manpower, sponsored by the Human Resources Department, Thammasat University, Bangkok, Nov. 26–Dec. 2.

Prasarn Trairatvorakoon. 1985. "Some Thoughts on the Rate of Return in the Informal Financial Market" (in Thai). A research report prepared for the Informal Financial Market Project, Bank of Thailand, Bangkok.

Rangsan Thanapornphan. 1989. "The Regulatory Process of Economic Policy in Thailand: A Historical Political Economy Analysis" (in Thai). Bangkok: Faculty of Economics, Thammasat University.

"Soi Bikes." *Thailand Business* (October, 1983): 6–10.

Sompong Padpui. 1984. *Rights of Slum Residents* (in Thai). Bangkok: Thailand Development Research Institute.

Somsak Tambunlertchai and Chesada Loohawenchit. 1980. "Labor-Intensive and Small-Scale Manufacturing Industries in Thailand." A paper presented at a seminar on ASEAN Comparative Study of the Development of Labor-Intensive Industry organized by the International Labor Organization, Chonburi, Thailand, Oct. 20–31.

———. 1983. "Small-Scale Manufacturing Enterprises in Thailand." Bangkok: Thammasat University.

Sopon Pornchokchai. 1985. *1020* (in Thai). Bangkok: School of Urban Community Research and Actions.

Sorayuth Meenaphan and Tanai Suwankanit. 1988. "Underground Economy in Thailand: Size and Significance of Developing Economy" (in Thai). *Thai Journal of Development Administration* 28, no. 1 (January): 1–43.

Subbiah Kannappan. 1984. "Tradition and Modernity in Urban Employment in Developing Nations." *Regional Development Dialogue* 5 (Autumn): 55–62.

Sullivan, John D., ed. 1987. *Building Constituencies for Economic Change*. A report to an international conference on the informal sector. Washington, D.C.: Center for International Private Enterprise.

Surakiat Sathienthai. 1986. "Legal Problems in Exporting" (in Thai). *Chulalongkorn Law Journal* 10 (July/Sept.): 180–97.

Teilhet-Waldorf, Sarah, and William H. Waldorf. 1983. "Earnings of Self-Employed in an Informal Sector: A Case Study of Bangkok." *Economic Development and Cultural Change* 31 (April): 587–607.

Thamrong Pattanarat. 1985. "A Campaign toward Orderly Vending Activities in Bangkok" (in Thai). Unpublished.

Thienchai Keeranan et al. 1982. "Report on the Economic, Social and Population Situation of Bangkok" (in Thai). Bangkok: Chulalongkorn University.

Tokman, Victor E. 1978. "An Exploration into the Nature of Informal-Formal Sector Relationships." *World Development* 6, no. 9/10: 1065–75.

Vargas Llosa, Mario. 1987. "The Silent Revolution." *Journal of Economic Growth* 2, no. 1: 3–7.

Viboon Vongpakdiban. 1976. "Survey of Illegal Small Mini-Buses in Bangkok" (in Thai). *Thailand Transportation Journal* 11 (September): 15–47.

World Bank. 1978. *Thailand: Bangkok Traffic Management Project.* Washington, D.C. Mimeo.

———. 1980. *Thailand: Industrial Development Strategy in Thailand.* Washington, D.C.

———. 1983. *Growth and Employment in Rural Thailand.* Report no. 3906-TH. Washington, D.C.

——. 1984. *Report: Employment, Incomes, Social Protection, New Information Technology*. Washington, D.C.

——. 1986. *Thailand: Growth with Stability—A Challenge for the Sixth Plan Period.* Report no. 6036-TH. Washington, D.C.

——. 1989. *Thailand: Country Memorandum. Building on Recent Success: A Policy Framework.* Report no. 7445-TH. Washington, D.C.

Chapter 6   Muzammel Huq and Maheen Sultan, " 'Informality' in Development: The Poor as Entrepreneurs in Bangladesh"

References

Amin, A. T. M. 1987. "The Role of the Informal Sector in Economic Development." *International Labour Review* 126, no. 5.

Ashe, Jeffrey, and Christopher E. Cosslett. 1989. "Credit for the Poor." United Nations Development Program Policy Discussion Paper. New York: United Nations.

Bangladesh. Bureau of Statistics. 1989. *Statistical Pocket Book of Bangladesh*. Dhaka.

——. Ministry of Industries. 1982. *Report of the Task Force for the Handloom Sector*. Dhaka.

——. 1986. *Industrial Policy*. Dhaka.

——. Ministry of Planning. 1989–1990. *Memorandum for the Bangladesh Aid Group*. Dhaka.

Bangladesh Small and Cottage Industries Corporation (BSCIC). 1988. "Programme of Subcontracting and Ancillary Development in Bangladesh." Dhaka: BSCIC.

Centre for Urban Studies (CUS). 1989. "The Urban Poor in Bangladesh." Dhaka: CUS. Draft.

de Soto, Hernando. 1989. *The Other Path: The Invisible Revolution in the Third World*. New York: Harper and Row.

Economic Impact. 1988. "The Role of Microenterprises in Development." No. 63. Washington, D.C.: U.S. Agency for International Development.

Grameen Bank. 1981–1990. *Annual Reports*. Dhaka: Grameen Bank.

Hossain, Mahabub. 1984. "The Impact of Grameen Bank of Women's Involvement in Productive Activities." Dhaka: Bangladesh Institute of Development Studies. Mimeo.

——. 1988. "Credit for Alleviation of Rural Poverty: The Grameen Bank in Bangladesh." Research Report no. 65. Washington, D.C.: International Food Policy Research Institute.

Huq, Muzammel. 1985. "Grameen Bank: An Innovative Credit Programme for the Poor." Paper presented at Expert Group Meeting on Institutional Innovation, Asia Pacific Development Centre, Kuala Lumpur, Malaysia.

International Labor Organization (ILO). 1988. *Employment and Poverty in Bangladesh: Rural and Urban Informal Sector Programme Formulation Mission—Final Report*. Geneva: ILO.

Kalambu, Faustin T. 1987. "Rickshaws and the Traffic Problems of Dhaka." *Habitat International* 11, no. 2: 123–31.

Mann, Charles K. C., Merilee S. Grindle, and Parker Shipton. 1989. *Seeking Solutions: Framework and Cases for Small Enterprise Development Programs.* A Harvard Institute for International Development Study. Hartford, Conn.: Kumarian Press.

Masum, Muhammad. 1988. "Report of a National Consultant." Report prepared for the International Labor Organization, BGD/79/028. Dhaka: ILO. Mimeo.

———. 1989. "Report of a National Consultant." Report prepared for the ILO. Dhaka: ILO. Mimeo.

Ministry of Industry. 1986. *New Industrial Policy.* Dhaka.

Rahman, Atiq. 1989. "An Overview of the Informal Financial Markets in Bangladesh." Dhaka: Bangladesh Institute of Development Studies. Mimeo.

Streeten, Paul. 1989. "Mobilizing Human Potential: The Challenge of Unemployment." United Nations Development Program Policy Discussion Paper. New York: United Nations.

Yunus, Muhammad. 1982. "Grameen Bank Project in Bangladesh: A Poverty Focused Rural Development Programme." Dhaka: Grameen Bank. Mimeo.

———. 1987a. "Credit for Self-Employment: A Fundamental Human Right." Dhaka: Grameen Bank. Mimeo.

———. 1987b. "The Poor as the Engine of Development." *Washington Quarterly* 10, no. 4.

Chapter 7   A. Lawrence Chickering and Mohamed Salahdine, "The Informal Sector's Search for Self-Governance"

Notes

1. We are grateful to Robert B. Hawkins, Jr., for assisting us with this recommendation.

2. There is a vast foundation of both research and practice, especially in the United States, that can assist governments in developing countries experiment with their own models for these organizations and institutions.

References

Benham, Lee, and Alexandra Benham. 1991. "Transaction Costs and Economic Growth." Working Paper no. 6. San Francisco: International Center for Economic Growth.

Castañeda, Tarsicio. N.d. *Innovative Policies for Reaching the Poor: The Case of Chile.* San Francisco: ICS Press. Forthcoming.

Huq, Muzammel. 1988. "The Grameen Bank Approach in Reducing Poverty." Paper presented at the workshop "New Direction to Eradicate Poverty in Sabah," Kundasang, Indonesia, December 12–14.

Toubar, Samir. 1991. "The Informal Sector in Egypt." Unpublished paper.

Yunus, Muhammad. 1984. *Jorimon of Beltoil Village and Others: In Search of a Future.* Dhaka: Grameen Bank.

About the Contributors

A. Lawrence Chickering is associate director and founder of the International Center for Economic Growth (ICEG) and executive director of the Institute for Contemporary Studies' Project on Economic Growth in the Soviet Union. He has written widely on issues related to economics and politics and was the editor of *The Politics of Planning: A Review and Critique of Centralized Economic Planning* (1976).

Mohamed Salahdine has been a professor of socioeconomy at the University of Fes in Morocco since 1981. He received his doctorate from the University of Paris in 1981. From 1982 to 1989 he directed a research group on labor, training, and small-scale enterprises. Salahdine has been a consultant to the World Bank on female economic activities in agro-industrial production and to the U.S. Agency for International Development on the informal sector. He is the author of three books and numerous articles.

Ruperto P. Alonzo is professor of economics at the School of Economics, University of the Philippines. He served as chairman of the department from 1986 to 1988. In winter and spring 1991 he was a visiting research scholar at the Center for Southeast Asian Studies, Kyoto University. From 1981 to 1990 he was editor of the *Philippine*

Economic Journal. In 1987 he was named Outstanding Young Scientist for Economics by the National Academy of Science and Technology of the Philippines. Alonzo has written many articles on the informal sector, public finance project evaluation, and the economics of human resources.

Muzammel Huq is director of Training and Special Programmes at the Grameen Bank in Bangladesh, where he has worked since 1982. Huq received an M.A. in political science from the University of Dhaka in 1965, a diploma in rural development in South Asia from Michigan State University in 1971, and an M.A. in political science from the University of Michigan in 1972. He taught political science at Gordon College in Pakistan from 1966 to 1970, was a senior research scholar at Oxford University from 1972 to 1977, and was a visiting fellow at the International Peace Research Institute in Oslo, Norway, from 1977 to 1981.

Nipon Poapongsakorn teaches at the Faculty of Economics, Thammasat University, Bangkok. He received his Ph.D. in economics from the University of Hawaii in 1979. He has written extensively on employment, education, and behavior in labor markets. His latest research has been on the structure and functioning of the rural informal credit market and, more recently, on-the-job training in the Thai manufacturing and service sectors. In 1985 Nipon was a research fellow at the Population Institute of the East-West Center. He has served as a consultant to the World Bank and the Asian Development Bank.

Nimal Sanderatne is senior research fellow at the Institute of Policy Studies in Colombo, Sri Lanka. He was formerly chairman of Sri Lanka's largest commercial bank, the Bank of Ceylon; chairman of the Merchant Bank of Sri Lanka; and director of several companies and government organizations. He has also served the Central Bank of Sri Lanka as director of economic research and director of statistics. Sanderatne holds a Ph.D. in development studies and an M.A. in political science from the University of Wisconsin, an M.Sc. in agricultural economics from the University of Saskatchewan, and a B. Sc. in economics from the University of London.

Maheen Sultan received a *licence en sciences sociales* from the University of Geneva and a postgraduate certificate from the Institut Universitaire d'Etudes de Développement (IUED) in Geneva in 1984. She worked as a research assistant at the University of Geneva for two years and studied social change and social movements. Since 1986 she has been working in Bangladesh in the field of development, first as a national professional in the local United Nations Development Program office and since 1990 as a senior principal officer with the Grameen Bank.

Index

Abrera-Mangahas, Maria Alcestis, 44, 63
ACCION, Latin America, 6, 179
ADB. *See* Asian Development Bank (ADB)
Agencies, multilateral and bilateral, 40–41, 206–7
See also World Bank
Agricultural sector in developing countries, 186
Bangladesh
employment in, 151, 154–55
expected growth rate in, 167
importance to economy of, 145
Sri Lanka
estimate of contribution to GDP of, 89
size of informal sector in, 71–72, 89
Agustin, Elsa, 42
Aid agencies. *See* Agencies, multilateral and bilateral
Alonzo, Ruperto P., 44, 54, 56, 58, 63
Amin, A. T. M., 153
Ammar Siamwalla, 136
Aquino (Corazon) government, Philippines, 40
Asian Development Bank (ADB), 52
Associations, Philippines, 63–65, 69, 195

Badan Kredit Kecamatan (BKK), Indonesia, 179, 204
Bangkok Metropolitan Transport Authority (BMTA), 114, 116–17
Bangladesh Bank (central bank), 168
Bangladesh Small and Cottage Industries Corporation (BSCIC), 164, 166
Banking system
Bangladesh, 168
See also Credit market; Grameen Bank
Indonesia, 204
Morocco, 21

Sri Lanka, 73, 99–101
Thailand, 135–37
Bank of Thailand (BOT), 136–37
Bank Rakyat Indonesia, 6, 204
Barangay clearance, Philippines, 47, 60, 65
Barantes, Alfonso, 8
Barriers to entry
into formal sector, 40
Morocco, 21–22
Philippines, 45, 46–51
Sri Lanka, 94
Thailand, 129–32
See also Discrimination; Regulatory system
Bautista, Romeo M., 44
Bawarnsak Uwanno, 138
BDT. *See* Bureau of Domestic Trade
Benham, Alexandra, 209
Benham, Lee, 209
BIR. *See* Bureau of Internal Revenue
BMTA. *See* Bangkok Metropolitan Transport Authority
Board of Investment (BOI), Thailand, 132, 133
Board of Investments (BOI), Philippines, 49–50
BOT. *See* Bank of Thailand
Boundary system, Philippines, 57–59, 60
Bribery
Peru, 7
Thailand, 121–22, 132–33, 190
Brokering business, Sri Lanka, 83
BSCIC. *See* Bangladesh Small and Cottage Industries Corporation
BTT. *See* Business Turnover Tax
Bureaucratic model of development, 1–2, 5
Bureau of Customs, Philippines, 50
Bureau of Domestic Trade (BDT), Philippines, 47–48, 62–63
Bureau of Internal Revenue (BIR), Philippines, 48

ICEG Academic Advisory Board